Cultural Sustainability and the Nature–Culture Interface

As contemporary socio-ecological challenges such as climate change and biodiversity preservation have become more important, the three pillars concept has increasingly been used in planning and policy circles as a framework for analysis and action. However, the issue of how culture influences sustainability is still an underexplored theme. Understanding how culture can act as a resource to promote sustainability, rather than a barrier, is the key to the development of cultural sustainability.

This book explores the interfaces between nature and culture through the perspective of cultural sustainability. A cultural perspective on environmental sustainability enables a renewal of sustainability discourse and practices across rural and urban landscapes, natural and cultural systems, stressing heterogeneity and complexity. The book focuses on the nature–culture interface conceptualised as a place where experiences, practices, policies, ideas and knowledge meet, are negotiated, discussed and resolved. Rather than looking for lost unities, or an imaginary view of harmonious relationships between humans and nature based in the past, it explores cases of interfaces that are context-sensitive and which consciously convey the problems of scale and time.

While calling attention to a cultural or 'culturalised' view of the sustainability debate, this book questions the radical nature–culture dualism dominating positive modern thinking as well as its underlying view of nature as pre-given and independent from human life.

Inger Birkeland is Professor in Human Geography at the Department of Culture, Religion and Social Studies at University College of Southeast Norway, where she researches cultural and learning aspects of sustainability in local and regional development.

Rob Burton is a Research Professor at the Centre for Rural Research in Trondheim, Norway. He focuses on farmer agency and, in particular, the influence of identity and cultural factors on decision-making.

Constanza Parra is Assistant Professor in the Department of Earth and Environmental Sciences, at the University of Leuven, Belgium. She researches and writes on social sustainability, nature–culture interactions, governance of socio-ecological systems and sustainable tourism.

Katriina Siivonen is Adjunct Professor in Cultural Heritage Studies and Senior Lecturer and Discipline Coordinator in Futures Studies at the University of Turku, Finland. She focusses on cultural sustainability, semiotic theory of culture, traditions, cultural heritage, heritage futures, cultural identities and ethnography as well as qualitative and participatory futures methodology.

Routledge Studies in Culture and Sustainable Development

Series Editors:

Katriina Soini

University of Jyväskylä, Finland and Natural Resources Institute Finland

Joost Dessein

Institute for Agricultural and Fisheries Research (ILVO) and Ghent University, Belgium

Culture as an aspect of sustainability is a relatively new phenomenon but is beginning to attract attention among scholars and policy-makers. This series opens up a forum for debate about the role of culture in sustainable development, treating culture and sustainability as a meta-narrative that will bring together diverse disciplines. Key questions explored in this series will include: how should culture be applied in sustainability policies; what should be sustained in culture; what should culture sustain; and what is the relationship of culture to other dimensions of sustainability?

Books in the series will have a variety of geographical foci and reflect different disciplinary approaches (for example, geography, sociology, sustainability science, environmental and political sciences, anthropology, history, archaeology and planning). The series will be addressed in particular to postgraduate students and researchers from a wide cross-section of disciplines.

Form, Art and the Environment
Engaging in sustainability
Nathalie Blanc and Barbara Benish

Culturally Responsive Education
Reflections from the Global South and North
Elina Lehtomäki, Hille Janhonen-Abruquah, George Kahangwa

Design for a Sustainable Culture
Perspectives, Practices and Education
Edited by Astrid Skjerven and Janne Beate Reitan

Cultures of Sustainability and Wellbeing
Theories, Histories and Policies
Edited by Paola Spinozzi and Massimiliano Mazzanti

Cultural Sustainability and the Nature–Culture Interface
Livelihoods, Policies, and Methodologies
Edited by Inger Birkeland, Rob Burton, Constanza Parra and Katriina Siivonen

Cultural Sustainability and the Nature–Culture Interface

Livelihoods, Policies, and Methodologies

Edited by Inger Birkeland, Rob Burton, Constanza Parra and Katriina Siivonen

First published 2018
by Routledge

2 Park Square, Milton Park, Abingdon, Oxfordshire OX14 4RN
52 Vanderbilt Avenue, New York, NY 10017

Routledge is an imprint of the Taylor & Francis Group, an informa business

First issued in paperback 2019

British Library Cataloguing-in-Publication Data
A catalogue record for this book is available from the British Library

Library of Congress Cataloging-in-Publication Data
A catalog record has been requested for this book

ISBN: 978-1-138-65049-7 (hbk)
ISBN: 978-0-367-85579-6 (ebk)

Typeset in Times New Roman
by Wearset Ltd, Boldon, Tyne and Wear

Contents

Illustrations

Figures

Tables

Contributors

Chrystalla Antoniou is a PhD graduate of the Department of Multimedia and Graphic Arts, Faculty of Fine and Applied Arts, of the Cyprus University of Technology. She holds a Master's degree from the Department of Culture and Communication at the Linköping University (Sweden). Chrystalla works as a primary school teacher and museum educator, employed by the Ministry of Education and Culture of Cyprus. As a museum educator, collaborating with state and municipal museums and galleries, she designs and implements educational programmes as well as educational material for students and teachers. Chrystalla is also a Research Associate of the Visual Sociology and Museum Studies Lab (Cyprus University of Technology). Her research interests include outdoor education in authentic learning contexts, education for sustainability, museum education, environmental education, experiential learning and place-based education.

Inger Birkeland is a Professor in Human Geography at the University of South-east Norway. A human geographer by training, with a PhD from the University of Oslo (2002), her research interests are nature–society relations, human relationships to place and landscape, place pedagogies, gender and women's studies, heritage-making and cultural sustainability and the overall greening of cultural and social theory. Her latest book, *Kulturelle hjørnesteiner* (2014), presents results from research on the role of culture in heritage-making and climate change transformation in a post-industrial region in Telemark, Norway.

Nathalie Blanc is a Research Scientist and the Managing Director of the LADYSS, laboratory of the CNRS (France). After studying fine arts and urban geography, she earned her PhD with a dissertation on Nature in the City, focusing on the role of living species in urban spaces. Her research interests are nature in cities, environmental aesthetics and environmental mobilisations. She is also an artist and an art commissioner, currently working on the theme of ecological fragility.

Cláudia Brites is doing a PhD in Geography and Spatial Planning in the New University of Lisbon, Portugal. She is a researcher at Cernas (PC-ESAC). Her research interests are related to sustainable rural development, multifunctional agriculture and social farming. Her current research is the evaluation of the impact of social farming initiatives in sustainable development. Her latest paper is on organic agriculture values and practices in Portugal and Italy and aims to identify the factors that influence the choice of organic farmers for more sustainable practices.

Rob Burton is a Forsker I (Research Professor) with 20 years experience in research. His PhD in human geography looked at the role of farmer self-identity in their engagement with woodland planting, and much of his subsequent research has been on the influence of cultural factors on farmers' behaviour (particularly the adoption of agri-environmental policy). He currently works at the Centre for Rural Research in Trondheim, Norway, but has also worked in Scotland and New Zealand. He is currently leading a major project into the transition of Norwegian society away from its reliance on oil towards a bio-economy, as well as working on projects on crowdfunding local on-farm CO_2 reductions and transitioning towards a more sustainable dairy/beef sector.

Annalisa Cicerchia is a Cultural Economist. She serves as Senior Researcher at the Italian National Statistical Institute. She teaches management of creative enterprises at the Faculty of Economics, Roma Tor Vergata University. Her research areas include cultural economics, cultural indicators, social impact of culture, culture and wellbeing, cultural and creative economy, cultural sustainability, cultural participation, cultural heritage and museums. She has carried out extensive research in Italy, the United States, various European Countries, Egypt, Lebanon and Kosovo. She is the author of books and articles on these topics.

Karoline Daugstad is a Professor in Human Geography at the Department of Geography, Norwegian University of Science and Technology (NTNU). Her research interests cover studies of values, attitudes and policies attached to landscapes, cultural heritage linked to tourism, management of protected areas and issues related to the participatory dimension in managing landscape. Within her core topics she has undertaken studies in Norway as well as studies with a comparative approach, more specifically, studies of mountain communities in Northern Spain and Austria.

Knut Fageraas is a Research Scientist at the Norwegian Institute for Cultural Heritage Research (NIKU), Oslo. He is about to finish a PhD focused on the productive process of creating a World Heritage site by institutional polices and how this affects the cultural production of local values, human practices and animal behaviour using The Vega Archipelago in northern Norway as a case. At NIKU he works primarily with issues on environmental management policies, cultural heritage economics, non-expert heritage appreciation and cultural heritage in nature preservation areas. His research interests comprise cultural history, critical heritage studies, rural studies, nature–culture relationships and animal studies.

Katharina Gugerell is a trained landscape architect and planner. She is appointed as Assistant Professor at the Department of Spatial Planning and Environment at the Faculty of Spatial Sciences, University of Groningen, the Netherlands. Her academic work focuses on urban and landscape governance, living labs and co-creation and gameful approaches to participatory action.

Thomas Hammer is a human geographer and Professor at the interdisciplinary Centre for Development and Environment of the University of Bern, Switzerland. He directs the centre's interdisciplinary study programmes in sustainable development. In addition, he heads several research projects on sustainable regional, landscape and large protected area development.

Viðar Hreinsson grew up on a farm in Northern Iceland and completed a Mag Art degree in literary studies at the University of Copenhagen. He is an independent literary scholar and has taught and lectured on Icelandic literary and cultural history at universities in Canada, the United States and Scandinavia. He is the General Editor of the acclaimed *The Complete Sagas of Icelanders* I-V (1997) and wrote a two-volume biography of Icelandic-Canadian poet Stephan G. Stephansson (2002 and 2003), rewritten in English as *Wakeful Nights* (2012). Both versions received nominations and awards. He has been an environmental activist and served as the director of the Reykjavík Academy. At present, he is working on various projects within environmental humanities and cultural sustainability. His latest work is a 760-page monograph, *Jón lærði og náttúrur náttúrunnar* ('Jón the learned and the Natures of Nature', 2016).

Suvi Huttunen is a social scientist currently working as a senior lecturer in social sciences at the University of Jyväskylä and as an external researcher at the Finnish Environment Institute (Syke). Her work focuses on rural development and natural resource management with a particular interest in sustainability, including its cultural dimension. In particular she has studied questions related to renewable energy production and forestry. Currently she analyses sustainability transitions in agriculture from the perspective of practice theory.

Ásthildur Jónsdóttir is an Assistant Professor at the Iceland Academy of the Arts. Her research interests include arts and cultural movements that support sustainable development and Education for Sustainability at all levels, within both formal and informal contexts. She has curated exhibitions, developed curricula and taught in public and private schools at both lower and upper secondary level, colleges, community centres and with people of all ages and backgrounds both in Iceland, Geneva and New York. She is also a Doctoral Candidate at the University of Iceland, School of Education and University of Lapland, Finland. She holds a Master's degree from New York University, Steinhardt School of Culture, Education and Human Development and a Master of Education from the University of Iceland.

Pia Kieninger (landscape planner, with a PhD in Rural Development) is a Senior Researcher at the Department of Economics and Social Sciences (BOKU, University of Natural Resources and Life Sciences, Vienna, Austria) and a visiting researcher at the Faculty of Geosciences and Environment (University of Lausanne, Switzerland). Her scientific interests are human-nature concepts, landscape governance, collective action, UNESCO heritage sites, migration and demographic change.

Lydie Laigle has initially dedicated her research to urban sustainable policies of European cities. Focusing progressively on the adaptation of cities to climate change and issues related to environmental justice, her work has introduced her to the field of environmental ethics and the societal questions raised by local/global environmental changes. These questions contribute to a renewed notion of sustainability by stressing the cultural dimensions of human-environment relations. In cooperation with Nathalie Blanc, she has recently studied why the 'capabilities' approach offers new insights to analyse citizen participation in climate change adaptation and nature–culture based sustainability solutions. She is a Director of Research at CSTB-University of Paris-East. For six years, she was a member of the scientific evaluation committee of the ANR (French National Agency of Research). She is co-director of the national scientific council on sustainable neighbourhoods (Built-Environment Ministry).

Marion Leng is a Research Scientist at the Centre for Development and Environment of the University of Bern, Switzerland. After studying history, French, forestry and forest ecology, she earned her PhD with a dissertation on education for sustainable development in European protected areas. She directs the university's Certificate of Advanced Studies in Sustainable Development study programme. Her research interests are sustainable regional and landscape development, sufficiency and 'the good life' and education for sustainable development.

Pedro Mendes Moreira is an Assistant Professor at Coimbra College of Agriculture of Coimbra Polytechnic, Portugal. He is an agronomist with a PhD in Quantitative Genetics at ITQB/UNL, Lisbon. His research interests are strategies of genetic resources conservation, pre-breeding and participatory plant breeding. He is responsible for the VASO Program, a participatory maize breeding programme which started in 1984 in Sousa Valley, Portugal, and focused on maize for human consumption from seed to maize bread. He is also responsible at PC-ESAC for national and international level projects (e.g. FP7 SOLIBAM, H2020 DIVERSIFOOD and LIVESEED) that have been fundamental for the continuation of the VASO Program.

Constanza Parra, Assistant Professor at the University of Leuven, is an environmental social scientist with interdisciplinary interests in the ways societies relate to the environment and deal with contemporary sustainability challenges. Since 2014, she has worked at the Division of Geography, Department of Earth and Environmental Sciences at the University of Leuven. Before moving to Belgium, she was a Rosalind Franklin Fellow at the University of Groningen, the Netherlands, and an AFR/Marie Curie postdoctoral fellow at the University of Luxembourg. Her research focuses on social sustainability, social innovation, nature–culture nexus, governance of social-ecological systems and protected areas.

Marianne Penker is Associate Professor in Regional Development at the Department of Economics and Social Sciences at the University of Natural Resources and Life Sciences Vienna, Austria. She is an acknowledged researcher in the field of collective action, socio-ecological systems and landscape and food governance. She is the vice chair of the UNESCO National Committee, 'Man and the Biosphere', Academy of Sciences Austria.

Bettina Scharrer is a historian and Research Scientist at the Centre for Development and Environment of the University of Bern, Switzerland. Her research interests are environmental, agricultural and economic history, sustainable development pathways in agriculture and the food sector, social and solidarity economy and sustainable regional and landscape development. Her current research focuses on the role of the solidarity economy in the development of organic farming in Europe.

Katriina Siivonen has a PhD in European Ethnology and is Adjunct Professor in Cultural Heritage Studies at the University of Turku, Finland. She is currently working as a Senior Lecturer in Futures Studies at the Finland Futures Research Center at the University of Turku. Previously she has worked as a professor and in other different positions in ethnology and futures studies in Finland at the University of Turku, University of Helsinki and Åbo Akademi University. Her main research interests are cultural sustainability, semiotic theory of culture, traditions, cultural heritage, cultural identities, ethnography and qualitative and participatory futures methodology.

Katriina Soini is a cultural geographer working as a Principal Research Scientist at the Natural Resources Institute, Finland and Sustainability Science Fellow at Helsinki University, Finland. Her research has focused on social and cultural sustainability in particular in the context of rural development. Cultural sustainability has been an underlying topic in her research for many years. She has been particularly interested in the conceptual framing of culture in sustainability.

Kirsi Sonck-Rautio is an ethnologist and cultural anthropologist, specialising in environmental ethnology. She graduated with a Master of Arts from the University of Oulu, Finland, majoring in cultural anthropology, and is now a Doctoral Candidate in European Ethnology in the University of Turku, Finland. She has studied the fishermen and the environment of the archipelago of southwestern Finland for years and a few years ago she became the resident of one of the islands herself.

Nina Svane-Mikkelsen is a visual artist, photographer and media scholar associated with the Department of Information Science and Media Studies at the University of Bergen, Norway. Svane-Mikkelsen researches nature communication as it unfolds across a wide range of media, from museum exhibitions, wildlife photography and documentary film to art works and fictional work. She often includes practical work in her research method, thus exploring the aesthetics of nature communication through participation in developing stories of nature. For instance, through developing exhibitions and digital games for children on themes of maritime research.

Miroslav Taşcu-Stavre is a Professor at the Faculty of Letters, Department of Cultural Studies, at the University of Bucharest, Romania. He earned a PhD in Political Science and his main academic work focuses on transition and democratisation in Post-Communist regimes. He is acknowledged for contributions in fields such as sustainable development and cultural policies and he also supports environmental activism.

Series introduction

Katriina Soini and Joost Dessein

Finding pathways to ecological, social and economic sustainability is the biggest global challenge of the twenty-first century and new approaches are urgently needed. Scholars and policy-makers have recognised the contribution of culture in sustainability work. 'Cultural sustainability' is also being increasingly discussed in debates in various international, national and local arenas, and there are actor-driven initiatives. Yet despite the growing attention there have only been a very few attempts to consider culture in scientific and political discourses of sustainability in a more analytical and explicit way – probably as a consequence of the complex, normative and multidisciplinary character of both culture and sustainability. This difficulty should not, however, be any excuse for ignoring the cultural aspects of sustainability.

The series, 'Routledge Studies in Culture and Sustainable Development', aims to analyse the diverse and multiple roles that culture plays in sustainability. It takes as one of its starting points the idea that culture serves as a 'meta-narrative' which will bring together ideas and standpoints from an extensive body of sustainability research, currently scattered among different disciplines and thematic fields. Moreover, the series responds to the strengthening call for inter- and transdisciplinary approaches which is being heard in many quarters, but in few fields more strongly than that of sustainability, with its complex and systemic problems. By combining and confronting the various approaches in both the sciences and the humanities and in dealing with social, cultural, environmental, political and aesthetic disciplines, the series offers a comprehensive contribution to the present-day sustainability sciences as well as related policies.

The books in the series take a broad approach to culture, giving space to all the possible understandings and forms of culture. Furthermore, culture is not only seen as an additional aspect of sustainability – as a 'fourth pillar' – but rather as a mediator, a cross-cutting transversal framework or even as new set of guiding principles for sustainability research, policies and practices.

The essence of culture in, for and as sustainability is being explored through the series in various thematic contexts, representing a wide range of practices and processes (e.g. everyday life, livelihoods and lifestyles, landscape, artistic practices, aesthetic experiences, heritage, tourism). These contexts concern urban, peri-urban or rural settings, and regions with different socio-economic trajectories. The perspectives of the books will stretch from local to global and cover different temporal scales from the past to present and future. These issues are valourised by theoretical or empirical analysis; their relationship to the ecological, social and economic dimensions of sustainability will be explored, when appropriate.

The idea for the series was derived from the European COST Action IS1007 'Investigating Cultural Sustainability', running between 2011 and 2015. This network was comprised of a group of around 100 researchers from 26 European countries, representing many different disciplines. They brought together their expertise, knowledge and experience, and in doing so, they built up new inter- and transdisciplinary understanding and approaches that can enhance and enrich research into culture in sustainable development, and support the work of the practitioners in education, policy and beyond.

The relationship between society and nature has engaged philosophers and scientists for centuries. Wide ranging perspectives have emerged. At one end of the spectrum are those who see society and nature as entirely separate, and, at the other, those who see the two as inextricably entwined. Current sustainability concerns have led to our understanding of this relationship becoming critically important to the future of our planet: how can we sustainably manage our natural resources while guaranteeing the wellbeing of society and respecting the intrinsic value of nature and culture?

This book addresses this question from a cultural sustainability perspective, exploring cultural sustainability in differing contexts and across livelihoods, landscapes and everyday practices. The chapters address how culture can be understood and constituted as a separate dimension in sustainability, explore the implications of cultural sustainability on policies and planning, and introduce new methodologies that can be applied to help us understand this complex relationship. They enrich the scientific debate in two key ways: first, by offering new insights for understanding and addressing the relationship between society and nature, and second, by extending our conceptual understanding of culture as a separate dimension in sustainability. Overall, the book invites the reader to rethink the meaning and role of culture within sustainable development.

Introduction to culture, sustainability and the environmental realm

Constanza Parra, Inger Birkeland, Rob Burton and Katriina Siivonen

The road towards the materialisation of the sustainability ambition has been the subject of many books and articles published in the last few years. This ambition has been interpreted and re-interpreted in a variety of ways and by different scholarship streams, which have usually highlighted social, economic and environmental aspects of sustainable development. Contributors to and readers of this book are probably well acquainted with the existing academic and policy debate revolving around the sustainability field. Some might be convinced of the need for individuals and societies to find ways to collectively act and reorganise in response to pressing sustainability imperatives. Others, following a self-emancipatory political path, might already be engaged in the large variety of social experiments and practices striving for the concrete materialisation of the sustainability ambition (Manier, 2012; Parra and Walsh, 2016).

Long overshadowed by more utilitarian and economically-centred methodological approaches to sustainable development, the relationship between culture and sustainability can be considered an under-studied aspect within the sustainability and more recently resilience literature. In cases where culture and sustainability are put into dialogue, analyses and contributions vary in terms of the definitions of culture that are mobilised as well as the types of sustainability and places they are referred to. For example, literature on culture and sustainability has focused on heritage as a process for human wellbeing (see Auclair and Fairclough, 2015) and also on the role of culture, artistic expression and creativity in the sustainability of cities (see Hristova *et al.*, 2015). Other approaches address the interaction between sustainability and cultural policies (Hawkes, 2001; Pascual, 2006) and regional development, sustainability and territorialisation (Dessein *et al.*, 2015a). From the perspective of resilience, sustainability and adaptive capacity, culture has been put into dialogue with climate change effects and responses to risk across populations and communities (Adger *et al.*, 2012).

This volume engages with contributions from various social science and humanities disciplines in the quest for further connecting culture and sustainability (Soini and Dessein, 2016), through the perspective of the dynamic interrelations between nature and culture. In other words, the contributions of this book look at what we call the interface between societies and the environmental realm, as an invitation to rethink the meaning and role of culture within sustainable development. This invitation involves at least three important assumptions that underlie the different contributions to this volume. First, that sustainability has an intrinsic cultural dimension and therefore the role of culture in sustainability is manifold, i.e. as a driver of meanings and values, mediator, transformative process, among others (Dessein *et al.*, 2015b). Second, that nature is not an outsider or external agent that can be managed or controlled rationally by human beings or technology but a partner that deserves praise and full respect. As such, nature has an intrinsic value that goes beyond the value that humans can confer. Third, there is no single 'sustainability' but rather different ways in which culture has accommodated the natural environment and vice versa, leading, in combination, to a large variety of developmental paths which might be more or less sustainable (Parra and Moulaert, 2011a, 2016).

The interface between nature and culture, together with its relationship with sustainability and development, can be seen from various interrelated angles that are explored throughout the chapters of this book. Different cultures and human modes of living have related, used and transformed territories and nature in variegated ways. Human beings depend on (healthy) ecosystems, land, soil, water and air among many others to guarantee the reproduction of social life. Distinct types of landscapes, geographies, presence or absence of non-human living forms, availability of resources, cycles and forces of nature and other features of ecosystems have moulded, through the course of history, the naissance, flourishing, development and decline of different cultures, social relationships and groups of humans. More extractive and devastating uses and transformations of nature by human communities have impacted on nature and ecosystems, leading in many cases to water depletion, vulnerability of various kinds, biodiversity loss and many other examples of ecological unsustainabilities. Furthermore, the social, cultural and economic sustainability of human groups is also exposed to changes in the functioning of ecosystems – or let us call them social-ecological systems (Ostrom, 2007) – as reflected for example in the unprecedented scale and pace at which today's (unexpected) hazards can transform into (socially constructed) disasters (Oliver-Smith and Hoffman, 1999). Reflecting on the possibilities of and for the materialisation of the sustainability ambition, including the required system of production, consumption and regulation to make this transition possible, calls for enhancing interdisciplinary progress (Pretty, 2011) and dialogue among different communities of practices, cultures and worldviews in their relation to the environment. This book offers various perspectives from which to engage with the nature–culture nexus metaphor from a sustainability-culture perspective.

What is culture?

The use of the term 'culture' in multiple contexts has generated a variety of interrelated meanings and definitions. In simple terms, the dictionary defines culture as the set of ideas, customs and social behaviour of a particular people or society. A second definition provided by the dictionary relates culture to the arts and to intellectual achievements or improvement (i.e. cultural festival) (Oxford English Dictionaries, 2017). Elaborating on Cuche (2004), Parra and Moulaert (2011a) recall that since its first uses in the western world, the word culture has been related to development. In this context Cuche (2004) refers to a variety of uses of the word at different moments of history, ranging from definitions of culture as 'action' to an understanding of culture as a particular 'state'. These understandings and definitions comprise culture as the action of cultivating the land (thirteenth century), culture in the figurative sense (i.e. 'la culture des letters' during the eighteenth century), culture as education or spiritual instruction (eighteenth century) and culture as progress or evolution as in the Enlightenment.

The uses of the word culture nowadays denote in many cases a relation to social progress or development. Nevertheless, culture signifies much more than this 'evolutionary' understanding. Goody (1994) distinguished two different yet interrelated ways to define culture. On the one hand, culture can be seen as a structure and a system of meanings, which shapes social action and interaction. In this line of thought, Geertz (1973: p. 33) defined culture as 'the framework of beliefs, expressive symbols, and values in terms of which individuals define their world, express their feelings, and make their judgements'. On the other hand, culture is defined in its capacity to reproduce and recreate through social relations and human interaction (Goody, 1994: p. 250). Culture is, from this angle, conceived as a dynamic and fluid process from which cultural structures emerge, transform and disappear in specific periods of time, places and scales.

Material components, including biodiversity at the level of genes, species and ecosystems, are also part and parcel of the definition of culture in general, and within a sustainability context, in particular. As further discussed in this book, material or biophysical components characterising the natural environment play a fundamental role in the reproduction and recreation of culture and human interaction. Bearing this in mind, we bring on board Pilgrim and Pretty's definition of culture as

> a set of practices, networks of institutions and systems of meanings. Cultural systems code for the knowledge, practices, beliefs, worldviews, values, norms, identities, livelihoods and social organizations of human societies. Different cultures value nature in different ways and thus have different connection with their natural environments.
>
> (2010b: p. 3)

Several contributions by Pretty, Pilgrim and colleagues further elaborate different aspects of this definition of culture by highlighting four bridges connecting culture and nature which are presented below.

How do culture and nature relate?

Pretty and Pilgrim (2008) identify four bridges connecting nature and culture which provide a useful framework for understanding the interaction between culture and sustainability. These bridges comprise beliefs and worldviews, livelihoods and practices, knowledge bases and norms, institutions (and governance).

'Beliefs and worldviews' refers to the systems by which people interpret, explain and give meaning to the world (Geertz, 1973). A crucial aspect within these systems of values concerns the ways human beings have looked at and related to nature in the course of history. On one side of the spectrum, we find social groups acknowledging and showing deep appreciation for the multiple interconnections between biodiversity and cultural diversity. This was usually the case of pre-industrial societies and indigenous groups (Pretty, 2011). On the other side on the spectrum, we find multiple efforts to separate nature from culture, reproducing the modernist and anthropocentric nature–culture divide fallacy that places humans and human progress in a position of superiority vis-à-vis non-human living forms (Haila, 1999, 2000). Within a range between eco-/biocentrism and anthropocentrism, particular combinations of values, beliefs and worldviews have led over time to changing interpretations of the challenges contained within the sustainability ambition. From this perspective, we call attention to the contemporary emergence of two collectives with the audacity to challenge the nature–culture divide and its value underlying anthropocentric ethics and values. 'Voluntary simplicity', as introduced by Richard Gregg in 1936 and discussed by Alexander (2015), constitutes an interesting example from which to think on the diverse beliefs, values and worldviews bridging nature and culture. Voluntary simplicity is a way-of-life or degrowth plea heading towards needs, satisfactions and the construction of meanings through non-materialistic sources as expressed in the following quote:

> Variously defended by its advocates on personal, social, political, humanitarian, and ecological grounds, voluntary simplicity is based on the assumption that human beings can live meaningful, free, happy, and infinitely diverse lives, while consuming no more than an equitable share of nature.
>
> (Alexander, 2015: p. 133; see also Alexander and Ussher, 2012)

Beliefs and worldviews held by the inter-cultural Latin American alliance Buen Vivir constitute another interesting critique to the modern-times myth of progress and duality separating culture from nature (Haila, 1999, 2000; Gudynas, 2015). The Buen Vivir view of the world, together with the alternative development goals pursued by this inter-cultural alliance, have moved beyond a mere criticism of the unsustainabilities of contemporary economic growth to focus attention on a development discourse and socio-political struggle for a more holistic social, cultural and environmental flourishing. As such, the beliefs and worldviews of Buen Vivir strive for changing or improving present-day cosmovisions and worldviews regarding the interactions between humans, society, culture and nature (Gudynas, 2015: p. 204).

Livelihoods and practices, the second nature–culture bridge depicted by Pretty and Pilgrim (2008), refers to the different forms of production, consumption and reproduction of socio-ecological interrelationships leading to distinct forms of place attachment, place shaping and place keeping (Spijker and Parra, 2017). History is rich with different forms of production and survival strategies chosen by humankind and social groups. From hunting and gathering to industrialisation, and more recently attempts to go back to more circular socio-economic alternatives in cities, each practice and collective construction of livelihood has had a different impact or footprint on the planet. The concept of landscape covered by several contributions to this volume is meaningful from this perspective. Landscapes are the living result of extensive human uses and transformations over centuries and consequently they embody a plurality of localised cultural practices entangled with distinct ecological materialities (Pilgrim and Pretty, 2010a; Koster and Denkinger, 2017). Chapters in this volume by Gugerell and colleagues, Scharrer and colleagues and Burton provide interesting insights on sustainability venues observed in European parks which are characterised by the co-existence of practices and livelihood strategies based on a more balanced (or sustainable) relationship between nature and culture.

Knowledge, the third bridge connecting culture and the environmental realm, comprises

> a non-static compilation of observations and understandings contained within social memory that constantly evolve to try and make sense of the way the world behaves, and which societies can use to guide their actions towards the natural world.
>
> (Pretty *et al.*, 2009: p. 109)

From this perspective, knowledge includes the process of learning about, using and accommodating nature. Knowledge also refers to the stock of cultural knowledge of nature gathered throughout what Berkes *et al.* (2000) call the 'knowledge-belief-practice' complex. This complex can comprise facts, information and skills acquired through experience, education and research but also spiritual beliefs, traditional practices and alternative worldviews. The interconnections between culture and knowledge cannot be fully understood without referring to power dynamics and power systems. Beliefs, worldviews and knowledge are embedded in power systems that have usually positioned traditional, indigenous and lay knowledge in a lower range compared with knowledge and learning processes that proceed from experts and science (Cannon and Shipper, 2014). The question of how to articulate and combine the knowledge and value systems proceeding from different cultures in such a way that democratic imperatives of a project striving for sustainability are met, continues to challenge the different communities of practice, policy-makers and citizens.

Norms and institutions are the fourth bridge discussed by Pretty and colleagues. Norms and institutions emerge from the different values, practices and knowledge types mediating the nature–culture interface. According to Pretty (2011), norms and institutions 'govern human interactions and behaviours towards the natural environment, and have often co-evolved to sustain both people and nature'. Examples of norms and institutions include common property rules regulating use and access rights to different resources (Ribot and Peluso, 2003).

This institutional level, which includes norms concerning institutional regimes, structures and agency, can be also analysed from the perspective of the governance of the nexus between nature and culture (Parra and Moulaert, 2016). Within this context, Parra and Moulaert (2011a, 2011b) analytically discussed and examined the different components of the governance system, mediating and recreating the nature–culture nexus or pressing for an artificial dichotomy. These components comprise:

- First, the main social actors and their own sustainability visions, value systems and behavioural norms affecting sustainable development decisions and therefore the institutionalisation of distinct governance systems.
- Second, the main governance modes that are co-constructed and used, including, the development of joint projects, communication and decision-making principles, synergies between communication and decision-making channels, among others.
- Third, the multi-scalar socio-political nature of governance systems in general, and social-ecological systems in particular.
- Fourth, the nature–culture nexus itself and its fundamental role in shaping governance systems, rules, norms and institutions, and notably their missions, objectives and their modes of expression.

One of the central aims of this volume is to unravel how nature and culture co-evolve to produce sustainability. This comprises disentangling ongoing cultural transformations vis-à-vis the sustainability problematic and aspects of distinct cultures that remain or transform very slowly. This question also relates to the pluralities contained within the confines of existing communities and human groups, including internal hierarchies, leadership and power relationships as well as gender, age group and levels of instruction, among others. From the different chapters of this book one could conclude that cultures seeking sustainability are socially constructed from below, through history and in dynamic interrelation with non-human living forms (Haila, 2000; Inglis, 2004; Parra and Moulaert, 2016). Different types of nature–culture co-evolutions spring from the ground, and this ground is inhabited by a boundless cultural diversity that is dynamic and changing at a variety of different life tempos. Nonetheless, it would be a mistake to think of the nature–culture interface(s), including those striving for enhanced sustainability, as being comprised of separate islands or silos. The nature–culture interface is socially embedded in a dynamic multi-scalar system of socio-political and cultural relationships (Parra and Moulaert, 2016). In other words, entanglements and levels of interactions are not only dynamic but also multifarious. These comprise the nature–culture nexus, cultural diversity and biodiversity and plurality of socio-political relationships at different temporal and spatial scales, as reflected in the richness of this world in terms of landscapes, practices, communities, worldviews, governance modes of the nature–culture nexus and of course roads towards the sustainability ambition.

On culture, nature and the realisation of the sustainability ambition

A crucial question discussed and illustrated through case-studies in the different chapters of this book concerns the relationship between the nature–culture interface and the realisation or materialisation of the sustainability ambition. The variety of approaches depicted in the book show that there is more than one possible interpretation and action plan towards this pressing ambition which depends on and is mediated through diversity in culture, worldviews, knowledge and nature–culture entanglements.

Within this context, relating culture to sustainability from the perspective of the nature–culture interface becomes meaningful. Elaborating on Birkeland (2008, 2014), the concept of cultural sustainability can be related to a continuous process of inspiring and optimistic self-development having sustainable development as a goal (Stefanovic, 2000). Here the essential ingredients are dialogue and meaning-making, the negotiation of meanings, setting up shared goals and co-constructing visions for a present and future that are socially and environmentally just and democratic. Such an approach relates sustainable development and cultural sustainability to a movement or motion ensuring the soundness of entangled biodiversity and cultural diversity.

The content of this volume

The following chapters focus on the nature–culture interface using a diversity of approaches and taking a range of perspectives to examine cases from many parts of the world. Most of the chapters build on research work carried out by past members of COST Action 1007 Investigating Cultural Sustainability (2011–2015).

Part I of this volume concerns human livelihoods, cultures and practices in diverse environments and contexts and focuses on the ways the nature–culture interface is embedded in the human quest for securing the basic necessities of food, water, shelter and clothing from the environments. Themes covered by this section comprise the co-existence and co-evolution of humans and nature, including cultural and ecological sustainability; the role of culture, collective action and institutions in the sustainability and governance of protected areas; the relevance of biocultural diversity for sustainable agricultural practices; the redesign and reuse of waste and resources to form new businesses and institutions; and the rediscovery of pre-modern ideas and practices of sustainability.

Chapter 1 of this book, written by Katriina Siivonen, builds on a study carried out in the Southwest Finland Archipelago. Siivonen problematises the balance between environmental and cultural sustainability, by reflecting on where and in which forms traces of ecological (un)balance in the livelihoods of the current archipelago can be found. She argues that cultural sustainability can be seen as a support to environmental sustainability, as nature is an important element in human identities. A strong cultural coexistence with nature is often seen to mean ecologically sustainable human lifemodes and livelihoods. This coexistence – an example of the nature–culture interface – can be defined as one element of tangible and intangible cultural heritage. For Siivonen the core to achieving combined environmental and cultural sustainability is to understand that culture (as nature) is a process, and more precisely an interactive cultural process arising from a mix of intangible and tangible traditions in continuous development and change.

Katriina Soini and Suvi Huttunen explore agricultural practices and their sustainability with reference to Finnish farming practices in Chapter 2, asking what we can learn about cultural sustainability from farmers' views of sustainability in agriculture. They argue that agriculture is dependent on natural resources such as soil and natural processes (photosynthesis and procreation), as well as on human activities such as ploughing, seeding, harvesting and breeding. Consequently, the essence of agriculture is co-production between humans and nature. Soini and Huttunen have identified three core qualities of sustainability in farming as stressed by the farmers; namely fertility, diversity and continuity. These insights are used to understand how sustainable agriculture can provide a deeper and more profound understanding of culture in sustainability: what does it really mean to speak of culturally sustainable development? The authors contend that there is no one answer. Rather, this question must be raised again and again as the answer will vary depending on the particular context within which the question is asked. The need for a reflexive approach that focuses on practices and their conditions is thus one of the most important lessons we can learn from farmers.

In Chapter 3 Constanza Parra makes a plea for restoring the centrality of human beings, collective action and culture in sustainability. The focus on human action, individual and collective, speaks to the problematics of sustainability in a wide sense but also more specifically to transformations in the governance of protected areas, or rather to the way human societies have cared for the natural environment through protection or conservation. The case of protected areas illustrates the challenges of protecting biodiversity, as a particular domain in which the nature–culture interface as a worldwide phenomenon comes to the fore. Parra argues for the centrality of human beings in sustainability and institutions for nature protection but with an understanding that nature protection should occur in a dialogic and dynamic manner for the sustainability of biodiversity and cultural diversity. For Parra, the relevance of culture for and in sustainable development cannot then be separated from nature. This implies protected areas should be looked at as territorial expressions of a specific nature–culture interrelationship and not just as simple spaces of nature, wilderness or natural resources.

Cláudia Brites and Pedro Mendes Moreira show in Chapter 4 that culture cannot be dissociated from agriculture in rural areas. They argue that a stronger focus on biocultural diversity is a way to promote sustainable development. The authors discuss, from cross-cultural perspectives, cultural aspects of existing traditional farming systems as a means to better understand their adaptation to particular environments. They argue against the problematic tendency in research and policy to separate biological and cultural diversity. In reality, there exists a reciprocal relationship between the biological and cultural diversity which needs to be acknowledged. The authors show that despite the threat of a gradual process of industrialisation, some traditional farming systems still resist industrialisation while maintaining crop diversity and local landraces. The conservation of the tacit knowledge associated with traditional farming systems is essential to ensure long-term cultural sustainability, which means that it is very important to explore how culturally diverse practices are fundamental in the maintenance of biocultural diversity.

Moving to a historical and philosophical perspective on cultural sustainability, Viðar Hreinsson discusses pre-enlightenment conceptualisations of the relations between nature and culture in Chapter 5. He argues that cultural sustainability, the embeddedness of sustainability in culture, is a modern concept. Through a critique of science and philosophy he finds that unsustainability – which is a deep-seated problem – is a product of consumer-driven market ideology infiltrated in Western myths of progress. According to Hreinsson, it is possible to reach behind the myths and investigate earlier and pre-enlightenment conceptions of the relations between humans and nature. Modern ideas of domination over nature are based on a mechanical worldview that replaced an organic one in the seventeenth century. The chapter investigates the former concepts of nature and cultural sustainability that can be compared with current ideas of sustainable development, and suggests a shift towards a worldview that acknowledges the limits of human knowledge as well as actions and recognises diversity and complexity in a dialogic manner and thus responsible relations with nature.

Today's economic crisis contributes to a worsening of the ecological crisis but also represents an opportunity for a more profound renewal, according to Annalisa Cicerchia. In Chapter 6 she discusses how an instrumental view of nature, deeply rooted in anthropocentrism, has led to critical levels of unsustainability on a global scale. There is, however, a great interest today in creating economic growth from creative and cultural enterprises. Working from a multidisciplinary perspective, and drawing from economic anthropology and cultural economics, this chapter explores the role played by a small but growing number of cultural and creative enterprises that challenge unsustainable production and consumption patterns. The enterprises are ongoing, and deal with waste upcycling, design and production of environment-friendly food and the rediscovery of sustainable use of natural resources. These examples build their activity on innovative and sustainable redefinition and redesign of the relationship between nature and culture in their processes. The products are discussed with reference to demonstration potential and their relevance for households, businesses and cultural institutions alike around the world.

The second section of the book discusses planning and policies – at different spatial scales and in different sectors – for culture and for sustainable development. Landscape management practices in various settings and contexts, including United Nations Educational, Scientific and Cultural Organization (UNESCO) world heritage status, and the role of agriculture in the shaping and reshaping of landscapes are a central theme of concern. Among the topics covered by the different contributors, we highlight the challenge of better understanding adaptive capacity in social-ecological settings; the need for policy-makers and policies that are sensitive to the cultural component of sustainable development, including planning and management styles to enhance sustainability of coastal areas through tourism; and how UNESCO world heritage status are utilised, understood and appreciated locally.

Katharina Gugerell, Marianne Penker and Pia Kieninger discuss landscape co-management practices at the UNESCO world heritage site of Wachau in Austria in Chapter 7. These authors are interested in the involvement of local communities, power dynamics and ongoing conflicts, which are often ignored. Research shows that active citizenship and co-management practices, through which the government shares power with local communities, have the potential to support landscape sustainability. New co-management platforms offer more pluralistic perspectives, power-sharing and possibilities for improved decision-making. Central here is the strong bond between people and their landscape, which is important for driving landscape governance. The bond is often expressed in the collective memory of communities and shared narratives that can form the basis for sustainable development and governance of cultural landscapes. The authors stress however the importance of unravelling the power dynamics underlying the co-existence of different values and knowledges, given the fact that it is impossible to avoid contradictions, differences between interests and values concerning landscape.

Winter-seining has been an economically and socio-culturally important livelihood in the community of Rymättylä in southwestern Finland for centuries. Kirsi Sonck-Rautio's chapter (8) discusses local adaptation processes and the capacity to adapt, and resilience at the local level in order to improve community cultural sustainability in the face of global change. Her chapter examines the role of culture within adaptive capacity indicators, by taking the perspective that communities are formed by lifestyles, traditions and identities, just as much as by economic factors. The author argues that we need to develop a better understanding of the nature of cultural sustainability in order to identify the adaptive capacity indicators needed for studying the vulnerabilities to improve adaptation processes of social-ecological systems. The example of winter-seining – a form of fishing which is conducted under ice cover with a large seine and which requires a large amount of manpower – in the community of Rymättylä provides a good example to learn more about adaptive capacity and community resilience because of a rapid decline in winter-seining in the past few decades.

In Chapter 9 Rob Burton examines the preservation of cultural landscapes with a particular focus on upland farmers in the Lake District National Park in

Cumbria, United Kingdom. This, along with many unique cultural landscapes across Europe are under threat because of an inability of traditional agriculture to attract the next generation of family farmers. The author contends that the main problem is that policy efforts attempt to preserve the environmental structure of the region (e.g. stone buildings, fences, biodiversity) without considering that these structures are inextricably linked to the continuation of the culture. Factors such as limiting the building of new farm residences, a move to contracting out stone wall construction and minimising sheep numbers to preserve the environment – while intended to preserve the cultural landscape – can interfere with the ability of the younger generation to become culturally embedded in the region and thus, paradoxically, may contribute to its eventual decline or 'disneyfication'. For the author, cultural sustainability relates to the ability of these cultural landscapes to maintain themselves, not as historical artefacts, but as living examples of a culture-environment nexus.

Demographic and structural changes of cultural landscapes are also in focus in Chapter 10 written by Bettina Scharrer, Thomas Hammer and Marion Leng. They have studied the significance of a living agricultural heritage associated with terraced landscapes in the Parc Naturel Régional des Monts d'Ardèche, a protected region in south-central France. Their chapter discusses the significance of terraced landscapes for a region and its identity, and how inhabitants in the region deal with the heritage of terraced landscapes, for example, how they preserve, revive and develop knowledge of dry-stone walling and cultivation. This chapter shows how terraced landscapes – which are a particularly sustainable, long-lasting form of co-evolution of nature and culture – can be preserved, kept alive and developed thanks to innovative and participative management strategies. Preserving such terraced landscapes is only possible when desired and supported by the local community, and when the terraces continue to be used. Close co-operation between the park management, residents, professional dry-stone wallers and, last but not least, cultural workers and creative artists, is crucial to success.

Miroslav Taşcu-Stavre discusses tourism and sustainable development by comparing the recent historical development of two rural communities on the Black Sea coastline in Romania (2 Mai and Vama Veche) in Chapter 11. His chapter shows how rural communities in the coastal zone can successfully maintain their characteristic identities while also developing an environmentally friendly tourism sector – this despite the expansion of mass tourism during the 1990s. The chapter explores how development was able to fulfil both the host community's aspirations and the tourists' needs simultaneously. However, the two communities followed different development pathways. While one (2 Mai) preserved the environment by adopting the tourists into a sense of family membership, the second community (Vama Veche) represents a door to relaxation. In both cases, tourists needed the tourist landscape to be sustained, and intervened when it was necessary to ensure a positive outcome.

Karoline Daugstad and Knut Fageraas discuss the contrasting heritage management between farmers and fishermen at Vega, an island in Northern Norway in Chapter 12. Vega was classified in UNESCO's World Heritage List in 2004 as a cultural landscape as it reflects the ways in which generations of fishermen and farmers over the past 1500 years have maintained a sustainable living close to the Arctic Circle. Of special importance is the production of eiderdown, a particularly interesting example of the nature–culture interface where inhabitants protected and sheltered the birds while gathering down feathers – a cherished good – for processing and sale. The chapter focuses on how farmers and fishermen utilise, understand and value the UNESCO status, and shows how there is a significant difference between these two groups. While the fishermen consider the World Heritage Status to be of little value, the farmers saw possibilities for new income generation and benefits for the community. Fishermen's experiences mirror the negative development of coastal fisheries in particular but also show how particular land-based practices and traditions, such as down production, have been given a higher UNESCO status compared with the fisheries, which nevertheless has been equally important as farming in the development of the island historically.

The third part of the book deals with methodologies and focuses on some examples of systematic, theoretical analysis of possible methods applied to study cultural sustainability and the nature–culture interface. Research into the nature–culture interface is challenging, and as is pointed out by many of the chapter authors, scholarship on the relationships between the environment, sustainability and culture is scarce. There is a need for further methodological work on this, and the chapters in section three provide three different examples. These chapters deal with diverse domains, including climate research, arts education for sustainability and media and communication studies.

Nathalie Blanc and Lydie Laigle explore how narrative methodologies can be used to untangle the complex cultural construction of climate change in Chapter 13. They discuss the contribution of the 'capabilities approach' to the analysis of constraints and resources that people have in their daily lives and analyse how the formulation of relationships, knowledge and experiences with the environment can influence the ability of citizens to adapt to climate change. Capabilities-based analyses applied to environmental issues focus on the possibilities provided by the environment and on the capacity of individuals and groups to harness these possibilities. The approach thus focuses on the things that individuals and groups want to mobilise to maintain, i.e. health, subsistence and mobility, provided through the narratives they tell. The authors show how the exploration of ordinary stories from everyday life can provide learning about climate change adaptation. Such stories may reveal ways that citizens adopt environmentally friendly practices as they are advised in public life. The question for the authors is whether the exploration of capabilities through narratives is a path towards cultural sustainability. In their concluding discussion, the authors argue that we cannot leave the responsibility for addressing climate change to the scientific realm alone. Climate change must be part of the way we live our everyday lives. By exploring the co-construction of societies and their environments through capabilities as an intermediary, built through narratives, the authors illustrate how researchers and practitioners alike can explore the importance of a co-emergent nature–culture, where the environment is a foundation for life, and not only a place offering resources for life.

In Chapter 14, Ásthildur Jónsdóttir and Chrystalla Antoniou discuss artistic actions for sustainability in a contemporary art exhibition. The authors describe and explain how an art exhibition can raise awareness of sustainability issues and provide examples of the benefits of arts education for sustainability. The methodological reflections are particularly relevant for teachers, cultural workers and researchers interested in action- and participative-methods and action learning. Contemporary art exhibitions have the potential to play a key role for cultural sustainability, as they can build bridges between different community members, as well as encouraging self-awareness, values and decision-making. Many contemporary artists deal with issues that are disregarded in mainstream culture and politics. In this chapter, an Icelandic art exhibition called 'Challenge' is examined for the potential it offers in understanding the importance of sustainability and the ethical issues involved. The chapter explains and discusses some theoretical perspectives on art exhibitions in relation to learning processes based in arts-based environmental education and presents results that focus on participant experiences and learning from participating in the art exhibition. Methodologically speaking, the potential of working with art for sustainability is based in its experiential and cultural approach to learning. When making educational use of art and art exhibitions, sustainability issues can be considered through the working methods of both artists, researchers and teachers.

The final chapter is written by Nina Svane-Mikkelsen who explains and shows the possibilities of media aesthetic methodologies. The starting point is that media and communication studies can contribute to sustainability by providing insights into the interface between culture and nature that reveal deeper knowledge about cultural interpretations of how nature and wildlife are mediated. The chapter focuses on the visual media of documentary film and photography, where stories of nature are explored. It discusses the framing of nature through examples of widespread and popular media stories. Furthermore, the chapter details 'walk-through'-analyses, showing how media aesthetic analysis can be a useful analytical tool for researchers, politicians, NGOs and nature communicators of different kinds (e.g. media producers, teachers, museum employees and nature guides). The cases discussed are photographer Steve Bloom's wildlife photography with accompanying texts and the BBC's and David Attenborough's popular non-fiction nature-television shows.

References

Adger, W. N., Barnett, J., Brown, K., Marshall, N. and O'Brien, K. (2012) Cultural dimensions of climate change impacts and adaptation. *Nature Climate Change* 3(2): 112–117.

Alexander, S. (2015) Simplicity. In: G. D'Alisa, F. Demaria and G. Kallis (eds) *Degrowth: a Vocabulary for a New Era*. Routledge, London and New York:133–136.

Alexander, S. and Ussher, S. (2012) The voluntary simplicity movement: A multi-national survey analysis in theoretical context. *Journal of Consumer Culture* 12(1):66–86.

Auclair, E. and Fairclough, G. (eds) (2015) *Theory and Practice in Heritage and Sustainability: Between Past and Future*. Routledge, London and New York.

Berkes, F., Colding, J. and Folke, C. (2000) Rediscovery of traditional ecological knowledge as adaptive management. *Ecological Applications* 10:1251–1262.

Birkeland, I. (2008) Cultural sustainability: Industrialism, placeless-ness and the re-animation of place. *Ethics, Place & Environment* 11(3):283–297.

Birkeland, I. (2014) *Kulturelle hjørnesteiner: Teoretiske og didaktiske perspektiver på klimaomstilling*. Cappelen Damm Akademisk, Oslo.

Cannon, T. and Schipper, L. (eds) (2014) *World Disasters Report 2014: focus on culture and risk*. International Federation of Red Cross, Geneva.

Cuche, D. (2004) *La Notion de Culture dans les Sciences Sociales*. la Découverte, Paris.

Dessein, J., Soini, K., Fairclough, G. and Horlings, L. (eds) (2015a) *Culture in, for and as Sustainable Development. Conclusions from the COST Action IS 1007 Investigating Cultural Sustainability*. University of Jyväskylä, Jyväskylä, Finland.

Dessein, J., Battaglini, E. and Horlings, L. (eds) (2015b) *Cultural Sustainability and Regional Development: Theories and Practices of Territorialisation*. Routledge, London and New York.

Geertz, C. (1973) *The Interpretation of Cultures* (Vol. 5019). Basic Books, New York.

Goody, J. (1994) Culture and its boundaries: A european view. In: R. Borofsky (ed.) *Assessing Cultural Anthropology*. McGraw-Hill, New York:250–261.

Gregg, R. B. ([1936]2009) *The Value of Voluntary Simplicity*. The Floating Press, Auckland, New Zealand.

Gudynas, E. (2015) Buen vivir. In: G. D'Alisa, F. Demaria and G. Kallis (eds) *Degrowth: A Vocabulary for a New Era*. Routledge, London and New York:201–204.

Haila, Y. (1999) Biodiversity and the divide between culture and nature. *Biodiversity and Conservation* 8(1):165–181.

Haila, Y. (2000) Beyond the nature–culture dualism. *Biology and Philosophy* 15(2): 155–175.

Hristova, S., Šešić, M. D., Evi, M. D. and Duxbury, N. (eds) (2015) *Culture and Sustainability in European Cities: Imagining Europolis*. Routledge, London and New York.

Hawkes, J. (2001) *The Fourth Pillar of Sustainability. Culture's Essential Role in Public Planning*. Cultural Development Network & Common Ground Press, Melbourne.

Inglis, F. (2004) *Culture: Key Concepts in the Social Sciences*. Polity Press, Cambridge, UK and Cambridge, USA.

Koster, U. and Denkinger, K. (2017) *Living Landscapes: Europe's Nature, Regional, and Landscape Parks – Model Regions for the Sustainable Development of Rural Areas*. Verband Deutscher Naturparke e. V. (VDN), Bonn, Germany.

Manier, B. (2012) *Un Million de Révolutions Tranquilles*. Editions Les Liens qui Libèrent, Paris.

Oliver-Smith, A. and Hoffman, S. M. (eds) (1999) *The Angry Earth: Disaster in Anthropological Perspective*. Psychology Press, London.

Ostrom, E. (2007) *Sustainable Social-Ecological Systems: An Impossibility? Paper presented at the Annual Meetings of the American Association for the Advancement of Science, San Francisco, 15–19 February*. www.mcleveland.org/Class_reading/Ostrom_Sustainable_Socio-Economic_Systems.pdf (Accessed 27 November 2017).

Oxford English Dictionaries. (2017) *Culture*. https://en.oxforddictionaries.com/definition/culture (Accessed 12 December 2017).

Pascual, J. (2006) *Culture et développement durable: exemples d'innovation institutionnelle et proposition d'un nouveau cade pour les politiques culturelles. Commission de cultures de Cités et Gouvernements Locaux Unis – CGLU.* http://reseauculture21.fr/wp-content/uploads/2015/07/z_report-4_Resum-FR-copie.pdf (Accessed 15 May 2017).
Parra, C. and Moulaert, F. (2011a) La nature de la durabilité sociale: contributions pour une lecture socioculturelle du développement territorial durable. *Developpement Durable et Territoires* 2(2). http://developpementdurable.revues.org/8970 (Accessed 27 November 2017).
Parra, C. and Moulaert, F. (2011b) Why sustainability is so fragilely 'social'. In: S. Oosterlynck, J. Van den Broeck, L. Albrechts, F. Moulaert and A. Verhetsel (eds) *Strategic Spatial Projects: Catalysts for Change*. Routledge, London:163–173.
Parra, C. and Moulaert, F. (2016) The governance of the nature–culture nexus: Lessons to learn from the San Pedro de Atacama case. *Nature+Culture* 11(3):229–238.
Parra, C. and Walsh, C. (2016) Socialities of nature beyond utopia. *Nature+Culture* 11(3):229–238.
Pilgrim, S. and Pretty, J. N. (eds) (2010a) *Nature and Culture: Rebuilding Lost Connections*. Earthscan, London and Washington.
Pilgrim, S. and Pretty, J. N. (2010b) Bridging the gap: interdisciplinarity, biocultural diversity and conservation. In: S. Pilgrim and J. N. Pretty (eds) *Nature and Culture: Rebuilding Lost Connections.* Earthscan, London and Washington: 1–20.
Pretty, J. (2011). Interdisciplinary progress in approaches to address social-ecological and ecocultural systems. *Environmental Conservation* 38(2):127–139.
Pretty, J. and Pilgrim, S. (2008) Nature and culture. *Resurgence: Indigenous Intelligence: Diverse Solutions for the 21st Century* 250. www.resurgence.org/magazine/article2629-nature-and-culture.html (Accessed 27 November 2017).
Pretty, J., Adams, B., Berkes, F., De Athayde, S. F., Dudley, N., Hunn, E. and Sterling, E. (2009) The intersections of biological diversity and cultural diversity: Towards integration. *Conservation and Society* 7(2):100–112.
Ribot, J. C. and Peluso, N. L. (2003) A theory of access. *Rural sociology* 68(2):153–181.
Spijker, N. and Parra, C. (2017) Knitting green spaces with the threads of social innovation in Groningen and London. *Journal of Environmental Planning and Management* www.tandfonline.com/doi/full/10.1080/09640568.2017.1382338 (Accessed 27 November 2017).
Soini, K. and Dessein, J. (2016) Culture-sustainability relation: Towards a conceptual framework. *Sustainability* 8(2):167.
Stefanovic, I. L. (2000) *Safeguarding Our Common Future. Rethinking Sustainable Development.* SUNY Press, New York.

Part I

Livelihoods, cultures and practices

1 Sustainable everyday culture from glocal archipelago culture

Katriina Siivonen

Problematizing the harmony between humanity and nature

A strong cultural coexistence with nature is often understood as living one's life in an ecologically sustainable way. This coexistence can be defined as one element of a tangible and intangible cultural heritage, and the relationship between cultural heritage and sustainable development has been discussed in the heritage work of The United Nations Educational, Scientific and Cultural Organization (UNESCO), for example. The work that has been conducted by UNESCO has aimed towards searching for practices where cultural heritage could be defined as sustainable by nature, not only by its intrinsic value of cultural heritage, but also as a guarantee for maintaining or reaching ecological sustainability, as well as other dimensions of sustainability. Investments towards safeguarding cultural heritage, transmitted from generation to generation in the different corners of our globe, have thus been suggested as being an essential element that will lead to, for example, ecological sustainability (see e.g. Boccardi and Duvelle, 2013).

This is also the situation in the Baltic Sea area, in the Nordic countries (and in Finland as one of these countries) and in one of the Finnish maritime regions, the Southwest Finland Archipelago. As an example, the Archipelago Sea Biosphere Reserve, which is an organization working in a part of this archipelago area for sustainable development and culture, emphasizes the current and past relationship between man and nature in the archipelago as a strength, by claiming that '[p]eople in the archipelago have lived in *harmony* with nature for centuries' (author's emphasis; Archipelago Sea Biosphere Reserve 2016a, 2016b). However, there is alarming evidence of the deteriorated condition of the natural environment in the Archipelago Sea. In particular, the addition of excess nutrients as a result of human activities is leading to a dramatic increase in the growth of plants and algae, causing oxygen depletion in the sea. This phenomenon is called eutrophication, and it is only one indicator of human pressure on nature in this area (Lindholm, 2000; Mattila, 2000).

The aim of this chapter is to problematize the idea of harmony between humanity and nature as an expression of ecological sustainability used, for instance, in cultural heritage activities. My focus is on an area where this harmony is seen as an essential part of local identities and culture, the Southwest Finland Archipelago. However, it seems that culture does not always guarantee harmony. There is thus a need for a better understanding of what elements of culture could function as a resource for ecological sustainability and what elements do not constitute strong tools for reaching sustainability (cf. Birkeland, 2014). I will focus on two main questions: first, what expressions of the relationship between humans and nature exist and are valued in the everyday culture of the Southwest Finland Archipelago? Second, what lessons can be learned from this region that could assist us in achieving ecological and cultural sustainability?

In order to answer to these questions, I will analyse two main sources: the results of an analysis by the ethnologist Nils Storå (1993) on the adaptive strategies of the people living in the Åland Archipelago in the eighteenth and nineteenth centuries together with an analysis of the current ways that people identify with their home area in the Southwest Finland Archipelago. The latter analysis is based on interviews and observations conducted in the archipelago area during the years 1997–2001.[1] The interviewees represent men and women of different ages and professional backgrounds from the inner and outer archipelago, including those with long family roots in the area and those who have settled only recently. Through qualitative ethnological research, their descriptions of both the archipelago area and the important elements of their life inside its borders were analysed (Siivonen, 2008a, see also 2010).

Cultural sustainability as safeguarded cultural heritage

In this chapter, everyday culture is not defined as cultural heritage in its totality. Rather, cultural heritage is seen as selected elements of everyday culture that have been elevated to the special status of cultural heritage, taken into use as cultural resources in society or among a group of people. When different cultural phenomena are referred to as or officially nominated to the status of cultural heritage, they are always consciously defined as such for some specific purpose. Cultural heritage is a central concept with institutional power in both cultural and regional policies around the globe. When cultural heritage is employed instrumentally in this fashion by different administrational organizations representing a state, region or group of people, the goal is to create a strong common identity for a group of people and support social welfare, community cohesion and the economic or perhaps ecological development of the targeted area (Beckman, 1998; Shore, 2000; see also Auclair and Fairclough, 2015).

Recently, discussions on the relationship between culture and sustainability have highlighted the different interpretations of what cultural sustainability means. One established use of cultural sustainability is as a support for the intrinsic value of cultural heritage as a fourth pillar of the sustainability model in relation to the widely-accepted three pillars (ecological, economic and social). However, a broader view of cultural sustainability sees cultural heritage as 'the fundamental element of sustainability which supports, interconnects and overarches the traditional three pillars [of sustainability], all of which, of course, exist in a cultural context, and all of which can be seen as cultural constructions' (Auclair and Fairclough, 2015: p. 7). Either way, the longue durée, or continuity, of heritage is often emphasized when defining the relationship between heritage and sustainability – even though change and creativity are commonly seen as important parts of heritage (Auclair and Fairclough, 2015: pp. 1–3, 7 and *passim*; see also Dessein *et al.*, 2015). The UNESCO conventions for world heritage and intangible cultural heritage are examples of regulations for the safeguarding of cultural heritage (e.g. UNESCO, 1972, 2003). Different national and regional principles for the protection of heritage follow these conventions. Along the lines of these conventions and the like, cultural sustainability is mainly understood as a continuity of cultural heritage, and then as the fourth pillar of sustainability that also supports the other pillars of sustainability as well.

One way of defining cultural sustainability is to see it as a support structure for cultural elements that posit the relationship between people and nature as harmonious (see e.g. Archipelago Sea Biosphere Reserve, 2016b; Auclair and Fairclough, 2015: pp. 6–7). In the Nordic countries, an example of this form of cultural heritage is the Vega Archipelago in Norway, nominated for the UNESCO World Heritage List in 2004, and described as reflecting 'the way fishermen/farmers have, over the past 1,500 years, maintained a sustainable living' (UNESCO, 2016a; Daugstad and Fageraas in this volume: p. 181). Another example is the Kvarken Archipelago, a UNESCO World Heritage site that is shared between Sweden and Finland, which has been labelled as of natural heritage due to the geological uniqueness of the area. The impact of the people living in the area, 'engaged in small-scale traditional farming, forestry and fishing', is estimated to be 'negligible' for the geological value of the region (UNESCO, 2016b).

Defining local cultural elements as cultural heritage to support the ecological sustainability of a certain area takes the harmony between human beings and nature as an obvious determinant of these cultural elements and these cultures. From the perspective of safeguarding cultural heritage, it is then enough to simply identify examples where cultural heritage is understood as contributing to ecological sustainability. However, it is important to investigate whether this assumption is correct, in light of empirical evidence of everyday culture and its relationship to nature and natural resources. For this chapter, I will focus on the Southwest Finland Archipelago.

The Southwest Finland Archipelago

The Southwest Finland Archipelago covers an area of approximately 10,000 km^2, containing over 22,000 islands. The area is often seen as an idyllic, semi-natural environment (Figure 1.1). The large and fertile islands in the inner archipelago are suitable for farming, while the islands in the outer archipelago are less favourable. Over the entire archipelago, 75 per cent of the islands – mostly situated within the outer archipelago – have less than one hectare of surface area,

Figure 1.1 Kustavi, Isokari in the Southwest Finland Archipelago, 2012.
Source: Katriina Siivonen.

and many are largely devoid of any vegetation (Granö *et al.*, 1999: pp. 33, 38). The area is divided into eight municipalities (Figure 1.2) and contains a population of around 17,000 inhabitants (Tilastokeskus, 2005: pp. 92–94; Sisäasiainministeriö, 2007: pp. 56–57).

The living conditions in this archipelago have changed as a result of modernization processes in the twentieth century. Earlier sources of livelihood, mainly agriculture including animal husbandry, fishing, hunting and rural shipping, are no longer as profitable and have been replaced by other activities such as the service industries. The area also features some industry that is partly rooted in the seventeenth century. Nevertheless, livelihoods associated with primary production continued to play an important part in the local economy even during the era of modernization (Lukala, 1986: pp. 228–232; Andersson, 1998). During the twentieth century, the population fell steadily, especially in the outer archipelago, where fishing had been one of the dominant livelihoods. However, since the 1970s, the population has remained relatively stable (Vainio, 1981: p. 33; Bergbom and Bergbom, 2005: pp. 57–61).

Ecological adaptation in the archipelago

The ethnologist Nils Storå (1993) conducted his research in the Åland Archipelago, which forms a geographical continuum with the Southwest Finland Archipelago (see the location of the Åland Archipelago in Figure 1.2). The

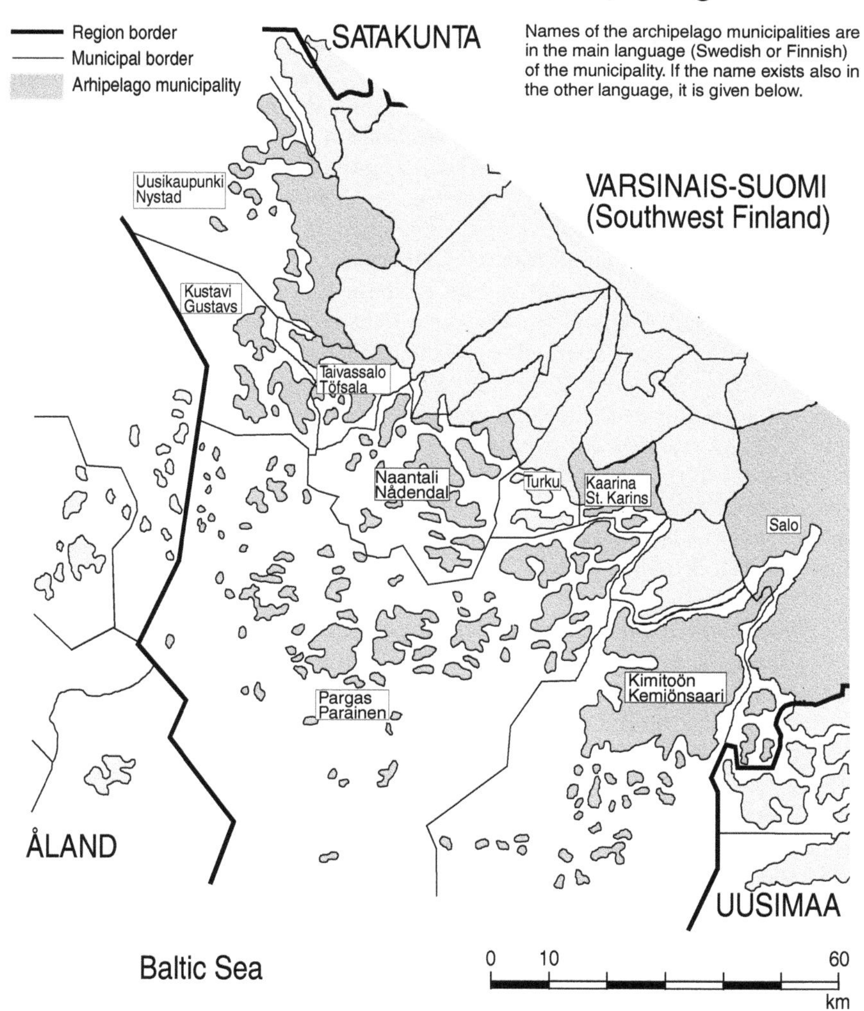

Figure 1.2 Southwest Finland Archipelago.

living conditions in these areas are and have always been similar from an ecological point of view, and Storå's analysis of the adaptive ecological dynamics in the Åland Archipelago is useful here for analysing the Southwest Finland Archipelago.

In his research, Storå analysed the adaptive strategies of the people who lived in the Åland Archipelago in the eighteenth, nineteenth and the beginning of the twentieth century in order to explore the relationship between humans and their environment. These strategies are expressed in multiple everyday living practices and, for instance, when communicating with children as part of their socialization process. In Storå's study, ecological adaptation was understood as a complex combination of ecological, cultural (including technology), demographic, social, legal and administrative aspects of the livelihood activities in the area. The culture of this area in the eighteenth and nineteenth centuries was shaped by a combination of local self-sufficiency and trade in both local and international markets (for necessities such as grain and salt, as well as iron used in building ships). As culture in this kind of ethnological meaning is located within a complex socio-ecological system, changes in one of these aspects in local culture often has implications for other parts of the system (Storå, 1993). As a consequence of this, the culture in these two neighbouring archipelago areas – the Åland Archipelago and the Southwest Finland Archipelago – has always been in a glocal, interactive process of change.

According to Storå, this local culture contains strongly embedded knowledge about nature, both as a living condition and resource, yet he also identifies a cultural tendency towards the overuse of natural resources in the archipelago in several ways. First, he argues that the human impact on the environment has been so significant that 'there was already a 'man-made' environment dominating the physical landscape' by the nineteenth century. Second, by referring to Mead and Jaatinen he notes that

> [e]ven early periods of population pressure could easily have led to overexploitation and strong impacts on the limited distribution of land. There already seems to have been a population pressure on land and natural resources by the end of the Middle Ages.
>
> (Storå, 1993: pp. 189, 225–226; ref. Mead and Jaatinen, 1975: p. 75)

The overuse of wood, pasture land and fish that occurred at the beginning of the twentieth century resulted in a need to limit pasture and logging, as well as hunting in the area (Lappalainen, 2004: p. 13). During the twentieth century, the overuse of natural resources was evident as fertilizers became increasingly necessary for agriculture, and the area also began featuring the cultivation of fish (one source of the current eutrophication of the Baltic Sea) to restore the area's diminished fish resources (Storå, 1993: pp. 189, 223; Hammer, 2000; Mattila, 2000; Vuorinen, 2000). Even since the number of inhabitants has decreased, human pressure on the environment continues to be significant, partly due to rising living standards.

The philosopher Ilkka Niiniluoto argues that the beginning of agriculture changed human beings from a creature that was at the mercy of nature to a creature that is consciously reworking, cultivating and culturalizing their own living environments (Niiniluoto, 2015: pp. 171–172). The period of cultivation in the Southwest Finland Archipelago began in the prehistoric era, even though fishing, hunting and foraging have maintained their popularity during the centuries – especially in the outer archipelago. Currently, the area's most extensive branch of industry is the service sector (Andersson, 1998), which includes tourism based on an idyllic image of an archipelago culture where humans live in harmony with nature (Siivonen, 2008a: pp. 299–305). This aims to incorporate the archipelago into a mobile and resource-hungry world, where more and more people, material resources and ideas move globally, faster than ever before. Cultural heritage is then used as a resource for promoting tourism. In particular, the romanticized view of nature and the cultural harmony with nature, which are defined by the spirit of eighteenth and nineteenth century Romanticism, are used as a core resource in tourism (Siivonen, 2008a; Niiniluoto 2015: p. 171). To achieve this goal, there is a need to tell a story about archipelago culture as an example of a form of culture that is in harmony with the natural world.

Overall, it is evident that the human population in the archipelago that is part of this socio-ecological system has not, and, in previous centuries, has never consciously lived in an ecologically sustainable manner. Ecological sustainability is defined here as the use of natural resources in a way that does not deplete the resources available for future generations (United Nations, 1987). Human life in the archipelago has always included qualities that can contribute to the overuse of natural resources, placing increasing pressure on the natural system. Currently, it can even be argued that this pressure has extended beyond the immediate environment to regional and global levels, in particular through the use of fertilizers that contribute to both global warming and the eutrophication of the Baltic Sea. The safeguarding of tangible and intangible cultural heritage with the goal of maintaining harmony between humans and nature in the archipelago thus does not represent a comprehensive solution for ecological sustainability.

According to the understanding above, cultural sustainability that is based on cultural heritage as a cultural continuity of different tangible and intangible cultural elements relies on a too-narrow interpretation of culture and leaves out relevant aspects of the relationship between human beings and their cultural and natural environments. Culture contains values, practices and meanings that can be in harmony with nature, as well as those that can be in conflict with nature – and this becomes highly evident when we analyse cultural and economic activities within a specific socio-ecological area. An ecologically sustainable approach would demand some cultural changes even in the areas where people have a strong relationship with their natural environment, such as in the Southwest Finland Archipelago.

Identification with current archipelago nature

My analysis of the current relationship between humans and nature in the Southwest Finland Archipelago utilizes the results of a study that I conducted in the Southwest Finland Archipelago during 1997–2001, concerning the ways that locals identified with the archipelago. The basis for these identifications is in the local understanding of the archipelago, or rather the different individual archipelagos within the archipelago. There are several different ways in which both the archipelago and its borders, as well as individual experiences of the archipelagos, take shape during everyday life in the archipelago (Siivonen, 2008a). This forms the basic defining factor for the human-nature relationship in the archipelago.

Overall, the different understandings of the local people in the archipelago on what areas should be identified as belonging to the archipelago can be defined as a continuum. In its largest sense, this continuum covers almost every island in the surrounding sea, from the large islands in the inner archipelago to the small islands in the outer archipelago. In this kind of understanding, the connection to the sea from the islands is the only necessary defining element for the archipelago. According to the strictest definition, the archipelago only includes those islands that can be reached with one's own boat or perhaps by a public ferry, but not by bridge. There the inner archipelago contains many bridges from the islands to the mainland, and these islands are commonly not included as part of the archipelago (Siivonen, 2008a).

In southwest Finland, the archipelago features many temporary residents. People spend part of the year, mainly the summertime, in these residencies, while holding their permanent residencies elsewhere in another municipality or town. In the strictest terms, to be classified as part of the archipelago by some of the local people, the area should be occupied by permanent residents who have family roots within the area. In addition, they should also be able to survive in the archipelago with the help of their own, hard work, as the archipelago is described as being a very demanding environment. All told, according to these criteria, for some people the outer archipelago is symbolically a more proper archipelago than the inner archipelago. At the same time, the archipelago in its largest sense – including the islands with a bridge connection to the mainland – constitutes a proper archipelago for others (Siivonen, 2008a).

Within this continuum of different understandings of the archipelago, there are several smaller, more individual archipelagos. Even the same person can define them in varying ways in different situations. Usually, the definition of an individual's own archipelago has been outlined with its familiar areas that are related to everyday activities, thoroughfares and waterways, while other areas in the archipelago may remain unfamiliar. These ideas about the archipelago continuously change, and especially a new bridge or ferry connection can cause a reappraisal of these definitions, sometimes even concerning what the very nature of a proper symbolic archipelago is (Siivonen, 2008a).

Many of the people who live in the Archipelago use their own boats or common ferries every day for their personal trips. Even though this happens on a daily basis, the exposure to the surrounding nature and the sea does not become an invisible and habitual part of life, but leads to a strong and conscious appreciation of the natural beauty of the archipelago. However, nature and the sea contain more than just beautiful elements. Many people also develop a conscious knowledge of the violent, temperamental and powerful nature of the sea. This leads to a perception that island life should not be taken for granted but that it is a privilege, and that survival requires the application of one's own skills and knowledge. Thus, it is common to experience a strong commitment to nature and the sea (Siivonen, 2008a).

The continuously changing nature of the environment is a major source of satisfaction for the inhabitants of the archipelago – whether seen from the kitchen window or from a fishing boat in the early hours of the morning, as the following quote from an interview with a professional, full-time fisherwoman suggests:

> The sea air in particular is something that I can't imagine being any greater, when spring comes, the ice breaks up and ... You see, when you get up with the sun and then go to your perch-pike nets, and the birds are singing and it's quite calm and you can be alone and in peace and ... That is what is most essential of all. Of course, sometimes the weather is bad. There're the gusts of wind and everything, but ... I don't know, I suppose people who aren't interested in fishing ... they would never do it, the weather is so bad sometimes, there's the weak ice and storms and everything. But, you see, you can actually do it, when you have an interest in doing it. But you must have this interest. I was a very small girl the first time I went, four or five years old, so.
>
> (TYKL/SPA/435; Siivonen, 2008a)

Nature is an organic part of everyday life in every sense – as a source of joy, fear and challenge. It is a necessary living condition that is familiar from childhood.

Many interviewees emphasized their ability to survive even in a harsh environment. One example of this is the ability to cross the ice-covered sea during the wintertime. It sometimes happens that people accidently fall through ice when it is too thin to support their weight, but some are also able to rescue themselves. This is not an easy task in the cold, deep water with the ice breaking around the hole. Such events provide tangible reminders of the power of nature and the sea. The stories that the people tell about them are symbolic expressions of the skills needed to survive in the archipelago areas, where communication is more often dependent on the capricious state of nature. These skills – and similar skills as well – become part of local archipelago identities, as the following quote suggests:

> KS: Aha, so this is a part of island life?
>
> [...]
>
> I: Yes, it is, this was one experience. The first time I fell through the ice with a sledge happened during my secondary school days one Wednesday afternoon, when we went home – we always went home on Wednesdays during the wintertime – and it so happened that we fell in with our sledges, the neighbour's girl and I. That was the first time that it happened to me.
>
> (TYKL/SPA/403; Siivonen, 2008a)

The transportation options in the area are so unreliable that some decades ago, during the childhood of this interviewee, pupils had special weekday accommodations near the school, and they went home on the weekends and, as in this case, every Wednesday. The experience of falling through the ice was important for the interviewee, who could clearly recall several details of his experience even in his adult days.

In everyday archipelago culture, nature and the sea are part of the everyday life of all inhabitants, tying people strongly to their own archipelago area. Identification with the archipelago is described through practices related to nature, but also as explicit discussions about their personal relationships with nature. Practices function as tacit knowledge, which, as an embodied form of knowledge, is sometimes difficult to describe in words. In some contexts, these practices and experiences become conscious identity symbols, such as the case of falling through the ice in the wintertime. These kinds of experiences – which are almost exclusive to year-round inhabitants – allow the construction of a very different relationship to the archipelago than what summer visitors are able to develop (Siivonen, 2008a).

The three most important elements of these archipelago identities are: the beautiful but destructive powers of nature and the sea; the freedom to work and define one's own way of life on the islands and in their own archipelago; and the skills and knowledge learned on the islands with which the inhabitants are able to best the administrative and literal knowledge of outsiders, including the knowledge of environmental authorities. Unlike outside human authorities, nature and the sea are perceived as strong controlling factors of the actions and identities of the people living in the archipelago and are accepted as authorities with a power over those who live and move there (Siivonen, 2008a).

However, sometimes these current everyday practices in the archipelago contain elements that are not in harmony with nature, i.e. when the islanders' perception of their close relationship with nature does not match reality. People find themselves in situations where survival is dependent not on a harmonious relationship with nature, but rather taking measures that are contradictory to this ideal. For example, when the economy of a family is dependent on fish farming (a known cause of eutrophication in the Baltic Sea), or when measures are taken against protected seal populations when they break expensive fishing tackles (Siivonen, 2008a).

The tacit knowledge described above – daily variations in routines, familiar elements in one's own surroundings, and the changing practices of communities with both positive and negative outcomes – can be better understood through the concept of tangible and intangible traditions than 'cultural heritage'. Traditions are continuously changing cultural elements and practices that are transferred from one individual to another through interaction (Bringéus, 1981). They are not necessarily conscious cultural elements, nor are they cultural strategies that are deployed deliberately in order to create a common identity by using cultural heritage. Traditions can function as part of an everyday strategy that local people use to survive in the archipelago, but cultural heritage that is utilized as a strategic resource for regional or cultural policy does not easily catch the core of this everyday strategy. Cultural heritage consists of selected elements of traditions that have become 'cultural heritage' by virtue of being identified and labelled as such. However, focusing on defined cultural heritage means that the significance of *change* within cultural traditions can be lost as the focus falls on preserving past cultural elements rather than preserving the interactive and creative process of culture (also see Burton in this volume: p. 137). Identities are a part of this process, and human-nature relations, materialized in human perceptions, knowledge and practices, are an important element of identities. Defining (or redefining) cultural identities is an act that can only be performed by the residents of the archipelago and, indeed, it is their will to determine how their tangible and intangible cultural environments change.

The uncultivated sea

The position of everyday practices, i.e. intangible and tangible traditions in the relationship between humans and nature, can be analysed with help of Philippe Boudes' concepts of cultivation and culturalization (following the ideas of George Simmel). Even though in cultivation, yield is a product of human activities, it is in part shaped by nature, and thus outside the direct control of culture and traditions. When people produce culturalized products, they use natural resources, but the form of the product is shaped according to cultural traditions (Boudes, 2011; ref. Simmel, 1988).

In archipelago traditions, agriculture is cultivation in its proper sense, where the products of agriculture are shaped as much by the natural environment as by human activity. For fishing, hunting and foraging – such as picking berries or mushrooms – nature plays an even more critical role in determining the outcome. Tangible and intangible cultural heritage generated by these traditional activities is produced and used to support other livelihoods, in particular such services as tourism. However, heritage is a culturalized product and, unlike the other forms of production in the archipelago, the 'yield' from heritage is not directly dependent on or shaped by natural forces. Instead, it is a cultural construction, within which nature can be redefined depending on the needs of the person involved. Following the thoughts of Niiniluoto (2015), in all of these instances, however, humans are creatures who more or less rework their own living environments. These products do not have a position of authority over human beings, like the sea has in the archipelago identities. In archipelago traditions, the relationship between humans and the sea can be defined as a relationship between culture and an uncultivated and unculturalized natural element, with the sea being accepted as having power over human beings.

The way in which the human-nature interface can best be understood is as part of the interactive, changing process of traditions described as the interactive and iterative process of 'anthroposemiosis' (Deely, 1994; Siivonen, 2008a: pp. 49–69, see also 2008b). This can be seen as an addition to Charles S. Peirce's theory of semiotics and semiosis, which proposes that our understanding of the world is based entirely on signs (Peirce, [1868] 1992). A sign is comprised of three interrelated elements: the interpretant, representamen and object (CP: 1.347;[2] Bergman, 2004: pp. 176–177). In the human context, an interpretant is a sign in the mind of a human being, to which one combines first a representamen (a material or immaterial manifestation of the sign outside of the human mind) and then the object of the sign (CP: 2.228, 2.274–2.302).

With the sign, the human being then remoulds their understanding of the world, and the world thus becomes a part of their understanding, i.e. a part of a new interpretant in their mind. In the presentations of signs, interpretants are used in the formulation of representamens, and interpreted with help of a new interpretant. Hence, interpretants and signs form chains during the process of presentations and the interpretations of signs. These chains of signs are called semiosis (Deely, 1994: pp. 22–49, 94–96; CP: 7.536, 7.587).

John Deely writes about semiosis as a universal network of which one part is an interactive network between human beings and their surroundings. Deely calls this 'anthroposemiosis' (Deely, 1994: pp. 22–31). Overall, anthroposemiosis is the constantly-changing relationship between human beings and their surroundings, through which these surroundings become a part of human understanding. The 'anthroposemiotic network' consists of the natural and human (physical) worlds, as well as concepts, thoughts and stories that people exchange with each other. When we combine Peirce's and Deely's ideas of semiosis with Boudes' and Simmel's cultivation and culturalization, the end result suggests that natural phenomena (e.g. resources) become a part of anthroposemiosis through the process of cultivation and culturalization. According to this view, in the human-nature relationship, nature in its cultivated and culturalizated form is part of the signs in the human mind. These signs can, in practice, be perceptions, interpretations based on different meanings and values, as well as the practices of human beings in relation to nature. However, semiosis is not a part of anthroposemiosis, and the area outside of anthroposemiosis remains a part of semiosis: nature in its uncultivated and unculturalized form.

In the archipelago, the sea and surrounding nature are not completely integrated through the process of anthroposemiosis. In archipelago identities and culture, an undefined part of the sea is unknowable and impossible to control with cultivation and culturalization, but its presence as such is still known. The sea is explicitly part of a larger unit, semiosis, which covers the whole physical and symbolic world, and includes anthroposemiosis. It is not only human beings who communicate in the world. Other living creatures also communicate with one another, with human beings and with the tangible and intangible, cultivated and culturalized, as well as uncultivated and unculturalized world. The communication of human beings is not separate to the communication of other species or inorganic nature; rather, they are tightly intertwined (Deely, 1994: pp. 6, 24, 41 and *passim*).

Sustainable development as conscious changes in the process of traditions

In his analysis of adaptive ecological strategies in the Åland Archipelago, Nils Storå highlights the conscious cultural practices with which people cultivated and culturalized their living environment by employing technology in their everyday practices. He did not, however, make any particular mention of the unknowableness of nature as a recognized part of ecological strategies. Current societal activities that aim to promote sustainable development focus on strategic practices that are culturalized, i.e. planned and formed by human beings (see Huutoniemi, 2014). These practices, activities and strategic understandings neither necessarily nor explicitly include the understanding of such parts of semiosis that are not cultivated or culturalized. Thus, they tend to look only at the impact that humans have on nature, and not nature as a power outside of human impact.

As this analysis of the Southwest Finland Archipelago has shown, even if daily practices include an understanding of the power and unpredictability of nature, the overuse of natural resources is still possible and even likely due to the process of anthroposemiosis. This process leads people to take a conscious risk and begin playing a dangerous game with nature and the sea while being fully aware of the authoritarian power of nature and the fragility of human life.

As noted earlier, to achieve sustainable development from a cultural perspective, we need to move beyond the instrumental use of cultural heritage. One particular concern is that equating cultural heritage with cultural sustainability is an act that simultaneously both fixes and limits what is viewed as culture – preventing it from adapting to changing circumstances. This narrow definition is likely to be too limited to ensure ecological sustainability. In particular, if the sustainability of culture is seen only as the protection of the continuity of cultural heritage, there is a risk of stagnation of a living culture and ultimately the development of something that, whilst once ensuring sustainability, simply ceases to do so. Cultural change is necessary to ensure both cultural and ecological sustainability.

Therefore, it can also be argued that culture should not be seen as a dimension of sustainability, but rather as a platform for all dimensions of sustainability. This platform is a process that involves the development of traditions, or anthroposemiosis, which, in turn, is part of the process of semiosis. It forms the basis for all human activities; economic activities, social structures, humanity's relationship with nature, and the instrumental use of cultural heritage are all defined and redefined through this process.

To better reach ecological sustainability, the relationship between humanity and nature needs to be uniformly redefined. We need cultural change to reach ecological sustainability, and thus we need changing and creative traditions. We cannot stop the inevitable change of culture or the process of anthroposemiosis. But the direction of change everywhere, especially in our technologized world, is not necessarily towards a more ecologically sustainable world. There are tendencies towards the overuse of natural resources, even in areas where human beings have a strong commitment to nature. What we must do is guide this change, and apply the understanding that nature exerts power over human systems to all aspects of our future development.

Notes

1 These interviews are archived with an archive code (TYKL/SPA/number of the interview) in the Archives of the School of History, Culture and Arts Studies, the Ethnology Archives, University of Turku, Turku, Finland. The archive code is used as reference to these interviews and they are found in the list of references by the archive code.
2 Following the accepted practice, the *Collected Papers of Charles S. Peirce* (CP) is referred to by volume and paragraph numbers, separated by a full-stop e.g. 1.347. In the list of references volumes are given in Roman numerals.

References

Andersson, K. (1998) *Näringsutveckling i sydvästra Finlands skärgård, Tolv kommuner i ljuset av offentlig statistik.* Rapporter och diskussionsinlägg 4/98. Svenska social- och kommunalhögskolan vid Helsingfors universitet, Helsinki.

Archipelago Sea Biosphere Reserve. (2016a) *What is a biosphere reserve?* www.skargardshavetsbiosfaromrade.fi/general-information/what-is-a-biosphere-reserve-2/?lang=en (Accessed 2 October 2016).

Archipelago Sea Biosphere Reserve. (2016b) *Man and nature.* www.skargardshavetsbiosfaromrade.fi/man-and-nature-2/?lang=en (Accessed 2 October 2016).

Auclair, E. and Fairclough, G. (2015) Living between past and future. An introduction to heritage and cultural sustainability. In: E. Auclair and G. Fairclough (eds) *Theory and Practice in Heritage and Sustainability. Between Past and Future.* Routledge, London and New York:1–22.

Beckman, S. (1998) Vad vill staten med kulturarvet? In: A. Alzén and J. Hedrén (eds) *Kulturarvets natur.* Brutus Östlings Bokförlag Symposion, Stockholm and Stenhag.

Bergbom, G. and Bergbom, K. (2005) Befolkningsförändringar och ägoförhållanden på utskären i Skärgårdshavet 1954–2004. *Skärgård. Tidskrift utgiven av Skärgårdsinstitutet vid Åbo Akademi* 1:57–67.

Bergman, M. (2004) *Fields of Signification. Explorations in Charles S. Peirce's Theory of Signs.* Philosophical Studies from the University of Helsinki 6. University of Helsinki, Department of Philosophy, Helsinki.

Birkeland, I. (2014) *Kulturelle hjørnsteiner. Teoretiske og didaktiske perspektiver på klimaomstilling.* Cappelen Damm Akademisk, Oslo.

Boccardi, G. and Duvelle, C. (2013) *UNESCO Background Note on Introducing Cultural Heritage into the Sustainable Development Agenda.* UNESCO – April 2013, Sessions 3A and 3A-a. www.unesco.org/new/en/culture/themes/culture-and-development/hangzhou-congress/introducing-cultural-heritage-into-the-sustainable-development-agenda/ (Accessed 2 October 2016).

Boudes, P. (2011) La nature au secours de la culture? Lecture simmelienne de la végétalisations des villes et de leurs fonctions. *Revue d'Allemangne et des Payes de langue allemande* 43(1):131–146.

Bringéus, N-A. (1981) *Människan som Kulturvarelse.* LiberLäromedel, Lund, Sweden.

CP: See Peirce, C. S. [1931–1935, 1958] 1994.

Deely, J. (1994) *The Human Use of Signs or Elements of Anthroposemiosis.* Rowman & Littlefield Publishers Inc., Lanham, Maryland, United States and London.

Dessein, J., Soini, K., Fairclough, G. and Horlings, L. (eds) (2015) *Culture in, for and as Sustainable Development. Conclusions from the COST Action IS1007 Investigating Cultural Sustainability.* University of Jyväskylä, Jyväskylä, Finland.

Granö, O., Roto, M. and Laurila, L. (1999) *Environment and Land Use in the Shore Zone of the Coast of Finland*. Publicationes Instituti Geographici Universitas Turkuensis N:o 160. University of Turku, Turku, Finland.

Hammer, M. (2000) Fiske och fiskodling i skärgården från ett ekosystemperspektiv. In: M. von Numers (ed.) *Skärgårdsmiljöer – nuläge, problem och möjligheter*. Nordiska ministerrådets skärgårdssamarbete, Stockholm.

Huutoniemi, K. (2014) Introduction. Sustainability, transcisciplinarity and the complexity of knowing. In: K. Huutoniemi and P. Tapio (eds) *Transdiciplinary Sustainability Studies. A Heuristic Approach*. Routledge, New York.

Lappalainen, M. (2004) *Skärgårdshavets nationalpark. En jungfrudans av öar*. Föreningen Konstsamfundets publikationsserie XX. Söderströms and Konstsamfundet, Helsinki.

Lindholm, T. (2000) Algblomningar och andra algproblem. In: M. von Numers (ed.) *Skärgårdsmiljöer – nuläge, problem och möjligheter*. Nordiska ministerrådets skärgårdssamarbete, Stockholm.

Lukala, M. (1986) *Dalsbruk 1686–1986*. Ovako, Dalsbruk, Finland.

Mattila, J. (2000) Eutrofiering i skärgården. In: M. von Numers (ed.) *Skärgårdsmiljöer – nuläge, problem och möjligheter*. Nordiska ministerrådets skärgårdssamarbete, Stockholm.

Mead, W. R. and Jaatinen, S. H. (1975) *The Åland Islands*. David & Charles, Newton Abbot, United Kingdom.

Niiniluoto, I. (2015) *Hyvän elämän filosofiaa*. Suomalaisen Kirjallisuuden Seura, Helsinki.

Peirce, C. S. ([1868]1992) On a new list of categories. In: N. Houser and C. Kloesel (eds) *The Essential Peirce. Selected Philosophical Writings. Vol. 1 (1867–1893)*. Indiana University Press, Bloomington, United States and Indianapolis, United States.

Peirce, C. S. ([1931–1935, 1958]1994) *The Collected Papers of Charles Sanders Peirce*. In: J. Deely (ed.) The electronic edition reproducing C. Hartshorne and P. Weiss (eds) Vols. I–VI, Harvard University Press, Cambridge, United States, and A. W. Burks (ed.) Vols. VII–VIII, Harvard University Press, Cambridge, United States.

Shore, C. (2000) *Building Europe. The Cultural Politics of European Integration*. Routledge, London and New York.

Siivonen, K. (2008a) *Saaristoidentiteetit merkkien virtoina. Varsinaissuomalainen arki ja aluekehitystyö globalisaation murroksessa*. Kansatieteellinen Arkisto 51. Suomen Muinaismuistoyhdistys, Helsinki.

Siivonen, K. (2008b) Culture is basically creative. What is the relationship between a culture as a whole, and heterogeneous cultural processes with individual traits, change, variation and creativity? In: M. Mäenpää and T. Rajanti (eds) *Creative Futures Conference Proceedings 10.-11. October 2007 in Pori, Finland*. Taideteollisen korkeakoulun julkaisu C 6. University of Art and Design, Pori School of Art and Media, Pori, Finland.

Siivonen, K. (2010) Local culture as a resource in regional development in the Southwest-Finland archipelago. *Journal of Ethnology and Folkloristics* 3(2):47–63.

Simmel, G. (1988) *La Tragédie de la Culture et Autre Essais*. Rivage, Paris.

Sisäasiainministeriö. (2007) *Saaristo-ohjelma 2007–2010, Saaret, meri, järvet, joet ja rantavyöhyke aluekehitystekijöinä*. Sisäasiainministeriö, Saaristoasiain neuvottelukunta, Helsinki.

Storå, N. (1993) Adaptive dynamics and island life. In: J. Hackman (ed.) *Resurser, strategier, miljöer. Etnologiska uppsatser av Nils Storå Utgivna den 29 maj 1993*. Åbo Akademi, Åbo, Finland.

Tilastokeskus. (2005) *Suomen tilastollinen vuosikirja. 100. vuosikerta (uusi sarja)*. Tilastokeskus, Helsinki.

TYKL/SPA/395–468 – *Katriina Siivonen's interviews and fieldwork material for her doctoral thesis*. TYKL – Archives of the School of History, Culture and Arts Studies, the Ethnology Archives, University of Turku, Turku, Finland.

UNESCO. (1972) *Convention Concerning the Protection of the World Cultural and Natural Heritage*. UNESCO, Paris.

UNESCO. (2003) *Convention for the Safeguarding of the Intangible Cultural Heritage*. UNESCO, Paris.

UNESCO. (2016a) *Vegaøyan – The Vega Archipelago*. http://whc.unesco.org/en/list/1143 (Accessed 13 March 2016).

UNESCO. (2016b) *High Coast/Kvarken Archipelago*. http://whc.unesco.org/en/list/898 (Accessed 13 March 2016).

United Nations. (1987) *Report of the World Commission on Environment and Development: Our Common Future*. United Nations, New York.

Vainio, J. (1981) *Flyttningsrörelse och avfolkning i syvästra Finlands skärgård (Korpo, Rimito och Merimasku 1950–1974)*. Turun yliopiston maantieteen laitoksen julkaisuja N:o 92. Turun yliopisto, maantieteen laitos, Turku, Finland.

Vuorinen, I. (2000) Fiskodlingen – en inkomstkälla och miljöhot. In: M. von Numers (ed.) *Skärgårdsmiljöer – nuläge, problem och möjligheter*. Nordiska ministerrådets skärgårdssamarbete, Stockholm.

2 Cultivating cultural sustainability in farming practices

Katriina Soini and Suvi Huttunen

Introduction

> Farming's essence is true to soil. Proper farming might be said to make concrete what is latent in humanity's dependence upon the provisions for human's sustenance. Farming is the activity that locates the human species most surely in the planetary ecosystem. It is on farming that we depend for food and in farming that what we take from the earth is returned to it.
>
> (Thompson, 1995: p. 3)

The excerpt above nicely captures the human-nature interface in agriculture and links it to sustainability: agriculture is dependent on natural resources, most notably soil and natural processes such as photosynthesis and procreation, but also on human activities, ploughing, seeding, harvesting and breeding. Consequently, the essence of agriculture may be considered as a co-production of 'Man' and 'Nature' (van der Ploeg, 2003). This co-production results in different tangible forms of culture, such as food products, landscapes and animal breeds (see Brites and Mendes Moreira this volume: p. 66). It also results in forms of culture that are intangible, like sensual, bodily and even religious experiences, aesthetics and learning. Agricultural practices shape both the farming environment and the farmers' values and appreciations through mutual adaptations. In that way, agriculture is essentially a mixture of different components of culture such as worldviews, materials and symbols, institutions, and dynamic spatial and temporal processes inherently connected with nature.

The etymology of the word culture suggests a connection between agriculture, culture and nature (Knobloch, 1996). 'Culture' is derived from the Latin word 'cultura' (noun) meaning 'cultivation, agriculture', and 'colere' (verb) meaning 'to tend, guard, cultivate, till' (Online Etymological Dictionary, 2017). However, the noun 'cultura' is only one out of two derrivations of the Latin verb. The other is 'cultus' (Fink, 1988 in Oltedal *et al.*, 2004). While 'cultura' is tied to the cultivation of land, 'cultus' is the worship of divinity. The two forms of culture were connected in earlier times as the cultivation of both the soil and divinity were life-giving, with no clear distinction between nature and culture (ibid.). Since then agriculture has, in many ways, been separated from natural processes, e.g. through various technological means, detaching nature and culture (Renting and van der Ploeg, 2001; see Hreinsson, this volume: p. 79).

Recently, we have seen new attempts at defining the challenging nature, role and meaning of culture in relation to sustainability (Throsby, 2008; Soini and Birkeland, 2014). Inspired, on one hand, by the co-productive character of agriculture and, on the other by the etymology of 'culture', we explore in this chapter how sustainable agriculture can provide insights for a deeper and more profound understanding of culture in sustainability. Consequently, we seek to explore how the nature-culture relationship can be better understood through farming, in order to inform the conceptual understanding of culture in sustainability. In particular, this involves addressing the questions: what should sustain in culture? What does culturally sustainable development entail?

The chapter is based on research conducted by the authors, which has concerned broadly Finnish farmers' values and attitudes to different aspects of sustainable agriculture as well as their actual farming practices in different contexts: biodiversity at genetic, species and landscape levels, fertilization and manure management and changes in cultivation practices (see Vuorio *et al.*, 2005; Soini, 2007; Soini and Aakkula, 2007; Takamaa and Soini, 2007; Soini *et al.*, 2012; Huttunen, 2015; Huttunen and Oosterveer, 2017; Huttunen and Peltomaa, 2016). The studies are based on broad empirical material in the form of quantitative surveys including open-ended questions and qualitative interviews of Finnish farmers, observations at farm- and landscape-levels, workshop discussions and mapping methods. The oldest datasets were collected in 2003 and the most recent are from 2014.

We combined a social practice theory (Reckwitz, 2002; Shove *et al.*, 2012) with a framework of culture and sustainability (Soini and Birkland, 2014; Soini and Dessein, 2016) which enabled us to understand what farmers wanted to sustain on their farms and how this was put into practice. As a result, we identified five key dimensions; diversity, fertility, continuity, appreciation and rationalization, which we considered central for the farmers. In the next section, we briefly discuss and define our approach to sustainable agriculture and agricultural practices. In the section thereafter, we introduce what we have identified from our empirical material and in the final section we explore our findings in respect to the existing definitions and frameworks of cultural sustainability.

Sustainable agricultural practices in cultural framework

Agriculture as a social practice

Social practice theory is commonly known as a framework for describing how individuals shape and are shaped by the culture in which they live, and in this way, aims at articulating ways in which identity and individual agency rely on and produce cultural forms. Following Reckwitz (2002: p. 249) a practice can be defined as 'a routinized type of behavior which consists of several elements, interconnected to one other', including most essentially 'forms of bodily activities, forms of mental activities, "things" and their use'. Hence, from the practice perspective agriculture becomes a set of interconnected practices: seeding, fertilization, feeding animals, maintaining fences and buildings and so on, constituting the way agriculture is understood and enacted. This theory is most often applied in consumption research, but there are also some examples of agri-environmental studies utilizing the framework (Huttunen and Oosterveer, 2017; de Kromm, 2015).

In this chapter, we define agricultural practices following Shove *et al.* (2012), who conceptualize practices as constituted of three interlinked elements: material, competence and meaning. The material element refers to physical objects related to farming in the natural environment (such as soil, water and wildlife), but also to the tools, machines and animals used in agricultural practices, as well as the material inputs (seeds and fertilizers) and outputs (harvest, other biomass) related to farming. Competence refers to the skills and know-how of farmers gained through education, experience or tacit knowledge transferred within the farming community. Many skills are mobilized during the range of procedures which constitute the actual farming practices, guiding the farmers on what, when and how to farm. Meanings refers to symbols, norms, values and collective conventions that govern actions. In the case of agriculture there are many unwritten social conventions associated with production actions that are important for cultural recognition as 'a good farmer' (Silvasti, 2003; Burton, 2004; Stock, 2007; Sutherland, 2013; Huttunen and Peltomaa, 2016).

Farming entails several interconnected practices and as such it can be regarded as a bundle of practices (Shove *et al.*, 2012) comprising, for example, seeding, feeding, breeding, ploughing, harvesting and fertilizing – all of which can be assessed as social practices (see Burton, 2004). Hence, we contend that agricultural practices are constituted by the three elements mentioned above. The elements are interconnected and form the general understanding of the practice as an entity, a culturally shared idea of what practice is. For example, fertilization is generally understood as including fertilizers and applying them to fields in order to enhance the growth of the plants. When the practice is performed, these elements are concretely brought together and the practice renewed by re-establishing the linkages between the elements. The same culturally shared general practice can be performed in varying ways depending on the details of the elements and ways of connecting them (Huttunen and Oosterveer, 2017). Sustainable agricultural practices involve somewhat different meanings, materials and competences compared with conventional intensive farming practices.

Sustainable agricultural practices

Given the multidimensionality and vagueness of the concept of sustainability, 'sustainable agriculture' can have several meanings. It has been seen, for example, as an end-goal: 'a normative framework for operationalizing desirable future end-states' (Renting *et al.*, 2009); a process of transforming agriculture based on sustainability principles, a process for learning (Pretty, 1995); and as a movement that balances concerns of environmental soundness, economic viability and social justice (Allen *et al.*, 1991). There is a vast amount of scientific literature that discusses 'sustainable' and 'unsustainable' agriculture, and a number of indicators have been developed to measure agricultural sustainability. Although the main focus of sustainable agriculture is on ecological sustainability, economic and social, cultural or ethical dimensions, as well as the interconnectedness of these dimensions, have also been recognized.

As with scientists studying agricultural sustainability, farmers determine the sustainability of their agricultural practices in relation to their everyday work environment. Farmers' perceptions of sustainable agriculture, which are rooted in the localized, context-specific nature of farmers' knowledge systems (see e.g. Kloppenburg, 1991), may differ from scientific understandings of sustainable agriculture. The agricultural practices also vary very much from place to place and time to time – from highly industrial forms to traditional and subsistence farming, reflecting different objectives, target levels (from subsistence farming to market oriented) and technologies. Obviously, the conditions for sustainability vary greatly between the scales of production. One should be careful not to make any generalizations or justifications about the sustainability of the practices based, for example, on the size of the farm, the way of farming (organic versus techno-chemical) or product end-users (subsistence versus market-oriented). Yet, based on the literature and empirical findings we assume that there exists a virtue of farming reflecting certain values linked to sustainability. These values, however, might be distinct from the actual performed farming practices that are shaped by materials, competences and other meanings provided by the agricultural policies, markets and the resources (land, economic resources) available to the individual farmers.

Sustainable culture – cultural sustainability

Culture has recently been introduced as an explicit fourth pillar or dimension of sustainability in parallel with the ecological, social and economic pillars (Hawkes, 2001; Throsby, 2008; Soini and Birkeland, 2014; Soini and Dessein, 2016; UNESCO, 2013). Yet, cultural sustainability is a broad discourse with many different perspectives. In a comprehensive review paper by Soini and Birkeland (2014) the authors discerned seven different storylines, or meanings attached to the concept of cultural sustainability, namely; heritage, cultural vitality, economic viability, diversity, locality, eco-cultural resilience and eco-cultural civilization. These storylines built on the three widely known pillars of sustainability: environmental, social and economic.

The relationship between culture and other pillars of sustainability have been further discussed and defined (Soini and Birkeland, 2014; Soini and Dessein, 2016). In the narrowest sense culture can be seen as a cultural capital that has to be sustained. This can be called 'cultural sustainability' or 'culture in sustainability' and in the farming context this refers, for example, to knowledge and skills as well as the landscape shaped by farming practices. Culture can also be understood in an anthropological sense as having a mediating role between the other dimensions of sustainability in a certain context (e.g. place). Here culture is defined *for* sustainability suggesting that it is the farming culture, for better or worse, which shapes ecological, social and economic sustainability. The third role of culture encloses the other pillars of sustainability and becomes an overarching dimension of sustainability, suggesting sustainability transformation that is driven by cultural change. This refers to culture *as* sustainability or 'sustainable culture' and in the farming context it could refer to a learning process towards more sustainable practices (Burton and Paragahawewa, 2011).

While the three ways of understanding cultural sustainability described above can be used to discern different perspectives of culture in sustainability, they do not take any position with respect to relationality and normativity of culture and sustainability. As for the normativity, 'culture' within agriculture does not necessarily promote sustainability, as some modern farming cultures have incorporated as cultural norms environmentally unsustainable practices, for example, providing cultural importance to activities associated with intensive agricultural production (Burton, 2004). As for the relationality, both 'culture' and 'sustainability' are context dependent and dynamic in space and time. Therefore, two important questions can be identified. First, do the three above representations of culture in agriculture contain common (cross-representational) meanings that are fundamental to assessing the role of culture in sustainability? Second, to the extent that these common meanings exist, what are the qualities they define and how are we best able to identify and assess them?

From a practice theoretical perspective, culture is produced and reproduced in social practices. When cultural sustainability is understood as driving a sustainability transformation, the social practices in which culture is reproduced become central for the analysis of its sustenance and change. Culture is visible in the meanings, competences and materials attached to practices and, hence, in identifying the elements of sustainable practice. How they are connected increases our understanding of what is essential and should be sustained in culture. For this chapter, we analysed how the farmers described their practices without observing how the practices are actually performed by the farmers. When the aim is to understand how sustainability appears in and is a result of practices, it is useful and relevant to analyse the farmers' talk and perceptions about these practices (Hitchings, 2012). This allows us to focus on the meanings while also providing an understanding of how meanings become intertwined with materials and skills and how this both restricts the full realization of sustainability goals and reshapes the goals. In this way, we can give new meaning to agricultural practices as a nature–culture interface, where nature is seen as both restricting and generating culture.

Sustainable agriculture practices – the farmers' view

From our research results we identified three interconnected qualities of culturally sustainable agriculture practices defined by the farmers: (Bio)diversity of the agricultural environment, fertility of the soil and continuity of farming – particularly at the farm level. In addition, we found that the practices are shaped by rationalization, which involves finding a balance between the qualities of the practices and rational decision-making of the farmers (e.g. organization of the work and economic profitability). Finally, there is a process of making social and moral judgements on the symbolic value of the practices. We call this process appreciation, which is partly a matter of pleasure and satisfaction, partly related to the meanings derived from their aesthetic representation and partly embedded in judgements about desirability and quality of the practices. These dimensions are presented in Figure 2.1. Agricultural practices are located in the nature-culture interface. The key qualities of sustainable agriculture – biodiversity, fertility and continuity – are shaped by rationalization and appreciation which are in a constant dialogue between themselves, but also with the aforementioned qualities. They are further defined and redefined by a broader cultural framework and natural conditions.

In the following section, we describe each of the key qualities using three criteria: (1) the way in which the key qualities were described by the farmers, (2) how these qualities contributed to 'sustainable' farming and how they are promoted/maintained through agricultural activities and (3) how the

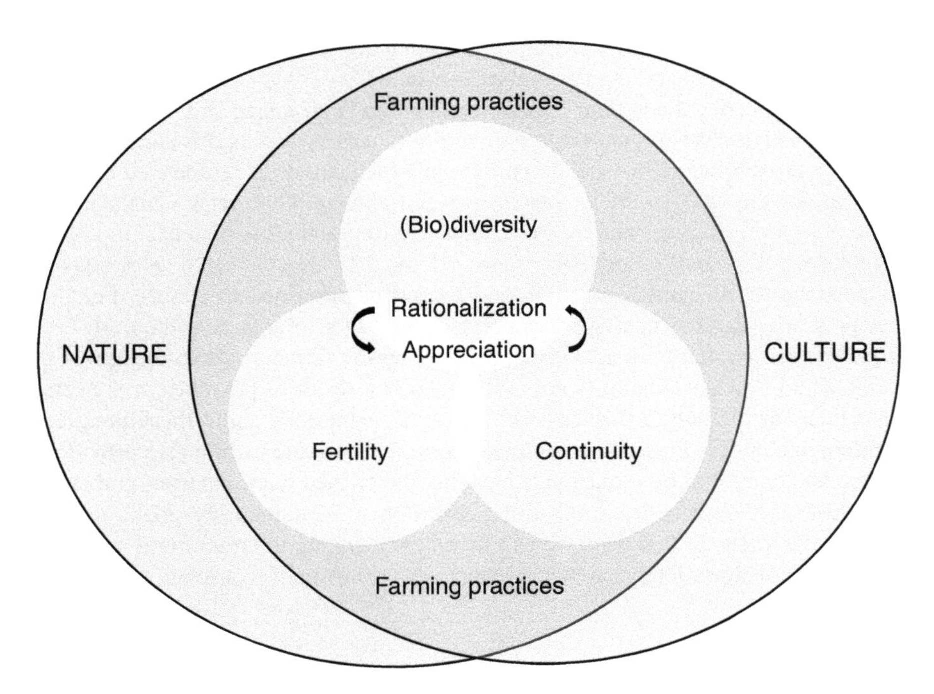

Figure 2.1 Agricultural practices are co-produced by nature and culture. The three qualities of farming practices (fertility, continuity and (bio)diversity) which are shaped by rationalization and appreciation.

rationalization and appreciation shape the practices related to these qualities. Finally, we discuss the understanding of cultural sustainability in particular in relation to nature-culture interface.

Fertility

Fertility relates essentially to the availability of nutrients within the soil and therefore shows a strong correlation with the ability of fields to produce good yields. In general, there are a number of different ways to ensure nutrition, including the provision of mineral and organic fertilizers, ensuring the presence of humic matter in the soil to retain moisture and the availability of clay particles to bind minerals and prevent chemical leaching.

For most farmers maintaining fertility in the long term was a critical factor in all agricultural practices related to cultivation – ranging from tilling, harrowing and sowing to harvesting. However, especially for conventional farmers, the addition of fertilizer in significant quantities was the key means of maintaining soil fertility. This was manifest in their common concern for the low fertilization limits in agri-environmental schemes, which the farmers saw as jeopardizing the quality of the yield (Huttunen, 2015; Huttunen and Oosterveer, 2017; Huttunen and Peltomaa, 2016). Besides actual fertilization, some farmers performed specific practices to improve the fertility of their fields. These included adding organic materials, cultivating green manure, using long-rooted and/or nitrogen binding plants in crop rotation or as undergrowth and crop rotation itself (Huttunen and Oosterveer, 2017).

Despite the shared goal of maintaining and improving the fertility of the soil, the farmers held different rationales behind the application of fertilizer – resulting in a variety of practices (Huttunen and Oosterveer, 2017; Huttunen and Peltomaa, 2016). For example, farmers could under-fertilize the fields as a result of beliefs concerning the cost-efficiency of fertilization (yield gain relative to cultivation cost) (Huttunen and Oosterveer, 2017). Another example is the application of increasingly popular no- or reduced-tillage practices. Farmers had mixed views on the impact of no-till on soil structure and fertility and, consequently, its application was mainly grounded in economic reasoning, including fuel savings and reduction in the amount of work (Huttunen and Peltomaa, 2016). Farmers also maintained fertility through crop rotation, not only with the intention of increasing fertility, but also to avoid some diseases and maintain the health of the soil. Paradoxically, another motivation for the application of fertilizer was as a means of disposing of animal manure rather than to improve soil fertility (Huttunen, 2015). Farmers judged fertility through observations of the soil and its composition, visual appreciation of growing crops and the actual yield of the crop (Soini and Aakkula, 2007). The visual symbols of fertility reinforced its importance in the minds of farmers and was a means of displaying 'good farmer' credentials to other farmers (see Burton, 2004), although the visual symbols tended to obscure the diversity of practices employed.

(Bio)diversity

Biological diversity in the farming context is understood as diversity at the genetic (farm animal breeds and crops), species (richness of the crop species) and landscape levels (diversity of different habitats). Conservation, preservation and sustainable use of biodiversity have been encouraged among the farmers through state funded agri-environmental programmes. Although the term 'biological diversity' itself was relatively unknown for many farmers, biological diversity and its importance for both agriculture and wildlife was widely understood by the farmers (Soini and Aakkula, 2007).

Most commonly the farmers understood biodiversity at the landscape level, as biological diversity embedded in different landscape elements, although it was sometimes perceived more broadly as 'multifunctionality' (Soini and Aakkula, 2007; see also Renting *et al.*, 2009) and even as a variety of rural livelihoods and activities. The interviewed farmers often considered fields and other agricultural areas (meadows, grazing lands) to be part of the wider rural ecosystem comprised of forest, lakes, rivers and marshes. Many farmers considered this mosaic of rural landscape characteristics as biodiversity rather than ecological hotspots, a perception that they often derived from or associated with game management and hunting (Soini, 2007; Soini and Aakkula, 2007). At the field level, farmers recognized single landscape elements (e.g. a few trees with some stones in the middle of arable land) as important for increasing the species and landscape diversity and contributing to its aesthetic value. However, the landscape elements were often in conflict with efficient farming as they represented a barrier to conventional field management practices. The farmers also criticized field margins required by the agri-environmental scheme from an efficiency point of view: they were termed 'weed margins' or 'trash hay margins', and perceived to both spread weeds and to be aesthetically unpleasing (Soini, 2007; Soini and Aakkula, 2007).

At the level of species, farmers were concerned about the increase of monoculture in agriculture, i.e. cultivation of only one or two crops (Vuorio *et al.*, 2005) and in particular barley (Soini and Aakkula, 2007). Monoculture was seen as a threat to soil and crop quality in terms of soil structure, fertility and crop diseases, but also as a threat to wildlife. Crop rotation and diversity in the cultivated crops was valued, but often in practice limited due to factors such as grain prices, available machinery, work time and the distribution of farming work as well as cattle feeding requirements. Agri-environmental subsidies aimed at increasing farmland biodiversity by promoting field management for game or nature, also engendered mixed feelings. Fields managed in this manner were not aesthetically valued and farmers practicing this type of cultivation were easily labelled as pseudo-farmers (Huttunen and Peltomaa, 2016) – implying that despite the high value placed on diverse farmland and landscape, many felt the diversity should occur outside the 'real' farming land.

The farmers widely acknowledged the genetic diversity of farm animal breeds and plants. Farmers who maintained genetically more diverse old local cattle breeds saw 'sustainable cattle breeds' as representing a more morally acceptable way to practice husbandry (Soini *et al.*, 2012). Due to their genetic diversity, farmers found these breeds more persistent, long lived, resistant to diseases, adaptive in relation to changing environmental conditions, aesthetically more pleasant and generally closer to humans than other breeds (Takamaa and Soini, 2007).

Overall, the farmers interviewed recognized the loss of biodiversity at genetic, species and landscape level. In particular, the decrease of cattle farming and grazing had led to a decline in the amount of grazing land, traditional meadows and woodlands. They experienced this decrease as a loss, but highlighted the rational aspects as new practices that had to be adapted to maintain continuity (Soini, 2007).

Continuity

Continuity involves the ability to transfer the farm to the future generation in as good as or better condition than it was received from the previous generation (Silvasti, 2003; Dessein and Nevens, 2007). It is regarded as a central feature of good farming practices and encompasses many agricultural practices on the farm. When continuity is eroded (i.e. there is no transfer to the next generation), it can strongly affect the way the land is managed, for example, by removing any incentive to maintain soil fertility or leading to farm abandonment.

The farmers expressed the value of continuity in a number of ways. For example, farmers appreciated multiple temporal layers in the cultivated landscape (traditional biotopes) and associated man-made features (old buildings), although they were not always able to maintain them due to economic or technical reasons (Soini, 2007). Continuity was also considered as a spatially diverse phenomenon. The farmers regarded the agricultural land immediately adjacent to the farmstead as most valuable, something that they wanted to maintain, even if they had to make hard decisions elsewhere (e.g. reforest the fields) (Soini, 2007). Continuity was also expressed by the farmers who were maintaining local breeds as a hobby. These farmers considered having a few cows of a native breed among imported breeds a symbol of the continuity either at the farm, regional or even national and international level. They saw maintenance of the local breeds as an investment in future livestock farming and food security (Takamaa and Soini, 2007). This kind of moral commitment was also observed among the organic farmers, who saw organic farming as best enabling the continuity of the farm in both environmental and economic terms (Huttunen and Peltomaa, 2016).

Despite the desire to maintain some type of continuity, ruptures in practices occurred (e.g. from conventional to organic farming) in order to maintain the overall continuity of the farm. Practices such as growing new crops and adopting new farming methods were introduced in order to maintain overall farm continuity. This led, on some occasions, to paradoxical situations. For example, low levels of fertilization due to high fertilizer costs could maintain profitability in the short term, but in the long term could lead to a decrease in fertility of the soil and thus threaten the continuity of the farm.

Discussion and conclusions

What can our analysis of farmers' views of sustainability in agriculture tell us about cultural sustainability? What should sustain in culture? First, our analysis shows that farmers' perceptions of sustainable farming practices illustrate some of the storylines on cultural sustainability identified by Soini and Birkeland (2014). Continuity is linked with the storyline of heritage because of a need to conserve and preserve some of the immaterial and material heritage of agriculture, both natural and cultural. It is a continuous, complex and iterative cultural and social process of definition and use that includes the creation as well as the preservation of heritage, i.e. the cultural aspects of inheritance and change (Auclair and Fairclough, 2015: pp. 7–9). Diversity has ecological, socio-economic and cultural meaning for the farmers. The farmers recognized the value of biological diversity for agriculture but diversity was also considered to have an important intrinsic natural, cultural and aesthetic value. Moreover, the diversity of farms, farming practices and ways of farming contribute to the biological diversity, which supports the notion of biocultural diversity (Blanc and Soini, 2015; Brites and Mendes Moreira, this volume: p. 66). Fertility is linked to and reflects predominantly the economic viability storyline, but also eco-cultural resilience, which highlights a holistic view on sustainability and the seeking of a balance between humans and nature by aiming for the wellbeing of nature (soil and wildlife) for the benefit of humans and nature.

Our analysis of agriculture and its underlying social practices shows that cultural sustainability entails at least these three key qualities; diversity, continuity and fertility, that are produced in interactions between the farmers and their farming culture and nature inherent in farming practices. The way farmers described these qualities can be interpreted as expressions of resilience and capability creating wellbeing for both the human *and* ecological systems in the long term. In their view, capabilities represent the ability and willingness to maintain diversity, continuity and fertility, while resilience relates to the content and explains why these qualities are important in relation to agriculture. The notions of capability and resilience are not new in sustainability literature, they have been acknowledged as a key issue both within the fields of ecology (Holling, 2001) and social sustainability (Burger and Christen, 2011). However, our analysis connects capability and resilience to cultural sustainability and suggests that these are the issues that should, in the end, sustain in culture rather than any single characteristic (tangible or intangible).

One of the problematic issues regarding cultural sustainability is how to deal with the dynamic and relational nature of culture in sustainability. Culture, whether conceived in a narrow or broad sense, is not static or universal. Rather, both the material and immaterial aspects are adapted according to the requirements set by place. The social practice approach revealed an important aspect of cultural sustainability by offering evidence of a transformation of qualities, e.g. regarding biodiversity or fertility perceptions (Huttunen and

Oosterveer, 2017; Huttunen and Peltomaa, 2016). Here, the identified rationalization and appreciation turned out to be mechanisms that are relational phenomena, shaping the practices and eventually also the identified qualities of sustainability. This was especially evident in tensions that appeared when making decisions on biodiversity management and fertility practices. Biodiversity management appeared to be a compromise between the appreciation of nature and technical and economic feasibility, and resulted in farmers gaining pleasure from small areas or some practices that focused on enhanced biodiversity. Fertilization meant compromising between fertility of the soil and short-term economic continuity of the farm. Rationalizing fertilization to the financial situation at the farm often meant decreased fertilization, which may lead to an unappreciated decrease in the fertility of the soil (Huttunen and Oosterveer, 2017). An additional component to the relationships between rationalization and appreciation came in the form of agri-environmental policies that did not necessarily fit with farmers' ideas of sustainable agriculture (Kaljonen, 2011) but forced them to change their practices.

These examples demonstrate how the rationalization and appreciation change along with the change of the materials, meanings and competences that constitute the practices. Simultaneously they draw together nature and culture in the practices. The interplay between nature and culture sets the direction for the change and suggests that paying closer attention to the ways this interaction is occurring in social practices, enables the unpacking of the dynamic nature of culture in sustainability.

Furthermore, the social practice approach applied in this study enables us to elaborate on the relationship between nature and culture in cultural sustainability. At first glance, nature is present in the material element of the social practice framework, conditioning the practices as well as the culture that the practices represent. Continuity, diversity and fertility exist in relation to nature. However, by being part of the practices, nature becomes part of culture, for example, in fertility practices, which are directed at looking after and maintaining soil and the natural environment. The meanings and competences, that are elements of the social practice framework, are defined in relation to nature. Furthermore, as fertility is practiced, nature in the form of soil is (re)produced. Yet, this reproduction of nature does not mean that nature becomes subsumed by culture. Farming practices can never totally control nature, but nature always conditions human practices. Hence, the focus on farming practices discussed in this chapter points out how nature and culture are in a dynamic relationship in defining cultural sustainability. The rationalization and appreciation processes conditioning the practices help to unpack this dynamic to reflect on the nature–culture interface. From a sustainability perspective, the critical point is, however, where the dynamics induced in the nature–culture interface is leading to. Cultural sustainability requires rationalization and appreciation to be able to maintain capability and resilience.

In this chapter, we have explored the relationship between agriculture and cultural sustainability. We conclude that agriculture as a model of sustainable agricultural practices informs our understanding of cultural sustainability. It is able to clarify the connections between the humans and the nature and conditions for a creating a new Natural Contract (cf. Serres, 1995) that is urgently needed in our times.

Acknowledgements

Dr Michiel de Kromm and Dr Joost Dessein contributed to this manuscript by designing the overall idea. The contribution of Suvi Huttunen was funded by the Academy of Finland, decision 277896.

References

Allen, P., Van Dusen, D., Lundy, J. and Gliessman, S. (1991) Integrating social, environmental, and economic issues in sustainable agriculture. *American J. Alternative Agriculture* 6(1):34–39.

Auclair, E. and Fairclough, G. (2015) Living between past and future. An introduction to heritage and cultural sustainability. In: E. Auclair and G. Fairclough (eds) *Theory and Practice in Heritage and Sustainability. Between Past and Future*. Routledge, New York and London:1–22.

Blanc, N. and Soini, K. (2015) Cultural and biological diversity: interconnections in ordinary places. In: C. De Beukelaer, M. Pyykkönen, J. Singh (eds) *Globalization, Culture and Development: The UNESCO Convention on Cultural Diversity*. Palgrave Macmillan, Basingstoke, United Kingdom.

Burger, P. and Christen, M. (2011) Towards a capability approach of sustainability. *Journal of Cleaner Production* 19:787–795.

Burton, R. J. F. (2004) Seeing through the 'good farmer's' eyes: towards developing an understanding of the social symbolic value of 'productivist' behaviour. *Sociologia Ruralis* 44:195–215.

Burton, R. J. F. and Paragahawewa, U. H. (2011) Creating culturally sustainable agri-environmental schemes. *Journal of Rural Studies* 27:95–104.

de Kromm, P. M. M. (2015) Governing Animal–human relations in farming practices: a study of group housing of sows in the EU. *Sociologia Ruralis* 55(4):417–437.

Dessein, J. and Nevens, F. (2007) 'I'm Sad To Be Glad'. An Analysis of Farmers' Pride in Flanders. *Sociologia Ruralis* 47(3):273–292.

Hawkes, J. (2001) *The Fourth Pillar of Sustainability: Culture's Essential Role in Public Planning*. Common Ground P/L, Melbourne, Australia.

Hitchings, R. (2012) People can talk about their practices. *Area* 44:61–67.

Holling, C. S. (2001) Understanding the complexity of economic, ecological and social systems. *Ecosystems* 4:390–405.

Huttunen, S. (2015) Farming practices and experienced policy coherence in agri-environmental policies: case land clearing in Finland. *Journal of Environmental Policy & Planning* 17:573–592.

Huttunen, S. and Oosterveer, P. (2017) Transition to sustainable fertilisation in agriculture, a practices approach. *Sociologia Ruralis* 57(2):191–210.

Huttunen, S. and Peltomaa, J. (2016) Agri-environmental policies and 'good farming' in cultivation practices at Finnish farms. *Journal of Rural Studies* 44:217–226.

Kaljonen, M. (2011) *Caught between Standardisation and Complexity. Study on the Institutional Ambiguities of Agri-environmental Policy Implementation in Finland. Acta Universitatis Tamperensis; 1594*. Tampere University Press, Tampere, Finland.

Kloppenburg, J. (1991) Social theory and the de/reconstruction of agricultural science: local knowledge for an alternative agriculture. *Sociologia Ruralis* 56(4):519–548.

Knobloch, F. (1996) *The Culture of Wilderness. Agriculture as Colonization in the American West*. The University of North Carolina Press, Chapel Hill, United States.

Oltedal, S., Moen, B-E., Klemp, H. and Rundmo, T. (2004) *Explaining Risk Perception. An Evaluation of Cultural Theory*. Rotund publikasjoner, no. 85. Norwegian University of Science and Technology, Trondheim, Norway.

Online Etymological Dictionary. (2017) *Culture*. www.etymonline.com/word/culture (Accessed 12 December 2017).

Pretty, J. (1995) Participatory learning for sustainable agriculture. *World Development* 23(8):1247–1263.

Reckwitz, A. (2002) Toward a theory of social practices. A development in culturalist theorizing. *European Journal of Social Theory* 5:243–263.

Renting, H. and van der Ploeg, J. D. (2001) Reconnecting nature, farming and society. Enviromental Cooperatives in the Netherlands as Institutional Arrangements for creating coherence. *Journal of Environmental Planning and Policy* 3:85–101.

Renting, H., Rossing W. A. H., Groot, J. C. J., Van der Ploeg, J. D., Laurent, C., Perraud, D., Stobbelaar, D. J. and Van Ittersum, M. K. (2009) Exploring multifunctional agriculture. A review of conceptual approaches and prospects for an integrative transitional framework. *Journal of Environmental Management* 90(Suppl 2):S112–S123.

Shove, E., Panzar, M. and Watson, M. (2012) *The Dynamics of Social Practice*. Sage, London:191.

Serres, M. (1995) *Natural Contact*. The Michigan University Press, Michigan, United States.

Silvasti, T. (2003) The cultural model of ‘good farmer’ and the environmental question in Finland. *Agriculture and Human Values* 20:143–150.

Soini, K. (2007) Beyond the ecological hotspots: understanding local residents’ perceptions of biodiversity of agricultural landscapes. *Annales Universtiates Turkuensis*. Serie A II 206: 102(11):100.

Soini, K. and Aakkula, J. (2007) Framing the biodiversity of agricultural landscape: the essence of local conceptions and constructions. *Land Use Policy* 24:2:311–321.

Soini, K. and Birkeland, I. (2014) Mapping the academic discourse of cultural sustainability. *Geoforum* 51:223–233.

Soini, K. and Dessein, J. (2016) Culture-sustainable development relations: towards a conceptual framework. *Sustainability* 8(2):167.

Soini, K., Diaz, C., Gandini, G., Martin-Collado, D., Pizzi, F., de Haas, Y., Lilja, T., EURECA-consortium and Hiemstra, S. (2012) Developing a typology for local cattle breed farmer in Europe. *Journal of Animal Breeding and Genetics* 129(6).

Stock, P. V. (2007) ‘Good farmers’ as reflexive producers: an examination of family organic farmers in the US Midwest. *Sociologia Ruralis* 47:83–102.

Sutherland, L.-A. (2013) Can organic farmers be ‘good farmers’? Adding the ‘taste of necessity’ to the conventionalization debate. *Agriculture and Human Values* 30: 429–441.

Takamaa, H. and Soini, K. (2007) Kuvaus maatiaislampaiden ja -karjan kasvattajista 2000 -luvulla. In: M. Karja and T. Lilja (eds) *Alkuperäisrotujen säilyttämisen taloudelliset, sosiaaliset ja kulttuuriset lähtökohdat. Maa- ja elintarviketalous 106*. LUKE, Helsinki: 136–159.

Thompson, P. (1995) *The Spirit of the Soil. Agriculture and the Environmental Ethics*. Routledge, London.

Throsby, D. (2008) Linking cultural and ecological sustainability. *The International Journal of Diversity in Organisations, Communities and Nations* 8:15–20.

van der Ploeg, J. D. (2003) *The Virtual Farmer*. Royal Van Gorcum, Assen, The Netherlands.

Vuorio, H., Soini, K. and Ikonen, A. (2005) Kenestä erikoiskasviviljelijäksi? Erikoiskasviviljelyn omaksujatyypit ja omaksumisen taustalla vaikuttavat tekijät. [Who will cultivate special crops? In Finnish with English Abstract]. *MTT:n selvityksiä* 102:68.

UNESCO. (2013) *Placing Culture at the Heart of Sustainable Development Policies. The Hangzhou Declaration*. www.unesco.org/new/fileadmin/MULTIMEDIA/HQ/CLT/images/FinalHangzhouDeclaration20130517.pdf (Accessed 28 November 2017).

3 What can culture in and for sustainable development learn from protected areas?

Constanza Parra

Introduction

Starting by criticizing the fragility of the social in past and present sustainability debates, this chapter looks at the relationship between culture and sustainable development through the perspective of the entangled nature–culture histories of protected areas. When looking at the historical transformation of institutions for nature custodianship, it is possible to recognize a variety of institutional models, ranging from those promoting strict conservation to those striving for more integrated sustainability synergies (Hanna *et al.*, 2008). Strict conservation models embody the discursive separation of nature and human life, including the views that society and environment are in constant conflict and that nature should be rationally managed and controlled through technical expertise. However, the contemporary sustainability quest of a growing number of parks and institutions for nature protection around the world reveals the first attempts to shift towards worldviews, discourses, policies and practices aimed at restoring the unity between nature and culture (Pilgrim and Pretty, 2010). In other words, people – meaning locals of different types, indigenous communities and newcomers, neo-rural people and the whole variety of communities of users – while sometimes conflicting with nature also have the knowledge and willingness to embrace a renewed sustainability culture for protected areas (see Gugerell *et al.* (p. 109), Burton (p. 137) and Scharrer *et al.* (p. 151) in this volume). Nonetheless, as many contributors in the field suggest, this is not an easy journey with, on the one hand, power conflicts related to land tenure and rights of ethnic communities, and, on the other, a large number of interpretations on how and for whom to construct more sustainable paths of development (Glaser *et al.*, 2010).

This chapter makes a plea for restoring the centrality of human beings, collective action and culture within the sustainability problematic in general, and in the arena of protected areas, in particular. This effort to reinstate the centrality of human beings in sustainability and institutions for nature protection is understood as in dialogic and dynamic interaction with nature. Culture is here defined

> as a set of practices, networks of institutions and systems of meanings. Cultural systems code for the knowledge, practices, beliefs, worldviews, values,

> norms, identities, livelihoods and social organizations of human societies. Different cultures value nature in different ways and thus have different connections with their natural environments.
>
> (Pilgrim and Pretty, 2010: p. 3)

Following Pilgrim and Pretty (2010), nature and culture cannot be separated. Both meet and interact across several levels from values, beliefs and norms to practices, livelihoods, knowledge and languages. Such a view brings to the fore a view of culture in and for sustainable development which cannot be separated from nature. This role and definition of culture in sustainable development implies looking at protected areas as territorial expressions of a nature–culture nexus and not just as simple spaces of nature, wilderness or natural resources. As such, protected areas are seen as 'territorially embedded socio-ecological systems delimited and legally regulated according to sustainability imperatives with the purpose of preserving their unique natural quality, exceptional biodiversity, and cultural heritage' (Parra and Moulaert, 2016: pp. 239–240).

This chapter proceeds in five main sections. Section two discusses the concept of sustainable development by critiquing and addressing its enduring social and cultural fragility. Further elaborating on culture and sustainable development from the perspective of the nature–culture interface, section three discusses different perspectives on nature, environmentalism and protected areas. Protected areas are considered as privilege arenas or domains from which to further develop the debate on the role and meaning of culture in sustainable development. As such, section four furthers the debate on the nature–culture interface in sustainable development with lessons learnt from the historical development of protected areas and their current challenges. Section five concludes on the importance of rethinking culture in sustainable development without forgetting 'nature', on the one hand, and critical socio-political issues including equity, justice, gender and diversity, on the other. These two layers cannot continue to be the great absentees in debates on culture and sustainability.

An effort to clear the nebulosity of the social and cultural dimensions in sustainable development

Much water has flowed under the bridge since the first debates on sustainability and sustainable development. Whereas the first wave of environmentalism in the 1970s is emblematic for triggering the first alarm denouncing the environmental costs of economic growth, i.e. *The Limits to Growth* (Meadows *et al.*, 1972), *Silent Spring* (Carson, 1962), *The Population Bomb* (Ehrlich, 1968), the late 1980s and 1990s represent a second wave of environmentalism characterized by a new quest for synergies between social, economic and ecological development aims until then considered incompatible. The contemporary stage of the sustainability journey is characterized by enduring political negotiations, debates and struggles on how to pursue sustainability. The last two years have been emblematic in this respect. The launch of Sustainable Development Goals, known as

Transforming our world: the 2030 Agenda for Sustainable Goals (United Nations, 2015), together with the celebration of the 21st session of the Conference of Parties at the 1992 United Nations Framework Convention on Climate Change are two events reflecting how sustainable development has become one of the most pressing challenges of the current century.

In the sciences, sustainable development has been investigated as opposing weak and strong sustainability, and emphasizing respectively economic and ecological sustainability logics (Neumayer, 2003). It is not only the limited dialogue between these two rationales that is problematic but also their dominance over social, political and cultural sustainability components, which have ended by slowly wiping out the original sustainable development mission searching for fair complementarities and a balance between human beings and nature (WCED, 1987; Parra and Moulaert, 2011b). This underrepresentation of the societal component has also contributed to the downplaying of crucial sustainability rights and values, including among others equity, justice, democracy and respect for diversity in the distribution and access to resources, notably between countries from the Global North and the Global South (Parra and Moulaert, 2011b; Parra, 2013). The complex chain of social, economic, ecological, political, scientific and technical reasons that could help to explain the world's still unachieved sustainability mission is very long and difficult to disentangle (Redclift and Springett, 2015). However, without a doubt the emergence of a more robust agenda for the sustainability transition will depend on the human willingness and socially innovative capacity of different social groups to trigger – in the near future – a deep transformation that re-embeds the sustainable development problematic within the complex social-ecological plexus from which change should flourish (Parra and Walsh, 2016). In the last few years, efforts have been made to re-establish the centrality of the societal side of this combined social-ecological plexus and process, as is the case with this volume, dealing with the cultural sustainability component of the nature–culture interface.

Both the social and the cultural dimensions have been the late newcomers to sustainable development. This social lateness is also observed in more recent debates on (social) resilience, as stated by Paidakaki and Moulaert (2017). Further elaborating on Parra and Moulaert (2011a), Table 3.1 summarizes a diversity of contributions that have connected sustainability and culture. For analytical simplification, contributions presented in the table are divided in five groups. A first group of contributions connect culture to sustainable development through social sustainability and development related concerns. This is the case with the ecodevelopmental theories (Sachs, 1984), contributions on the role of education for (sustainable) development (Ventakataram, 2009) and on the impact of tourism in local communities, identity (re)building and the process of acculturation (Proulx, 2006). A second perspective relates culture to sustainable development by stressing the relational character that connects nature, society and culture. Co-evolutionary approaches discussing tensions between anthropocentric and eco/biocentric discourses and worldviews are representative of this stream. As such, this perspective has also to do with the role of culture – as behaviour and knowledge – in the (un)sustainable use and management of natural resources (Norgaard, 1988, 2006; Pahl-Wostl *et al.*, 2008). A third group of contributions make a plea for restoring culture in sustainable development, either as a fourth or central pillar (Hawkes, 2001; Nurse, 2006). In the latter, culture is seen as the basis or epistemological centre to question the meaning and daily practice of sustainable development. A fourth body of literature draws attention to the material and artistic dimensions of culture, which also include heritage. Culture here is seen as a development tool but also as a key dimension of local policies. In addition to the material aspects of culture, diversity in forms of expression and cultural diversity are seen as fundamental, as portrayed by The United Nations Educational, Scientific and Cultural Organization World Heritage Convention (Titchen, 1996). In the words of the Adjuntament de Barcelona (2004) and United Cities and Local Governments Committee on Culture and World Secretariat (2010), 'cultural diversity is for humans as important as biodiversity for living species'. For Pascual (2006: p. 7), 'the role of culture in sustainable development is about including a cultural perspective in all public policies. It has to do with guaranteeing that all sustainable development process has a soul'.

Table 3.1 shows a variety of perspectives aimed at revealing the role and meaning of culture in sustainable development. Whereas some of these perspectives focus on connecting culture with the development component of sustainability, only a few exceptions are explicit in connecting in a dynamic way culture to nature as well as to the ecological component of sustainability (Parra and Moulaert, 2011a). In their critical synthesis and analysis of cultural sustainability approaches, the contribution by Dessein and colleagues (2015) goes a step further by making a distinction between culture 'in', 'for' and 'as' sustainable development, including an attempt to define culture as a holistic and transformative process in interaction with nature.

The section below further advances the natural dimension of culture as an effort to make more tangible or real the role of culture in sustainable development (Parra and Moulaert, 2011a). This is done by looking at protected areas and analysing their histories of nature–culture protection/conservation. Protected areas are regarded as guardians of a distinctive society-nature relationship (Parra, 2010a, 2010b, 2012; Parra and Moulaert, 2016), and as such their history of success and failure is a valuable support in the quest for making culture more explicit in sustainability academia and policy by enhancing its connection with nature.

The nature–culture interface through the perspective of nature, environmentalism and protected areas

From early civilizations and utopian environmental concerns to the foundation of the first national parks

The preoccupation of societies with their environment has a history of conceptual evolution that long precedes the well-known Brundtland Report (WCDE, 1987; see Mittler, 2001; Vivien, 2001; Matagne, 2003). The sustainability of the

Table 3.1 Contributions and literature on sustainable development referring to the concept of culture

Type of literature	*Role and conceptualization of culture within sustainable development debates*
Ecodevelopment	*Role*: Relational/contextual. The question about culture is linked to the social.
	Definitions: Links between development, territory and culture. Cultural context.
Management of natural resources	*Role*: Culture is functional to the management and norms of behaviour.
	Definitions: Set of cultural practices (water cultures, risk cultures, etc.).
	Cultural capital as *the capacity of a group to behave in a certain way* (Cochrane, 2006: p. 320).
	Culture as the set of socially constructed believes or behaviours (Cochrane, 2006: p. 322).
Role and impact of cultural infrastructures and cultural industries in cities	*Role*: Culture as a physical product, infrastructure. Material and artistic dimensions of culture, including heritage.
	Definitions: Culture – defined as cultural infrastructure and arts – as a development tool. Relevance given to public policies for territorial and cultural development.
	Cultural sustainable development (Thorsby, 2008): importance of cultural industries for sustainable development.
Education for sustainable development	*Role*: Culture as a normative action. Education as a means for human development.
	Definitions: Culture as the result of education. Development is more than economic growth; social indicators such as education defined in terms of access and quality are considered crucial.
Tourism and sustainable development	*Role*: Culture as a collective state and identity. Concept of acculturation (of traditional, autochthon, indigenous cultures) is used within the context of cultures through tourism. This reflection is also using the concept of civilization as a frame of reference.
	Definitions: Importance and *meaning* of socio-cultural sustainability. Are changes or deeper socio-cultural transformations or acculturations desirable?
	Role of sustainable development: to stop the transformation or destruction of a certain culture? To improve cultures? To keep culture stable? To preserve *cultural diversity*?

continued

Table 3.1 Continued

Type of literature	*Role and conceptualization of culture within sustainable development debates*
Philosophical and methodological approaches to nature	*Role*: Culture as a lifestyle, ethics and worldview. Anthropocentrism, utilitarian approaches, techno-utopians versus eco/biocentrism, conservationists, deep ecologists. *Definitions*: Anthropocentrism (techno-, utilitarian): culture as progress of humans and techniques. Approach referring to civilization and the central place of human beings in the universe. Biocentrism/ecocentrism/deep ecology: human beings have the responsibility of protecting ecosystems (land/earth ethics; Leopold, 1949).
Co-evolutionary analyses of sustainable development	*Role*: Culture in its relational and interdependent dimension. Circular interdependence and co-evolutionary nature of the interactions between society and environment (Opschoor and Van der Straaten, 1993: p. 4). *Definitions*: A co-evolutionary sustainability implies avoiding development paths, social structures and technologies that threaten seriously.
Culture as a fourth pillar	*Role*: Culture as the forth pillar of sustainable development (Hawkes, 2001). Culture as sustainability (action for sustainability) and culture as desired social state. Culture as a specific reference. *Definitions*: Cultural vitality is as essential as social equity, environmental responsibility and economic viability for a society striving for sustainability. Culture as a concept for describing the community creation of values, meanings and objectives in life (Hawkes, 2001).
Culture as the central or basic pillar	*Role*: Culture as the central pillar of sustainable development (non-determinist approach) (Nurse, 2006). *Definitions*: Culture as the basis or epistemological centre to question the meaning and daily practice of sustainable development. This approach highlights the importance of cultural identity, autonomy, social justice and ecological balance yet it ends by going back to a very conventional approach to culture reduced to cultural infrastructure.

Table 3.1 Continued

Type of literature	*Role and conceptualization of culture within sustainable development debates*
Culture, local policies and the UNESCO Agenda 21 of culture	*Role*: Culture as a key dimension of local policies (cultural policy at the municipality level). Focus on cultural diversity, diversity of cultural expressions, analogy between culture and ecology, cultural ecology, cultural ecosystem. *Definitions*: '*Cultural diversity is for humans as important as biodiversity for living species*' (Adjuntament de Barcelona and United Cities and Local Governments, 2004). '*The role of culture in sustainable development is about including a cultural perspective in all public policies. It has to do with guaranteeing that all sustainable development process has a soul*' (Pascual, 2006: p. 7).
Sustainable development and the nature-culture nexus	*Role*: Culture in and for sustainable development in dynamic interaction with nature (Parra and Moulaert, 2011a, 2011b, 2016). *Definitions*: Culture as an ensemble of tangible factors of social life which also includes nature.
Cost Action 1007 'Investigating cultural sustainability'	*Role and definitions*: • culture with a supportive and self-promoting role (culture in sustainable development); • culture as a more influential force that can operate beyond itself (culture for sustainable development); • culture as the essential foundation and structure for achieving the aims of sustainable development (culture as sustainable development) (Dessein *et al.*, 2015: p. 8).

Source: author (adapted from Parra and Moulaert, 2011a and based on various sources).

nature–culture nexus together with the question about how nature should be used and protected have been subjects of importance for almost all societies, ranging from ancient civilizations' preoccupation with forest depletion in Mediterranean areas, to the environmental catastrophe that pushed the Mayan Empire towards its decline (Wheeler, 2004). Further, authors such as Henderson (1991) and Estes (1993) stated that it is reasonable to link the conceptual origin of sustainable development with religious and magical rituals of the world's earliest people, and more specifically with ceremonies pleading to deities for environmental renewal, rain in case of drought and fructiferous harvests (Frazier, 1922 cited in Estes, 1993 provides several examples). These practices reveal a cosmology stressing the importance of living in harmonious balance with nature in order to guarantee the survival of human beings. Such cosmologies can still be observed in contemporary references to the earth as Gaia, a living goddess (Estes, 1993), in Shamanism and in other indigenous cultures.

However, it was during the industrial revolution, in the late eighteenth and nineteenth centuries, when the impact of human action on ecological limits became more dramatic, inspiring utopian and romantic worldviews highlighting the virtues of nature as an antidote to industrialization. For John Muir, different forms of nature were the terrestrial manifestation of God, as expressed in the following quote, 'Everybody needs beauty as well as bread, places to play in and pray in, where nature may heal and give strength to body and soul alike' (Muir, [1912]2003: p. 256). For John Keats, Percy Shelley and other Romantic poets, nature was seen as a spiritually rejuvenating alternative to industrial society (Wheeler, 2004). This vision relates to the term 'sublime', present in both the poetic and philosophical literature of the time, which captures a full of sense of wonder vis-à-vis the grandeur and power of nature. Sublime is a term with a long history, used either as an adjective or a noun to express a tension between an intense aesthetic pleasure that stems from the displeasure of fear or horror (Cronon, 1996). Romantics used the word sublime to elevate the taste for ancient ruins, the alpine, storms, deserts and oceans, as well as the supernatural and impressive. Keats in his letters to Richard Woodhouse named this sensibility towards nature as the 'wordsworthian or egotistical sublime' (see White, date unknown).

More specifically concerning the idea of sustainability and conservation of nature, the eighteenth-century forestry practices and the notion of sustainable yield appear as precursors (Mittler, 2001). In the book *Man and Nature* ([1864]1965), George Perkins Marsh intended to raise awareness of forest depletion in England and France, and the risk that this situation could result in a human decline (Wheeler, 2004). A few decades later, the European forestry ideas exerted an important influence in forging the basis of the conservationist movement in the United States, after Pinchot imported and promoted a utilitarian approach to the management of forests. In contrast, preservationists such as John Muir, a major force in the foundation of the Yosemite National Park and the Sierra Club organization (Weaver, 2001), adopted a biocentric perspective, rejected economic rationalization and tried to establish an alternative system of values for protecting nature (Vivien, 2005). An alliance between the two approaches, utilitarist and biocentric, came about with the foundation of the Yellowstone (1870) and Yosemite (1890) national parks in the United States (Hays, 1959 quoted in Vivien, 2005: p. 19).

Even if there exists a certain consensus that the first conservationist experiences were forged in North America, the processes leading towards the foundation of national parks seem to be more complex. The idea of protecting nature or the wilderness gained force in the 1830s as a reaction against industrialization. Nevertheless, the creation of the first parks in the United States also responds to the desire to forge a national identity (Richez, 1992). In contrast to the long years of Europe's history and cultural heritage, the United States appeared devoid of culture to protect and exhibit. Therefore, in the search for original national icons, from which to construct an identity, wilderness appeared as a strong image to exhibit. The context and process through which the first protected areas in the United States were created is still subject to controversy, discomfort and pain, notably regarding the legitimacy of the new conservationist role of the state and its unacceptable behaviour towards native populations living in these areas. The following quote from John Muir provides some insights on the violent socio-political reality in which parks such as the one in Yosemite were born:

> In the wild gold years of 1849 and '50, the Indian tribes along the western Sierra foothills became alarmed at the sudden invasion of their acorn orchard and game fields by miners, and soon began to make war upon them, in their usual murdering, plundering style. This continued until the United States Indian Commissioners succeeded in gathering them into reservations, some peacefully, others by burning their villages and stores of food.
>
> (Muir, [1912]2003: p. 226)

The creation of the first national parks in the United States did not generate an immediate echo in Europe. It was necessarily to wait until the beginning of the twentieth century to see the first European parks, first Lunenbourg (1903), followed later by Sweden (1909), Switzerland (1914), Spain (1918) and Italy (1922). Authors such as Richez (1992) explain this apparent tardiness by noting that unified conservation systems were not needed in Europe before then. To a large extent the continent was covered by dispersed rural settlements as well as inhabited by a deep-rooted farming society who lived from the land and also kept control of the nature–culture balance of rural landscapes.

A few years after the inauguration of national parks in Europe, countries such as France realized that this nature-conservation model did not fit the reality and needs of French rural areas, given their higher population density settled in dispersed, small rural towns. This mismatch between the local needs and the national park model led in Europe to a process of differentiation of institutions for nature protection, ranging from reserves regulated under strict preservation directives to semi-protected territories conceived to reinvigorate in a sustainable way declining rural zones. This is the case of the Parcs Naturels Regionaux in France (Parra, 2010a; Scharrer *et al.* in this volume: p. 151) and Parco Regionale in Italy.

The contemporary academic debate on protected areas and nature conservation

Literature on protected areas constantly reproduces an old debate that opposes conservationist scholars, considering the world history of protected areas as a testimony of human progress in contrast to critical voices counting this history as a record of failure (Brockington *et al.*, 2008; Stolton and Dudley, 2010; Oldekop *et al.*, 2016). On the optimistic side, authors such as Stolton and Dudley (2010) have described protected areas as a source of the many goods, merits and 'services' that these spaces of nature provide to humans (and non-humans).

Protected areas are seen and studied in their capacity to act as source of health, rejuvenation and enjoyment but also for their role in recreation, education and several other cultural ecosystem services. From an ecological perspective, the capacity of protected areas to store water and food, conserve biodiversity, mitigate hazards and to control/mitigate climate change is also highlighted – as well as the contribution of protected areas around the world to peace building and custodianship of cultural diversity and heritage (Stolton and Dudley, 2010).

On the more pessimistic side of the spectrum, sceptical voices have criticized protected areas in many different ways, pointing out many examples of a gap between protected areas' values in 'theory' and real world practices. This gap is seen as unacceptable. A first weakness concerns the incapacity of protected areas to slow down the alarming rate at which world biodiversity is declining, as shown by many international reports (Chape *et al.*, 2005). From this perspective, protected areas and the environmental institutions and laws on which they depend are said to be powerless vis-à-vis market imperatives and contemporary capitalism forces commodifying nature and land. For, as several social scientists have emphasized, conservation regulation has in many cases been part of coercive colonial strategies, violent displacement and disempowerment of indigenous groups (Rangarajan and Shahabuddin, 2006; West *et al.*, 2006; Brockington *et al.*, 2008). Protected areas have also become victims of land and nature grabbing, processes through which property rights and control over natural resources are transferred from 'poor' to powerful hands (Fairhead *et al.*, 2012; Busscher *et al.*, 2017).

A more recent discussion on parks and nature conservation has been framed within the debate on the Anthropocene. The recently published book *After Preservation* critically discusses the viability, relevance and timeliness of the nature preservationist tradition in the so-called Age of Humans (Minteer and Pyne, 2015: p. 7). The question as to whether the Anthropocene is understood as either

> … a liberating revelation proving that humans should get on with the business of smart planetary management and get over outmoded myths of a separate, pristine, wild nature that exists free from human influence (and an environmental politics that limits human manipulations of nature) [or as a sign] of the tragic consummation of the destructive domination of the earth, a last threshold crossed on the march to total ecological despotism
>
> (Minteer and Pyne, 2015: p. 4)

reveals opposed ways of thinking about nature–culture interactions and gives protected areas a different role. Marris (2015) makes a plea for humility in the Anthropocene and argues that talking about how humans 'control' and 'dominate' the planet is not only a mistake but also arrogance. In her words, 'when those who talk about the Anthropocene say "humans control the planet", they do not mean humans are in control. They just mean that we have become one of the primary drivers of change. And that's indisputably true' (Marris, 2015: p. 44). Humility and moral conviction are fundamental for accepting that nature has a value in itself that goes far beyond the value that humans can confer.

Summarizing, protected areas are living spaces of nature and culture and therefore the plurality of values that they contain is attached to both biological diversity and cultural diversity. Consequently, protected areas are seen

> not just as sites rich in biological diversity but also as rich sites of social interactions and social reproduction. By social reproduction we mean the maintenance and replication of social practices, beliefs, and institutions that would have been considered 'culture' in anthropology in the past.
>
> (West and Brockington, 2006: p. 609)

Cross-fertilization between protected areas and cultural sustainability

There are many signs showing the enduring unsustainable relations between human beings and nature, and therefore calling for broader socio-cultural perspectives capable of inspiring not only humility, as stated by Marris, but also creativity in the grounding of alternative modes of living (Manier, 2012; Parra and Walsh, 2016). Parks and protected areas were chosen in this chapter to reflect on their potential and limits for constructing more sustainable nature–culture interactions. On the one hand, protected areas and the history of nature conservation are full of unsustainable nature–culture interactions. On the other hand, these places of entangled nature–culture heritage also host inspiring, positive examples of socio-ecological collective action enhancing sustainability (Parra, 2010a, 2012).

The question about how to make culture and the social more explicit in the academic and policy debate on sustainable development is imperative. The life and history of protected areas are a powerful example on how culture in and for sustainable development can only be understood in dynamic interaction with nature. Here culture is not seen as an artefact or rigid architecture but as an ensemble of tangible vectors of social life which cannot be separated from nature. Culture, defined in relational terms, is the outcome of human diversity materialized from interactions of worldviews, values, identities, behaviours, social practices and other types of human institutions (Newing, 2010; Pilgrim and Pretty 2010; Parra, 2013). Furthermore, culture in and for sustainable development is rooted in the moral motivation and belief in 'humankind's responsibility for nature' (Pawlowski, 2008: p. 81).

Can culture in sustainable development learn more from the potential benefits and pitfalls of protected areas as observed along their history? Certainly, the answer is yes. Consider all those parks in the world that came into being after indigenous populations were violently displaced and seriously threatened in their human rights. In fact, bringing on board bio- or eco-centric values to reflect on the meaning and role of culture in sustainable development is not enough. Dignity, defined as the state or quality of being worthy of honour or respect, also has to do with a deep respect for human diversity and cultures. Regrettably, the discourse and discussion linking sustainability and culture has not paid much attention to this ethical issue.

The sustainability problematic is not only about reaching or protecting a certain environmental quality but also about equity, equality and respect among human beings. From combined intra- and inter-generational perspectives, this equity goal means, on the one hand, that sustainability cannot be pursued at the expense of 'others' and, on the other, that the roles of culture in sustainability cannot be fully grasped without considering current inequalities in society in terms of income and power distribution, access to and benefits of culture, satisfaction of human needs, and unequal sharing of environmental 'bads' (Parra, 2010a). Contributions from environmental justice scholars (Agyeman, 2013) draw attention to the social, political and cultural layers of combined social-environmental injustices. More precisely they discuss how certain social groups of society – minorities, non-white, excluded, and so on… – are usually the ones that have to support the weight of the different unsustainable human expressions as well as how progress in sustainability has first and foremost a positive effect on an elite. This is precisely where many protected areas around the world have failed in their mission to respect and care for both biodiversity and cultural diversity. Bearing this in mind, this chapter contributes to this volume by stating that a research agenda investigating cultural sustainability from the perspective of the human-nature interface is not fully complete till it links the culture-sustainability duo to critical issues of gender, diversity, race, democracy and coupled social-environmental (in)justice concerns (Agyeman, 2013).

Social innovation is another crucial component from which the culture-sustainability duo could learn from protected areas. The list of failures in the sustainability journey is long and despairing, as shown by many international reports (Butchart *et al.*, 2010). However, this critical situation does not mean that there is no one out there working and investing energy in constructing more sustainable paths of development. As stated by Parra and Walsh (2016), the sense of urgency in a variety of sustainable development-related issues has brought into being communities, individuals, practices and leaderships investing in a present and future that brings a more friendly relationship between human beings and nature to the fore. Building on Moulaert *et al.* (2013) and Wright (2010), Parra and Walsh (2016) described these practices as 'real utopias' and dynamic laboratories of social innovation that inspire more friendly nature–culture relationships. This socially innovative sustainability has been observed in different arenas of social reproduction (Gibson-Graham, 2008; Manier, 2012; Mehmood and Parra, 2013) as well as within the realm of protected areas (Parra, 2010a, 2012). Saving nature from threats, contesting different forms of anthropocentrism in styles of governing protected areas, restoring biodiversity, respect for cultural diversity and efforts to reconnect human beings with nature in a dignifying manner are a few examples of the 'intelligences of nature' (Descola, 2008) contained in protected areas. The socially innovative character of the collective action observed in many spaces of nature is not only innovative from an ecological sustainability perspective but also in its nature–culture nexus, values, knowledge and fight for enhanced environmental rights (Parra, 2010a, 2013; Mehmood and Parra, 2013).

Final reflections

By critiquing the persistent social and cultural fragility of sustainable development, this chapter has contributed to the reflection on the role of culture in and for sustainable development with the analysis of nature–culture interactions in protected areas. The overall aim of this chapter was to answer the following question: what can culture in and for sustainable development learn from protected areas? In simple terms, the answer to this question is a double plea for, first, (re)thinking culture in sustainable development without forgetting 'nature' and, second, bringing to the fore critical socio-political issues, including equity, solidarity, respect and justice, without which sustainable development loses its fundamental essence. In short, these two complementary claims cannot continue to be the great absentees in the debates on culture and sustainability. On the one hand, it is not only artificial to separate nature from culture (Haila, 2000) but also denigrating to ignore diversity in cosmologies, cultures and communities (Parra and Walsh, 2016). On the other hand, a truly dignifying nature–culture nexus is the one that not only respects nature but also those fundamental human values and rights that are prerequisite for a socially sustainable reproduction of our *vivre ensemble.*

References

Agyeman, J. (2013) *Introducing Just Sustainabilities. Policy, Planning and Practice.* The University of Chicago Press Books, Chicago.

Ajuntament de Barcelona and United Cities and Local Governments. (2004) *Agenda 21 for culture.* www.agenda21culture.net/ (Accessed 1 March 2017).

Brockington, D., Duffy, R. and Igoe, J. (2008) *Nature Unbound. Conservation, Capitalism and the Future of Protected Areas.* Earthscan, London and Washington.

Busscher, N., Parra, C. and Vanclay, F. (2017) Land grabbing for conservation and industrial tree plantations: contradictions in land governance in Los Esteros del Iberá, Argentina. (Under review at *Land Use Policy*).

Butchart, S. H., Walpole, M., Collen, B., Van Strien, A., Scharlemann, J. P., Almond, R. E. and Carpenter, K. E. (2010) Global biodiversity: indicators of recent declines. *Science* 328(5982):1164–1168.

Carson, R. (1962) *Silent Spring.* Houghton Mifflin Harcourt, Boston, United States.

Chape, S., Harrison, J., Spalding, M. and Lysenko, I. (2005) Measuring the extent and effectiveness of protected areas as an indicator for meeting global biodiversity targets. *Philosophical Transactions of the Royal Society of London B: Biological Sciences* 360(1454):443–455.

Cochrane, P. (2006) Exploring cultural capital and its importance in sustainable development. *Ecological Economics* 57(2):318–330.

Cronon, W. (ed.) (1996) *Uncommon Ground: Rethinking the Human Place in Nature.* WW Norton & Company, London.

Descola, P. (2008) *A qui appartient la nature? La vie des idées*. www.laviedesidees.fr/IMG/pdf/20080118_descola.pdf (Accessed 24 May 2017).

Dessein, J., Soini, K., Fairclough, G. and Horlings, L. (eds) (2015) *Culture in, for and as Sustainable Development. Conclusions from the COST Action IS 1007 Investigating Cultural Sustainability*. University of Jyväskylä, Jyväskylä, Finland.

Erhlich, P. R. (1968) *The Population Bomb*. Sierra Club-Ballantine, New York.

Estes, R. (1993) Toward sustainable development: from theory to praxis. *Social Development Issues* 15(3):1–29.

Fairhead, J., Leach, M. and Scoones, I. (2012) Green grabbing: new appropriation of nature? *Journal of Peasant Studies* 39(2):237–261.

Gibson-Graham, J. K. (2008) Diverse economies: performative practices for 'other worlds. *Progress in Human Geography* 32(5):613–632.

Glaser, M., Baitoningsih, W., Ferse, S. C., Neil, M. and Deswandi, R. (2010) Whose sustainability? Top–down participation and emergent rules in marine protected area management in Indonesia. *Marine Policy* 34(6):1215–1225.

Haila, Y. (2000) Beyond the nature–culture dualism. *Biology and Philosophy* 15(2):155–175.

Hanna, K., Slocombe, D. S. and Clark, D. A. (eds) (2008) *Transforming Parks and Protected Areas: Policy and Governance in a Changing World*. Routledge, New York and London.

Hawkes, J. (2001) *The Fourth Pillar of Sustainability. Culture's Essential Role in Public Planning*. Cultural Development Network & Common Ground Press, Melbourne, Australia.

Henderson, H. (1991) *Paradigms in Progress: Life Beyond Economics*. Knowledge Systems, Indianapolis, United States.

Leopold, A. (1949) *A Sound County Almanac*. Ballantine Books, New York.

Manier, B. (2012) *Un Million de Révolutions Tranquilles*. Editions Les Liens qui Libèrent, Paris.

Marris, E. (2015) Humility in the anthropocene. In: B. A. Minteer and S. J. Pyne (eds) *After Preservation: Saving American Nature in the Age of Humans*. University of Chicago Press, Chicago: 41–49.

Marsh, G. P. ([1864]1965) *Man and Nature*. University of Washington Press, Seattle, United States.

Matagne, P. (2003) Aux origines de l'écologie. *Innovations, Cahiers d'économie de l'innovation* 18(2):27–42.

Meadows, D. H., Meadows, D. L., Randers, J. and Behrens, W. W. (1972) *The Limits to Growth*. Universe Books, New York.

Mehmood, A. and Parra, C. (2013) Social innovation in an unsustainable world. In: F. Moulaert, D. McCallum, A. Mehmood and A. Hamdouch (eds) *International Handbook on Social Innovation: Collective Action, Social Learning and Transdisciplinary Research*. Edward Elgar Publishers, Cheltenham, United Kingdom: 53–66.

Minter, B. A. and Pyne, S. J. (2015) *After Preservation: Saving American Nature in the Age of Humans*. University of Chicago Press, Chicago.

Mittler, D. (2001) Hijacking sustainability? Planners and the promise and failure of local agenda 21. In: A. Layard, S. Davoudi and S. Batty (eds) *Planning for a Sustainable Future*. Spon Press, London: 53–60.

Moulaert, F., McCallum, D., Mehmood, A. and Hamdouch, A. (eds) (2013) *International Handbook on Social Innovation: Collective Action, Social Learning and Transdisciplinary Research*. Edward Elgar Publishers, Cheltenham, United Kingdom.

Muir, J. ([1912]2003) *The Yosemite*. Random House, New York and Canada.

Neumayer, E. (2003) *Weak Versus Strong Sustainability: Exploring the Limits of Two Opposing Paradigms*. Edward Elgar Publishing, Cheltenham, United Kingdom.

Newing, H. S. (2010) Bridging the gap: interdisciplinarity, biocultural diversity and conservation. In: S. Pilgrim and J. Pretty (eds) *Nature and Culture. Rebuilding Lost Connections*. Earthscan, London and Washington: 65–82.

Norgaard, R. B. (1988) Sustainable development: a co-evolutionary view. *Futures* 20(6):606–620.

Norgaard, R. B. (2006) *Development Betrayed: The End of Progress and a Coevolutionary Revisioning of the Future*. Routledge, London.

Nurse, K. (2006) Culture as the fourth pillar of sustainable development. *Working paper Commonwealth Secretariat Malborough House, London, UK*. https://pdfs.semanticscholar.org/92da/e4886a02f1fb27dd4131db5912aae6b7074f.pdf (Accessed 5 May 2017).

Oldekop, J. A., Holmes, G., Harris, W. E. and Evans, K. L. (2016) A global assessment of the social and conservation outcomes of protected areas. *Conservation Biology* 30(1):133–141.

Opschoor, J. B. and Van der Straaten, J. (1993) Sustainable development: an institutional approach. *Ecological Economics* 7(3):203–322.

Pahl-Wostl, C., Tabara, D., Bouwen, R., Craps, M., Dewulf, A., Mostert, E., Ridder, D. and Tailleu, T. (2008) The importance of social learning and culture for sustainable water management. *Ecological Economics* 64(3):484–495.

Paidakaki, A. and Moulaert, F. (2017) Disaster resilience into which direction(s)? Competing discursive and material practices in post-Katrina New Orleans. *Housing, Theory and Society* 1–23.

Parra, C. (2010a) *The governance of ecotourism as a socially innovative force for paving the way for more sustainable paths: the Morvan regional park case*. Unpublished PhD thesis Faculté de Sciences Economiques et Sociales, University of Sciences and Technology of Lille – Université Lille 1, France. https://ori-nuxeo.univ-lille1.fr/nuxeo/site/esupversions/5307442f-0346-43d4-ab0e-658037182d9f (Accessed 13 December 2017).

Parra, C. (2010b) Sustainability and multi-level governance of territories classified as protected areas: the Morvan regional park case. *Journal of Environmental Planning and Management* 53(4):491–509.

Parra, C. (2012) The vicissitudes of the French regional park model illustrated through the life history of the Morvan. *Environment and History* 18(4):561–583.

Parra, C. (2013) Social sustainability, a competitive concept for social innovation? In: F. Moulaert, D. McCallum, A. Mehmood and A. Hamdouch (eds) *International Handbook on Social Innovation: Collective Action, Social Learning and Transdisciplinary Research*. Edward Elgar Publishers, Cheltenham, United Kingdom: 142–154.

Parra, C. and Moulaert, F. (2011a) La nature de la durabilité sociale: contributions pour une lecture socioculturelle du développement territorial durable. *Developpement Durable et Territoires* 2(2):1–17.

Parra, C. and Moulaert, F. (2011b) Why sustainability is so fragilely 'social'... In: S. Oosterlynck, J. Van den Broeck, L. Albrechts, F. Moulaert and A. Verhetsel (eds) *Strategic Spatial Projects: Catalysts for Change*. Routledge, London: 163–173.

Parra, C. and Moulaert, F. (2016) The governance of the nature–culture nexus: lessons to learn from the San Pedro de Atacama case. *Nature+Culture* 11(3):239–258.

Parra, C. and Walsh, C. (2016) Socialities of nature beyond utopia. *Nature+Culture* 11(3):229–238.

Pascual, J. (2006) *Culture et développement durable: exemples d'innovation institutionnelle et proposition d'un nouveau cade pour les politiques culturelles.* Commission de cultures de Cités et Gouvernements Locaux Unis – CGLU. http://reseauculture21.fr/wp-content/uploads/2015/07/z_report-4_Resum-FR-copie.pdf (Accessed 15 May 2017).

Pawlowski, A. (2008) How many dimensions does sustainable development have? *Sustainable Development* 16(2):81–90.

Pilgrim, S. and Pretty, J. (eds) (2010) Bridging the gap: interdisciplinarity, biocultural diversity and conservation. In: S. Pilgrim and J. Pretty (eds) *Nature and Culture. An Introduction.* Earthscan, London and Washington:1–20.

Proulx, L. (2006) L'écotourisme: une activité d'épanouissement collectif et individuel? Impacts sociaux et culturels du tourisme. In: C. Gagnon and S. Gagnon (eds) *L'écotourisme entre l'arbre et l'écorce: de la conservation au développement viable des territoires.* Presses de l'Université de Québec, Québec, Canada: 13–42.

Rangarajan, M. and Shahabuddin, G. (2006) Displacement and relocation from protected areas: towards a biological and historical synthesis. *Conservation and Society* 4(3):359–378.

Redclift, M. and Springett, D. (eds) (2015) *Routledge International Handbook of Sustainable Development.* Routledge, London and New York.

Richez, G. (1992) *Parcs Nationaux et Tourisme en Europe.* L'Harmattan, Paris.

Sachs, I. (1984) The strategies of ecodevelopment… *Ceres. FAO Review on Agriculture and Development (FAO)* 17:17–21.

Stolton, S. and Dudley, N. (2010) *Arguments for Protected Areas. Multiple Benefits for Conservation and Use.* Earthscan, London and Washington.

Thorsby, D. (2008) *Culture in sustainable development: insights for the future implementation of Art. 13, UNESCO CE/08/Thorsby/Art. 13 Sydney, 14 January 2008.* http://unesdoc.unesco.org/images/0015/001572/157287e.pdf (Accessed 16 May 2017).

Titchen, S. M. (1996) On the construction of 'outstanding universal value': Some comments on the implementation of the 1972 UNESCO World Heritage Convention. *Conservation and Management of Archaeological Sites* 1(4):235–242.

United Cities and Local Governments Committee on Culture and World Secretariat. (2010) *Culture: fourth pillar of sustainable development.* Draft Proposal for Approval of the UCLG Executive Bureau, 16 September 2010. www.agenda21culture.net/sites/default/files/files/documents/en/zz_culture4pillarsd_eng.pdf (Accessed 30 May 2017).

United Nations. (2015) *Transforming our World: the 2030 Agenda for Sustainable Development.* https://sustainabledevelopment.un.org/post2015/transformingourworld (Accessed 28 November 2017).

Venkataraman, B. (2009) Education for sustainable development. *Environment: Science and Policy for Sustainable Development* 51(2):8–10.

Vivien, F. D. (2001) Histoire d'un mot, histoire d'une idée: le développement durable à l'épreuve du temps. In: M. Jollivet, (ed.) *Le développement durable, de l'utopie au concept: des nouveaux chantiers pour la recherche.* Éditions scientifiques et médicales, Elsevier SAS, Paris: 19–60.

Vivien, F. D. (2005) *Le Développement Soutenable.* Édition La Découverte (Collection Repères), Paris.

WCED. (1987) *Our Common Future. World Comission on Environment and Development.* Oxford University Press, Oxford.

Weaver, D. (2001) *Ecotourism.* John Wiley & Sons, Milton, Australia.

West, P. and Brockington, D. (2006) An anthropological perspective on some unexpected consequences of protected areas. *Conservation Biology* 20(3):609–616.

West, P., Igoe, J. and Brockington, D. (2006) Parks and peoples: the social impact of protected areas. *Annu. Rev. Anthropol.* 35:251–277.
Wheeler, S. (2004) *Planning for Sustainability: Creating Liveable, Equitable, and Ecological Communities*. Routledge, London and New York.
White, L. (date unknown) *A brief history of the notion of the sublime.* http://lukewhite.me.uk/sub_history.htm (Accessed 15 June 2017).
Wright, E. O. (2010) *Envisioning Real Utopias.* Verso, London.

4 Culturally sensitive agricultures and biocultural diversity

Cláudia Brites and Pedro Mendes Moreira

Introduction

In 2002 the United Nations Educational, Scientific and Cultural Organization (UNESCO) and United Nations Environment Programme (UNEP) organized a roundtable on Cultural Diversity and Biodiversity for Sustainable Development with an interdisciplinary panel during the World Summit on Sustainable Development (WSSD). There, the importance of respecting and integrating biocultural diversity as a prerequisite for sustainable development was underlined. The homogenization of cultural and biological diversity has been rising with globalization. Some of the least developed countries still have a rich biodiversity and diversified culture, especially in remote areas. Cultural diversity is the critical link between the intangible and tangible dimensions of sustainable development and therefore implementation plan of the WSSD calls for the promotion of culture in the three interdependent and mutually reinforcing pillars of sustainability (UNESCO, 2002).

The concept of culture is a complex one with multiple meanings and connotations that are accompanied by a diverse and pluralistic set of definitions. Consequently, the relationship between culture and sustainable development is not easy to demonstrate, in spite of being widely recognized (Dessein *et al.*, 2015). Culture can be a self-standing, fourth pillar of sustainable development, alongside the environmental, social and economic pillars. Culture can further be incorporated in the ecological, social and economic pillars of sustainable development along with other issues. Here culture is not an additional and fourth pillar, but has an intermediate role giving meaning to the various dimensions of sustainability. Third, culture is also at the core of deep social changes towards sustainable development, underlining the role of cultural values in ecocultural evolution (Dessein *et al.*, 2015).

Sustainable development has been defined as: development that meets the needs of the present without compromizing the ability of future generations to meet their own needs (WCED, 1987). The current unsustainable patterns of production and consumption compromise our future welfare and reduce the possibilities for intergenerational equity. To ensure sustainable development of agricultural production and rural areas it is important to extend the understanding of sustainable development by incorporating cultural aspects. The introduction of cultural aspects to the three pillars of sustainability allows the creation of frameworks that engage farmers and other stakeholders in the search for biocultural diversity-based solutions for increasing agricultural production in a sustainable manner (Jackson *et al.*, 2007).

In the last few decades many rural areas have experienced change in response to global societal developments. The rapidly changing patterns of food consumption in many countries are limiting ecological sustainability, while modern trends of living corrode biodiversity and the socio-cultural framework of which patterns of food consumption are a part. Johns and Sthapit (2004) define the concepts 'Biocultural' and 'Biocultural Diversity' as:

> *Biocultural* emerges conceptually from an anthropological consideration of the manner in which human societies adapt to the varied biological circumstances in which they live. *Biocultural Diversity* is concerned with the relationships among traditional knowledge, biological diversity, and cultural diversity.
>
> (Johns and Sthapit, 2004: p. 143)

International and national policies based on biodiversity and cultural strengths have focused on intrinsic characteristics of long established sustainable food systems. On the other hand, policies can lead susceptible communities in the direction of unsustainability just through a change of practices. A biodiversity-focused approach has significance in development and research that stresses complexity, and that involves several aspects or dimensions including enhanced and sustainable provisioning and cultural services. From a socio-cultural perspective, traditional understandings of biodiversity are potentially important in order to maintain and enhance wellbeing as they provide the motivation for positive practices and sustainable development.

This chapter presents an approach to culture and sustainable development in the context of rural areas and with relevance to the preservation of agricultural resources. First, the role of culture for rural societies will be discussed with a focus on the importance of local value systems. Next, the chapter discusses the need for sustainable agro-systems with a focus on long-term public policy, investments, and infrastructure with active management plans. Third, biocultural diversity is discussed as a particularly problematic but important concept, stressing the need for a co-thinking of biological and cultural diversity in the conservation and use of agricultural landscapes and environments. Conservation of natural environments requires knowledge and the understanding of the human cultures that shaped them. In conclusion, the need for more research on agrobiodiversity and its ecosystems services is emphasized, both to justify agrobiodiversity conservation in traditional agricultural systems, and as a potential source of innovation for sustainable agro-ecosystems.

Rural societies

It is essential to focus on local and cultural value systems when researching agriculture in rural areas. It is the local value system – in a process of constant change – that shapes ways of life, provides practical perspectives and knowledge, and gives meaning to everything important, from food cultures to consumption patterns. Cultural values systems shape and give meaning to local livelihoods. From a developing countries perspective, the farmers' relations to food cultures and local gastronomy often provide the motivation for growing a diverse range of crops, cultivars and local breeds. These contribute to a high dietary diversity and food variety, maintain local culture and ethnic traditions (through use in cultural ceremonies, feast and festivals) and support cultural diversity. Specific plant varieties have become a constituent part of the rural landscapes and cultures as they have considerable value in terms of social prestige and quality of life. Cultivation of some of the more important crops embody cultural activities for all major steps in the production systems that further encourage farmers to maintain different varieties.

The globalization of cultures, business development and the economy in general has promoted the westernization of food systems and diets. In developing countries globalization has consequences that sometimes fail to meet religious and sociocultural needs (Sthapit *et al.*, 2003). As the value systems vary geographically, it is essential to understand and identify cultural aspects of food systems, diets and agriculture more generally (Sthapit *et al.*, 2003). In farming-based communities the surrounding landscape is the source of those elements that contribute to sustainable livelihoods (Sthapit *et al.*, 2003). The key to sustainability depends on human principles and practices, which can be inspired by communities that maintain a strong link with landscape and the natural environment (Johns and Sthapit, 2004).

Societies draw their sustainability – their ability to sustain – from five different sources – physical, financial, human, social and natural capital assets (Granberg *et al.*, 2009). The landscape of a specific region is shaped by (and shapes) the biological diversity and, at the same time, reflects cultural, social and political aspects of the local community. However, the ability of these landscapes to support sustainable livelihoods depends on whether they are being used in appropriate ways.

Threats to the continued existence of some farm animals and plant varieties compromise indigenous communities' practices (e.g. traditional festivities) and values. This may lead to a lack of social meaning and to the loss of cultural niches (Granberg *et al.*, 2009). When cultural meaning is disconnected from these culturally important animals and plants, old traditions can be preserved through folklore but folklore does not, in itself, preserve and sustain the way of life of the community. In a study from Chukotka in northeast Siberia this attitude to indigenous culture was described as follows:

> Each indigenous Siberian nation was supposed to have its 'ethnic culture' manifested through folklore (...). This 'folklore-and-dancing' of native

> culture was quite attractive to many as an established channel for social mobility and prestige… the 'folklore-and-dancing' niche managed to some extent to preserve traditional ethnic cultures and to pass them on to the younger generation in Chukotka and elsewhere across Siberia. Krupnik and Vakhtin in.
>
> (Granberg *et al.*, 2009)

In historical times in agriculturally based societies, knowledge was passed on during socialization activities such as dance and music. In many societies, important knowledge was (and still is) conserved and developed on the agricultural fields, which were places for imparting personal views on living, traditions and knowledge to younger generations. The importance of on-field socialization into farming roles remains a feature of agricultural continuity to this day, even in an industrial agricultural context (Fischer and Burton, 2014).

Throughout history cultural exchange and cultural invasion have led to change, development and even complete abolishment of established local practices. The arrival of new social groups with new cultural values in a territory often required complete cultural and social change in order to maintain dominance (Granberg *et al.*, 2009). However, in many cases (such as in desert or permafrost environments) this led to problems because the incomers were not culturally adapted to the ecological and biological conditions they faced.

The imposition of rules and norms by invading people often failed because they were only specific cultural directives, not socio-cultural representations or ideal-type models that represent or influence changing conditions of the daily life. The real changes of living conditions are the ones that govern thought, behaviour and local ritual practices (Granberg *et al.*, 2009).

Many rural areas in developed and developing countries are in crisis as the local identity is neglected while changes in traditional activities are occurring without preservation of geographically distinct cultural phenomena, forgetting human-environment interactions and ways of sustainable farming. Strategically linked to place-based sustainable development of rural areas we have indigenous cultures, the recognition of local cultural values and promotion of cultural diversity, as well as the preservation and conservation of tangible and intangible cultural heritage. Ultimately this issue is a problem of policies and politics, policy planning and decision-making on sustainable development, sustainable livelihood, cultural democracy and cultural ecology. Due to the complexity of the social interactions and the human-nature relationships inherent to rural areas, the sustainable development of those places needs to look beyond addressing separate social or biophysical issues and adopt a holistic approach that incorporates both simultaneously (Jackson *et al.*, 2007).

In Europe, for example, there are some countries that already have sustainable agricultural development strategies for conservation and sustainable utilization of biodiversity. To ensure agrobiodiversity conservation it is necessary to regulate the use of resources to promote their sustainability. Regulations are also necessary for the maintenance of natural or artificial ecosystems and habitats that are managed by rural communities using traditional farming systems (Park *et al.*, 2005; Al-Atawneh *et al.*, 2008). Existing protected areas already have associated long-term conservation cultures with management plans that avoid problems associated with non-protected areas (such as private land or roadsides where conservation value and sustainability is not a consideration in spite of being present). What is required is a change from conservation to sustainable use for future generations (Maxted *et al.*, 2012) and to ensure cultural cohesion of rural communities.

Sustainable agro-ecosystems

Long-term sustainable development requires public policy, combined investment in rural projects and infrastructure with active management plans. In addition, it requires social-marketing and extension services to local communities and to the owners that offer conservation, nutritional and socio-cultural benefits to consumers. Policies for agrobiodiversity preservation promote the locally adapted crops and their cultural linkages to societies. They are an important means of ensuring sustainable food security. Local farmers adapt crops to their ecological needs and cultural traditions, not only for harvesting and exploitation (Al-Atawneh *et al.*, 2008). In many societies food possesses symbolic and religious significance, as it is a basis for cultural identity and social wellbeing. This cannot be forgotten by any approach (e.g. political, food system, agro-ecosystem) to traditional and modern food culture where the aim is to promote sustainable development (Johns and Sthapit, 2004).

The overall reduction of biodiversity in today's agro-ecosystems is causing great concern among many scientists who deal with the issue of sustainable agricultural production. A biodiversity-based paradigm for sustainable agriculture is a potential solution to many of the ecological problems associated with intensive agriculture. Conservation of existing biodiversity in agricultural landscapes and the adoption of biodiversity-based practices have been proposed as ways of improving the sustainability of agricultural production through greater reliance on ecological goods (Granberg *et al.*, 2009).

To do this, the European Union has made a commitment to conserve and sustainably use its native biological diversity. One example is a project supported by the European Commission's sixth framework programme, 'Networking on conservation and use of plant genetic resources in Europe and Asia' (DIVERSEEDS). Another example is the international treaty for plant genetic resources for food and agriculture. This programme focuses on the plants that are used in agriculture and which contribute to agricultural sustainability and crop improvement (Kell *et al.*, 2008) and which can be prioritized, according to Maxted (2003). Here, different criteria for selection and preservation of plants can be used such as socio-economic use, eco-geographic distribution, current conservation status, cultural importance, threat of genetic erosion, cost feasibility and sustainability, genetic distinctiveness, ethics and aesthetics, biological importance, priorities of the conservation agency and legislation.

This prioritization is needed to dynamically illustrate the importance of these resources to community networks and to promote their sustainable use. The reason is that conservation of biodiversity is fundamental to preventing the erosion of cultural diversity in rural societies that rely on natural resources to survive (Maxted, 2003; Granberg *et al.*, 2009).

The value of agricultural biodiversity is significant and plays an important role in providing for short-term needs (nutritional, health, social and cultural) of a population. In the long-term, agricultural biodiversity protects and enhances genetic resources for the sustainable development of rural areas (Sthapit *et al.*, 2003). These genetic resources can be maintained *ex situ* in gene banks, but besides the low sustainability of this system and the high-energy input required, many require specific indigenous knowledge or indigenous management systems that are not so easily stored and reconstructed. Sustainable development depends on using the landrace that is strongly associated with sustainable landrace conservation (Banterng *et al.*, 2008).

Farmer-developed populations of cultivated species in traditional cultures reliant on small-scale agriculture show a high genetic diversity. These populations are linked to traditional cultures in a complex intertwining of the biological and cultural contexts and have a major role in sustainability of traditional farming systems (Negri, 2005).

A landrace is a locally adapted variety that is linked with traditional farming and cultural systems and to the cultural heritage of the human population who developed it and its place of origin. Landraces are part of local knowledge and cultural systems, from proverbs to myths and larger symbols that bind communities together, and are thus relevant in many different cultural contexts. They continue to be maintained as a result of social preferences and practices, as well as economic and cultural factors (Banterng *et al.*, 2008). Negri (2005) defines a landrace as a variable population, which is identifiable and usually has a local name. It has distinctive features characterized by a specific adaptation to the environmental conditions of the area of cultivation (tolerant to the biotic and abiotic stresses of that area). In addition, it has a great cultural value for the community related to the traditional uses, knowledge, habits, dialects and celebrations.

Landraces are of considerable cultural importance. In particular, the cultural and familial substrates of landraces strengthen social identity and cohesion in rural communities and have a considerable impact on the local cultures, while biological and human-driven cultural evolution generates new resources for the future (Negri, 2005). Further, specific landraces are valued for local food culture and special occasions for social prestige and quality of life (Sthapit *et al.*, 2003) and have the potential to be used in sustainable agricultural intensification.

All these values and functions of the local breeds can be examined under the heading of sustainable development. It has been suggested that sustainable societies can only be constructed on the basis of locally relevant agriculture, utilizing the local resources and production culture, shaped by locally specific environmental conditions and cultural practices. They promote sustainable agricultures and a sustainable way of life at the local level and beyond (Granberg *et al.*, 2009).

To improve the income of farmers and to promote public awareness of local landraces some local governments have developed programmes for ecotourism, cultural development and education (Park *et al.*, 2005). Although it recently became an important theme in research aimed at improving the sustainability of modern agriculture, it is vital to realize that projects have costs. It is necessary to both guarantee funding (Al-Atawneh *et al.*, 2008; Kell *et al.*, 2008) and pay the farmers for the socio-cultural benefits that they provide to consumers (Park *et al.*, 2005). Nevertheless, in developing such programmes, it is also necessary to be aware of the risk of transforming the agricultural systems into a 'Disneyland' of rural areas (UNESCO, 2002).

Sustainable production is a concept that has broad cross-cultural transference, as is evidenced by the fact that countries with very distinct food cultures and dietary diversity support it. In small-scale and sustainable agriculture the agro-biodiversity conservation, socio-cultural and agronomic aspects are priorities (Johns and Sthapit, 2004). Therefore, it is of crucial importance for ecologically sustainable agriculture to focus on ways of achieving agrobiodiversity and to value the services farmers perform in enhancing the long-term sustainability of agro-ecosystems.

Biocultural diversity

The tendency in the research and policy spheres to separate biological and cultural diversity is problematic as it fails to appreciate the reciprocal relationship between the two. An understanding of both biological and cultural diversity and how they work together – as biocultural diversity – is thus necessary to ensure the resilience of social and ecological systems (UNESCO, 2002). Biological diversity can be a reflection of cultural diversity as different cultures and communities may produce different biological goods and services they require to meet their cultural needs (Sthapit *et al.*, 2003). On the other hand, it is also possible for specific cultural groups to require biologically diverse landscapes in order to provide for their cultural needs. In either case, the diversity of needs of the culture/s becomes the predominant driver for a biologically diverse agricultural landscape and the landscape is at once biological and cultural – biocultural.

To make changes in the landscape – for example to enhance biodiversity – consumption patterns and cultural change must be acknowledged as important drivers behind land use. The key role of culture further means that such changes must be handled sensitively as, to ensure resilience, an understanding of the relationship between the biological diversity and cultural diversity is required.

Genetic diversity resulting from local farming practices provides both direct and indirect support for cultural practices, satisfying for example, religious and ethnic needs directly. In a socio-cultural sense, some animal breeds can be compared with endangered wild animal species where conservation is necessary to meet not only environmental, but also cultural and social objectives as well (Granberg *et al.*, 2009). The big challenge is to find ways of meeting these different needs in a sustainable fashion.

'Food security' and 'health and environmental sustainability' are key concepts in official policies and declarations concerning both the conservation and use of the environment and the provision of adequate nutrition (regionally and globally) (Al-Atawneh *et al.*, 2008). Therefore, to achieve goals of conservation and sustainable use of traditional genetic resources and food-systems, it is essential to simultaneously meet the demand for future food security and sustainable agricultural development (Johns and Sthapit, 2004; Park *et al.*, 2005).

The use of traditional knowledge in innovation practices of indigenous and local farmers is essential to maintain the diversity of both local landscapes and cultures (Alvarez *et al.*, 2005; Park *et al.*, 2005). In this context, the sustainable livelihoods approach can be used to investigate human-nature interactions. This approach combines the concept of capability with the notions of equity and long-term environmental sustainability and makes it possible to analyse whether a form of livelihood is sustainable. Sustainability is judged to have been achieved if, after a stress event, the system can maintain or enhance its capabilities and assets and provide sustainable livelihood opportunities for the next generation (Granberg *et al.*, 2009).

Farmers in traditional home gardens often maximize the range of cultivated species by growing a diverse range of crops – a practice that is also integrated with traditional cultural practices. Attachment to the local food is often cited as a reason for this behaviour (Sthapit *et al.*, 2003). For example, Sthapit *et al.* (2003) reported that the high dietary diversity and food variety of Vietnamese people in both the lowland Mekong delta and Central Highlands are both associated with local food culture. Because of the value placed by farmers on rice there are cultural activities (such as religious ceremonies) involved in all the major steps of rice production. The ceremonial importance of rice production also illustrates how local food culture and festivals encourage farmers to maintain a wide range of the preferred rice varieties (Sthapit *et al.*, 2003).

In the same way, diversity determines the distribution of rice landraces, and especially those that are culturally or nutritionally valued. These tend to be grown by many households – albeit at a relatively small scale because of low productivity (Sthapit *et al.*, 2003). The production of multiple varieties promotes agricultural sustainability by reducing a farmer's economic dependence on a single crop. It also contributes to ecological sustainability through the ecosystem services that the enhanced biodiversity provides. The varieties cultivated in home gardens are commonly used in cultural ceremonies and feasts and contribute to the overall cultural diversity. Specific cultural values associated with the use of local varieties leads to the conservation of a variety of unique crops and cultivars in home gardens as farmers recognize that landrace diversity is closely linked to their cultural needs (Sthapit *et al.*, 2003).

A similar situation takes place with animal breeds used in traditional farming systems. For example, molecular genetic analysis has revealed that the Yakutian Cattle (cows and horses of Siberian regions) are important for the maintenance of bovine and equine genetic diversity (Granberg *et al.*, 2009). It is a common practice in remote villages and communities to cultivate crops and harvest wild species from natural areas in order to maintain or increase agricultural productivity, resilience and sustainability (Jackson *et al.*, 2007). This is very important because wild plants related to modern crops can be used to increase agricultural productivity. The disappearance of landraces leads to genetic erosion, and can also both erode local culture and hamper biological and cultural evolution (Negri, 2005).

Nature-based cultural events in rural areas take forms distinctly different from those happening in urban contexts. The development policies for rural areas (such as regeneration programmes) need to respect the cultural needs of the local communities that are dependent on the surrounding environment for their livelihoods, strengthening the local and regional value system. However, the diversity of values and meanings amongst rural communities and a lack of understanding of the importance of biocultural diversity means that such programmes are difficult to both establish and maintain. A participatory approach to the development of such programmes and policies could be an effective means of creating robust policies and programmes.

Assessments of folk culture can be used to evaluate the values and meanings and develop plans for the conservation and sustainable use of biodiversity in a specific agricultural landscape. In terms of youth involvement in particular, participation in events related to folk culture provides a means of motivating young people to engage with sustainable practices based on their cultural heritage. This promotes future sustainability by embedding sustainable practices into the living culture.

The Convention for Biological Diversity recognizes that knowledge, innovation and practices of indigenous and local communities (which embody traditional lifestyles) are relevant for the conservation and sustainable use of biological diversity. The mutual relationship between the cultural aspects of communities and biodiversity is reflected in these three components. Local breeds are seen as contributing to cultural diversity as one example of the preservation of a diverse range of cultural practices and values. The Convention for the Safeguarding of the Intangible Cultural Heritage (2003) and the Convention on the Protection and Promotion of the Diversity of Cultural Expressions (2005) should also to be taken into consideration in the context of conservation, as they emphasize the interdependence between the intangible cultural heritage and the tangible cultural and natural heritage (Granberg *et al.*, 2009).

Landraces and local breeds have shaped cultural systems while, at the same time, culturally based human activities have affected their evolution. From a cultural perspective, they are sources and stewards of cultural heritage. They also serve as a resource for the creation and transformation of intellectual and cultural capital through science and education. The cultural values of the local breeds and landraces have been viewed by western societies as a basis for economic activities (Granberg *et al.*, 2009).

Consequently, there exists a moral responsibility for us towards maintaining cultural diversity as a common heritage of humanity. It is a responsibility to take care of cultural traditions and cultural diversity as a value in itself, reflecting human goals and aspirations. Cultural diversity is also a means of ensuring the continuation of traditions and a range of cultural identities. If we examine the contribution of the Yakutian Cattle, for example, from a cultural point of view they influence the local way of life, local food culture, and local knowledge (Granberg *et al.*, 2009).

An increase in the cost of production is an issue commonly cited as a reason against a focus on sustainable agro-ecosystems. However, many authors argue that sustainable agro-ecosystems should be maintained and promoted (Granberg *et al.*, 2009) even if they are likely to increase the cost of production (Negri, 2005). The preservation of natural and cultural heritage has a higher intrinsic value than the immediate economic cost (Granberg *et al.*, 2009).

The cultural distinctiveness of ethnic groups is based on aspects associated with biocultural diversity. Landraces and local breeds can be considered local cultural assets or ‘capital’ generated by rural communities in sustainable ecosystems, in a deep relationship between biological and cultural contexts (Negri, 2005). Biocultural diversity represents preservation of the traditional way of life and conservation of cultural heritage, considered important for maintaining and strengthening the cultural identity of the indigenous people (Granberg *et al.*, 2009).

It is possible that a focus on cultural significance is the easiest way to convince politicians and ordinary people about the importance of conserving biocultural diversity. In this respect, we should bear in mind the most significant achievements of indigenous people: that they created and preserved their own culture, even in post-colonial times. Ethnic revitalization of a culture has taken place in many rural areas as indigenous people have rediscovered their ethnic roots and cultural traditions (Granberg *et al.*, 2009). Although, we should bear in mind that culture is not a thing, but a practice, which makes communication possible.

There exists thus a wide range of cultural values related to biocultural diversity. One question arises: what is the future for these cultural values and meanings? This question urges us to communicate widely the values of biocultural diversity found in local food production and local culture. If we want to keep villages settled and strengthen cultural identity, several important aspects of biocultural diversity must be acknowledged. Biocultural diversity represents the deepest cultural meanings and values related to identity (and in particular ethnic identity), it represents sense of place (in terms of regional identity) and it represents scientific and educational value (Granberg *et al.*, 2009). The cultural and socio-economic values are emphasized in our understanding of biocultural diversity. They are connected to the cultural identity of rural communities as places, therefore, biocultural diversity is extremely connected to the territory, in addition to being connected to the genetic resources.

Conclusions

In this chapter we have discussed how biocultural diversity promotes sustainable development. From a socio-cultural perspective, it provides a nexus for change in individual and group practices and, thus, is an essential factor to consider when promoting production and consumption changes at the household level. Such changes can be based on the experiences of multiple households cultivating landraces on a small scale for socio-cultural purposes (Sthapit *et al.*, 2003). At the community level, deep cultural change can be activated through practical programmes that balance environmental concerns and human wellbeing. Finally, at the policy-level, for example in cultural policies and development programmes or research, it is possible to introduce choices based on theoretical and moral considerations and socio-cultural values (Johns and Sthapit, 2004).

Food security and environmental sustainability in the twenty-first century depend on available genetic resources, resources that need to be conserved both *ex situ* and *in situ.* Preserving these genetic resources without also preserving the established cultural knowledge/practices concerning management diminishes the potential to use these resources to promote sustainability within rural communities. Having a material resource may not be sufficient without the cultural resources in place to use it sustainably, and economic motivation alone may not ensure the continued preservation and economic development of the resource (see the example of fell farming in Burton, this publication: p. 137). Therefore, management plans that consider conservation and sustainable use of biocultural resources for specific regions or communities are very important in order to maintain the close connection between cultural values and crops (Al-Atawneh *et al.*, 2008).

Cultural diversity also plays a role in in biodiversity conservation. A socially diverse system is likely to be more flexible and therefore more sustainable than a structure with a single type of production unit (Granberg *et al.*, 2009). Recognition of the important role that agriculture plays in ecological sustainability is a prerequisite for a sustainable development of rural areas. In particular, such recognition can harvest the determination of farming communities to preserve their own culture and way of life (Negri, 2005) (UNESCO, 2002) – something which may be absent if well-intended measures are simply imposed on people.

In terms of future developments, this chapter illustrates the need for more research on agrobiodiversity and its ecosystems services. In a rapidly changing world we face the potential loss of not only the world's genetic resources but also the cultures and environments in which they developed. Understanding the connection between culture and biodiversity is a critical step not only to preserve genetic resources, but also to understand how these resources can contribute to some of the major sustainability challenges facing the world at the moment. Cultural heritage is a critical motivating factor in this respect, and, when this is associated with the preservation of a diverse range of species (landraces), fostering pride in cultural practices could play an important role in promoting sustainability. Thus, future research on cultural and biocultural diversity is needed to shift the present systems towards more environmentally friendly agricultural and sustainable systems. It is of critical importance to connect to the past while looking to the future, in order to not have irremediable losses for all humankind.

References

Al-Atawneh, N., Amri, A., Assi, R. and Maxted, N. (2008) Management Plans for Promoting In Situ Conservation of Local Agrobiodiversity in the West Asia Centre of Plant Diversity. In: N. Maxted, B. Ford-Lloyd, S. Kell, J. Iriondo, M. E. Dulloo and J. Turok. (eds) *Crop Wild Relative Conservation and Use.* CABI, Wallingford, United Kingdom: 340–363.

Alvarez, N., Garine, E., Khasah, C., Dounias, E., Hossaert-McKey, M. and McKey, D. (2005) Farmers' practices, metapopulation dynamics, and conservation of agricultural biodiversity on-farm: a case study of sorghum among the Duupa in sub-sahelian Cameroon. *Biological Conservation* 121(4):533–543.

Banterng, P., Barazani, O., Engels, J., Ford-Lloyd, B., Hadas, R., Hager, V., Khoshbakht, K., Lam, N. T., Maxted, N., Ratanasatien, C., Schidt, M. and Wei, W. (2008) *DIVERSEEDS e-conference on conservation and sustainable use of plant genetic resources in Europe and Asia.* www.diverseeds.eu/forum/ (Accessed 26 August 2008).

Dessein, J., Soini, K., Fairclough, G. and Horlings, L. (2015). *Culture in, for and as Sustainable Development. Conclusions from the COST Action IS1007 Investigating Cultural Sustainability.* University of Jyväskylä, Jyväskylä.

Fischer, H. and Burton, R. J. F. (2014) Understanding farm succession as a socially constructed endogenous cycle. *Sociologia Ruralis* 54(4):417–438.

Granberg, L., Kantanen, J. and Soini, K. (eds) (2009) *Sakha Ynaga.* Finish Academy of Science and Letters, Helsinki.

Jackson, L., Pascual, U. and Hodgkin, T. (2007) Utilizing and conserving agrobiodiversity in agricultural landscapes. *Agriculture, Ecossystems and Environment* 121:196–210.

Johns, T. and Sthapit, B. R. (2004) Biocultural diversity in the sustainability of developing-country food systems. *Food & Nutrition Bulletin* 25(2):143–155.

Kell, S. P., Laguna, E., Iriondo, J. M. and Dullo, M. E. (2008) Population and Habitat Recovery Techniques for the In Situ Conservation of Plant Genetic Diversity. In: J. M. Iriondo, N. Maxted and M. E. Dulloo, *Conserving Plant Genetic Diversity in Protected Areas.* CABI, Pondicherry, India: 124–168.

Maxted, N. (2003) Conserving the genetic resources of crop wild relatives in European Protected Areas (E. S. Ltd., Ed.) *Biological Conservation* 113(3):411–417.

Maxted, N., Akparov, Z., Aronsson, M., Asdal, Å., Avagyan, A., Bartha, B., Benediková, D., Berishvili, T., Bocci, R., Cop, J., Curtis, T., Daugstad, K., Dias, S., Duarte, M.C., Dzmitryeva, S., Engels, J., Ferant, N., Freudenthaler, P., Frese, L., Hadas, R., Holly, L., Ibraliu, A., Iriondo Alegría, J. M., Ivanovska, S., Kik, C., Korpelainen, H., Jinjikhadze, T., Kamari, G., Kell, S. P., Kristiansen, K., Kyratzis, A., Labokas, J., Maggioni, L., Magos Brehm, J., Maloupa, E., Martinez, J. J. R., Mendes Moreira, P. M. R., Musayev, M., Orphanidou, P., Radun, M., Ralli, P., Sandru, D., Sarikyan, K., Schierscher-Viret, B., Stehno, Z., Stoilova, T., Strajeru, S., Smekalova, T., Tan, A., Vorosvary, G., Veteläinen, M., Vögel R. and Negri, V. (2012) Current and Future Threats and Opportunities Facing European Crop Wild Relatives and Landraces Diversity. In: N. Maxted, M. Dulloo, M. Ford-Lloyd, B. Frese, L. Iriondo and J. Pinheiro de Carvalho (eds) *Agrobiodiversity Conservation: Securing the Diversity of Crop Wild Relatives and Landraces.* CABI, Wallingford, United Kingdom: 333–353.

Negri, V. (2005) Agro-biodiversity conservation in Europe: ethical issues. *Journal of Agriicultural and Environmental Ethics* 18:3–25.

Park, Y. -J., Dixit, A., Ma, K. -H., Kang, J. -H., Rao, V. R. and Cho, E. -G. (2005) On-farm Conservation Strategy to Ensure Crop Genetic Diversity in Changing agro-ecosystems in the Republic of Korea. *Journal of Agronomy and Crop Science* 191:401–410.

Sthapit, B., Rana, R., Eyzaguirre, P. and Jarvis, D. (2003) *The Value of Plant Genetic Ddiversity to Resource-Poor Farmers*. Tri-societies Conference. ASA-CSSA-SSSA, Denver.

UNESCO. (2002) *Cultural Diversity and Biodiversity for Sustainable Development*. UNEP, Johannesburg.

WCED. (1987) *Our Common Future. World Comission on Environment and Development*. Oxford University Press, Oxford.

5 A matter of context and balance

Pre-industrial conceptions of sustainability

Viðar Hreinsson

Introduction: poetry and philosophy

The American poet and essayist Bill Holm (1943–2009) once wrote:

> BIRD POETRY ON SKAGAFJORD
> Seabirds arrange themselves into a sentence on the water.
> A crooked line of gulls and ducks
> bob into the slow tide for breakfast.
> Enough for everybody under here!
>
> They are spelling something – a message
> in white and gray, printed
> on blue textured paper.
> Much as I squint and mumble
> to myself, it still won't come clear.
>
> Every now and then, a letter or a whole
> syllable takes off into the air,
> rearranges itself in the dative case,
> or maybe a plural. It seems
> too certain to be subjunctive. The raven
> punctuates the sentence.
>
> The bird letter arrives
> for me to admire,
> but never understand.
>
> (Holm, 2004: p. 6)[1]

Apart from conveying the semiotic generosity of nature, the poem gently outlines the sheer impossibility of fully conceptualizing or understanding nature. Nature is converted into cultural terms, physical and mental food, messages, meaning, but we can only admire it from afar, without understanding it completely. Language is a sign-system that is never entirely systematic, it is elusive, it escapes definitions easily, it develops constantly and sometimes unexpectedly in an interaction with technology, as is obvious in the various electronic social media.

Literatures and sciences are in a quest for different kinds of truth, but no truth is absolute except the totality of being. All sign systems and methods of measurement come too short in one way or another. Scientific knowledge is fragmented, capturing only limited aspects of the reality or nature, and universal laws are predominantly theoretical. There is always an alienating gap between human expression and reality and some fill this gap in their knowledge with gods (according to Spinoza, 2002: p. 241). All forms of knowledge need to acknowledge these limitations and reflect upon a larger context. Literary studies, and even all humanities, operate in the vast field of meanings that escape 'exact' knowledge, claiming that there are truths and insights different from those of the assumed 'exact' sciences.

Cultural sustainability, the embeddedness of sustainability in culture, is a modern concept. Modern unsustainability is a product of consumer-driven market ideology infiltrated in Western myths of progress and growth. It is possible to reach behind the myths and investigate earlier conceptions of the relations between humans and nature. Modern ideas of domination over nature are based on a mechanical worldview that replaced an organic one in the seventeenth century (Merchant, [1980]1989). This chapter will investigate pre-enlightenment conceptions of nature and cultural sustainability that can be compared with current ideas of sustainable development.

Original concerns for technology and sustainability

Two prominent philosophers have addressed the dangers of unreflected knowledge and technology. Their ideas can be applied to current environmental threats in order to underpin the importance of cultural sustainability.

Hannah Arendt pointed to a split between technology and thinking nearly 60 years ago, in her 1958 classic *The Human Condition*:

> If it should turn out to be true that knowledge (in the modern sense of know-how) and thought have parted company for good, then we would indeed become the helpless slaves, not so much of our machines as of our know-how, thoughtless creatures at the mercy of every gadget which is technically possible, no matter how murderous it is.
>
> (Arendt, [1958]1998: p. 3)

This reflects a contention that technical achievements justify any action, without considering the consequences or context. This was written in the same year as Rachel Carson realized that she would have to write *Silent Spring*, a milestone in the environmental movement, because of its exposure of the harmful use of pesticides (Carson, [1962]2002: p. viii).

The Finnish philosopher Georg Henrik von Wright, has described as 'deadly' the alliance between science, technology and capital, that form the cornerstones of the conventional ideas of progress. This alliance is deterministic and tends to renounce the harmful consequences of 'scientifically' based human activities (von Wright, 2003: pp. 62, 106, 232–239; Hreinsson, 2014). He states boldly that the perilous quandary of the modern technocracy and belief in science is rooted in arrogant reductionism that followed the Enlightenment in the eighteenth century. He calls it the myth of progress, myth in the sense of unsubstantiated or false collective assumptions behind activities or institutions. Along with the Enlightenment, an idea developed that thought and knowledge had been liberated from the authority of the Word and religion, and it would be possible to reach ultimate truths by means of science (von Wright, 2003: p. 62). According to von Wright, the liberation that followed the Enlightenment, as well as the nineteenth and twentieth century positivism and belief in progress, is in fact leading to a new kind of slavery where technocracies replace political systems (von Wright, 2003: p. 106). He claims that one of the reasons for this impasse is a kind of a causal determinism, that claims reality to be in accordance with laws that make it basically comprehensible.

During the twentieth century, philosophers have increasingly realized that reality is not that simple, but is rather uncertain and chaotic, and consequently this old and simplistic, scientific worldview has been crumbling. Ideas about the predictability of natural processes are changing and the deterministic halo is gradually disappearing from the worldview of science. The arrogance of the old scientism is giving way to more modesty towards reality and everything that is unpredictable and chaotic (von Wright, 2003: pp. 232–239). Nature is essentially chaotic and complicated, escaping the old Newtonian physical mechanics. Carolyn Merchant, quoting Jennifer Wells' *Complexity and Sustainability* postulates a new paradigm shift that adopts complexity as a new framework for approaches to nature, in order to achieve sustainability (Merchant, 2016: pp. 2–4, 150–153). Wells wrote:

> Complexity has long been eschewed in pursuit of certainty, order, and control. Today, complexity is emerging onto the scene in all directions. Scientific and scholarly discoveries and analyses have been cracking open and exposing the dangerous simplicities of classical thinking. Finally, the dam of modernity has been broken.
>
> (Wells, 2013: p. 50)

Obviously, something has gone woefully wrong and mankind is dealing with the consequences of short-sighted human activities and environmental threats to all life on earth due to dominating instrumentality and mechanical frames of mind that have alienated organic life.

Nature, cultural history and sustainability

The problem described above is an aspect of deep changes in the conception of, or attitude to nature and resources, caused by the two fateful revolutions of science and industry. Both were at least ambiguous and possibly even paradoxical: having simultaneously greatly improved living conditions and caused the environmental threats of today. Both revolutions were deeply unsustainable, in regarding nature as a controllable and inexhaustible resource, often precluding the possibilities of harmful consequences.

Global pollution and unsustainable development is a consequence of the industrialization following the Enlightenment. Linear rationalism led to the domination of nature and the idea that it would be possible to reach ultimate knowledge. The material development was indeed a response to poor conditions, a development towards prosperity and consumption – and there is, indeed, nothing wrong with improving conditions and quality of life. But the Western world is now far beyond normal sustenance, and appears to be at a tipping point. Material progress was above all based on a vision of the future, a brave new world, but the journey towards this bright future has gone in the wrong direction. Humans have distanced themselves from nature in order to improve conditions, claiming to have conquered it on the path of what is often only imaginary progress.

Environmentally damaging activities that result from the capitalist, consumer-driven ideology of economic expansion and accumulation (Löwy, 2010) are justified among other things by the modern myths of progress described above. Although the idea of persistent economic growth has been subject to increasing criticism, it forms the basis of the rhetoric of politicians as well as mainstream economics; that is, the neoliberal economics that have dominated since the late 1980s based on open markets and free trade, deregulation and privatization as well as reduced government spending (Martin, 2016).

Growth is a metaphor in this context, and rather unfortunate, since it reveals how language blurs rather than clarifies. The metaphor is taken from living organisms. Nothing grows endlessly but the word connotes organic growth that is essentially self-regulated within larger ecosystems. The metaphoric usage indicates organic self-regulation in economic systems, thus indirectly postulating deregulation. Living organisms do not accumulate or grow endlessly in one direction. Life is rather a circulation of growth and decay in constant, tangled webs of life. Accumulation or expansion would be more appropriate terms. By using this metaphor, the meaning of growth has been banalized, reduced to a phenomenon that is inapplicable to organic life, becoming empty rhetoric that conceals the negative externalities. It requires cultural knowledge to reveal this production of meaning that disguises an unsustainable phenomenon. Another aspect of the culturally conditioned linking of economic thinking and language is that social or cultural phenomena acquire monetary meanings in terms such as human capital, to invest time or energy etc. which represents a kind of economical capturing of language (see Bourdieu, 1986).

The idea of sustainable development is a response to the increased impact of unsustainable human activities in modern times. The period from the mid-eighteenth century is now called Anthropocene and has been the subject of lively discussion since Crutzen and Stoermer proposed the term in the year 2000, in order to draw attention to the extent of the impact of human activities (Crutzen and Stoermer, 2000). Although climate change has greatly overshadowed other aspects of this impact, such as pollution and resource depletion, it might be more fruitful to observe the world's environmental problems as a whole. The global environmental crisis has traditionally been regarded as a subject for the natural sciences but there has been an increasing recognition of the need to involve the humanities and social sciences to a much greater extent, in order to view the problem in a larger, more comprehensive context (Palsson *et al.*, 2013: pp. 3–4). Ultimately this requires a greater involvement of culture in sustainability.

Sustainable development is a meaningful concept based on reason but has to some extent been deprived of its meaning – turned into a handy slogan for politicians and business leaders, often only as an obligatory affix in speeches and policies. Although sustainable development is a necessary and progressive idea, it reflects the rationalism described above and can therefore be problematic and in need of reconsideration in acknowledgement of complexity and chaos, the uncontrollability of nature (Merchant, 2016: pp. 149–150). This is where the cultural aspect, cultural sustainability, enters the scene in order to add such necessary dimensions. Studies into the relations between humans and nature throughout history can shed light on the ideologies behind the domination of nature inherent in conventional reason, or the assumed rationality of a variety of activities, such as instrumental or technical rationalism. Nature has for a long time been a reified object for human operations or exploitation, and thus oppressed, without any sense of humans being part of nature.

The 'ship of rational fools' is a metaphor that Val Plumwood uses to introduce her analysis of the deep crisis of Western reason and rationalist culture. She argues: 'The ecological crisis we face then is both a crisis of the dominant culture and a crisis of reason, or rather, a crisis of the culture of reason or of what the dominant global culture has made of reason'. These forms of reason, she argues, are behind the domination of and disengagement from nature and consequently are directly responsible for the environmental crisis (Plumwood, 2002: pp. 1, 5). Plumwood sees this corrupt form for reason as linear, and an aspect of the Cartesian turn, the rationalist way of thinking. It might be fruitful to browse through the cultural history and discover the past in the present, in order to understand better the grand narratives and the shallow myths of progress that have led to the modern ecological crisis. It is interesting, in this context, to look into the pre-enlightenment concept of nature, in order to examine some ideas in traditional pre-industrial societies, that, *mutatis mutandis*, might shed light on modernity. It might be useful to try to reach behind modern society and culture, and investigate earlier cultures, earlier conceptions of the interface between humans and nature. It is possible to develop a more pluralist concept of the human-nature interface, as the current ideas of sustainable development are still too strongly dominated by conventional rationalist and mechanical perspectives. There might be a good reason to reconsider the meanings of the past, the ways of thinking and acting in the past, in the same way as it is necessary to redefine humans in nature – to create dialogues with past cultures and try to understand their ways of thinking, patterns and processes of thought. The past is an important component of cultural diversity, an important response to the hegemony of instrumental rationalism.

The fall and the original sin?

Culture is, in the broad, anthropological sense, ways of life and networks of conceptual systems that determine human behaviour and social relationships (Geertz, 1973: pp. 3–30) and connect material development with the development of knowledge and ideas. In that sense, it is the crisis of Western rational culture that has resulted in the environmental crisis. The most important aspect of the changes that led to the present situation is perhaps the subsumption of nature under humans, the emergence of the modern ideas of domination over nature from the seventeenth century and onwards, the objectification of nature that also included reductionism and fragmentation of knowledge. In somewhat simplified terms, the mechanical worldview that replaced to a large extent an organic one (Merchant, [1980]1989).

This is a variation of the biblical fall of man and the subsequent original sin, an eternal loss of innocence. It is, however, not that simple and straightforward, not a question of a return from the modern, fragmented realities back to the natural innocence of the beginning of times, from the fearful symmetry of the Tiger to the innocence of the Lamb, to refer to well-known poems by William Blake. All kinds of viral wisdom in this vein circulate in cyberspace. Native American Indian wisdom is quite common, providing messages about humans and the living Earth. Some of these stress sustainable ways of living – and may well be true and authentic, for instance, at the core of sustainable development, the story of how the earth is not given to us by our parents but loaned to us by our children. That, however, does not necessarily mean that all Native Indian cultures were sustainable in every respect. Environmental movements have often labelled Native Indians as 'ecologically noble' but the reality is a bit more complicated as this slogan indicates: 'Save a whale, harpoon a Makah' – seen when militant environmentalists protested against whaling by Makah Indians in the Pacific (Nadasdy, 2005: quotation p. 291).

The same counts for assumed wisdoms of past, pre-industrial societies. Although we nostalgically observe the holistic or organic worldviews that yielded for the mechanic, modern outlook, and revere figures like St Francis of Assisi preaching to birds, it cannot be taken for granted that ancient views on nature and the environment are ideal. Sustainable ways of life in the pre-industrial past may well be due to technological shortcomings. For instance, when the Basques were pioneers in developing industrial whaling in the sixteenth century and sailed to Newfoundland, due to bigger and better ships, they overharvested from the stock in a few years around 1600 and went on to Iceland instead (Miglio, 2015). The improved technology immediately made the whale hunting unsustainable and there was nothing inherent in the whalers' mindset that prevented it.

Cultural sustainability is a question of relations to nature and its resources, especially the closeness to or distance from nature. Ever since tools replaced the teeth and fingernails in the eating and processing of prey, humans have distanced themselves from nature and lost some sense of it, but at the same time gained new skills and knowledge instead. It is impossible to return to nature, in order to regain a long-lost affinity. But, having distanced themselves from nature or lost this presumed, immediate affinity, humans must reflect upon it and extract knowledge and insights from the past. Human relations to nature are a prominent theme throughout our cultural history, all the way from ancient myths and legends to modern times. Old myths, being Greek or old Scandinavian, deal precisely with distance or closeness to nature and the moral implications thereof. The well-known story of the Rheingold in old Scandinavian legend has themes of this kind, a mythical logic of closeness to and distance from earth or nature. In the tale the hero kills the dragon Fáfnir and takes hold of the gold that had grown along with the dragon. The gold was thus a kind of a natural or savage element and becomes an evil force in the story, an earthly element that prevents people from establishing healthy relations between themselves (Hreinsson, 1999). This myth reveals deep moral ambiguities in the relations between humans and nature, i.e. humans are incapable of distancing themselves completely from nature.

The Renaissance

How was nature, and human relations to nature, cognitively understood in the Middle Ages and Renaissance? What was the mentality, what were the reflected views, in philosophy, theology, sciences and cosmology? Traditional environmental history deals with tangible realities and experiences, daily life and work, but how did people conceive the world and was there any concept resembling cultural sustainability?

The period from the late Middle Ages through the Renaissance to the Enlightenment is a crucial period of a paradigm shift in human approaches to nature, the shift from the organic to the mechanical outlook (Merchant, [1980]1989). Late medieval 'Western culture distinguished sharply between nature as cognitively understood essence and nature as experienced physical environment' (Siewers, 2009: p. 20) and perhaps a similar distinction is needed today, as a cultural or philosophical foundation for more holistic sustainable development. With regards to the 'experienced physical environment', overexploitation of resources on economic grounds will gradually be replaced by restrictions on practical grounds in order to maintain human life on earth. But perhaps one comes too short in sorting out the 'cognitively understood essence', that is, some generally accepted metaphysical qualities (Siewers, 2009: p. 20).

Nature was to a large extent conceived as mysterious and marvellous – full of wonders that were sometimes collected into cabinets ('Wunderkammer'). Nature was a complicated web of signs and meanings from which it was possible to decode the meanings that God had implanted. Everything was connected in an organic whole, where microcosmos reflected the macrocosmos. It was recognized that there was much still to be discovered (Merchant, 1980: pp. 99–126; Asworth, 2003). Philosophical and theological approaches were inseparable and the conduct of the two main powers, the worldly (royal/feudal) and the spiritual (the church) was intertwined. Nature, or Earth was to a large extent conceived of as a living being, inhabited by hidden beings who were increasingly demonized by the church. Natural magic was common, consisting mainly of attempts to get to grips with nature and understand it. Many of the greatest Renaissance innovators of science were magicians (Kieckhefer, [1989]2000; Russell and Brooks, 2007: pp. 13–14; Siewers, 2009).

The conception of nature was purely qualitative in the Middle Ages, not partly quantitative as it is today, where it is, in some influential fields or power centres of society, such as politics, business and economics, conceived as a manipulable, external object. The Latin meaning of the term nature was dynamic and organic, related to birth and creation (Hreinsson, 2018: p. 67). Isidore of Sevilla defined nature in the seventh century like this: 'Nature (*natura*) is so called because it causes something to be born … for it has the power of engendering and creating. Some people say that this is God, by whom all things have been created and exist' (Isidore, 2006: p. 231). Later in the Middle Ages, natural law meant simply striving for God and perfection, since all creatures seek the fulfillment of their natures but only man is aware of it (McInerny and O'Callaghan, 2014).

In the early seventeenth century, a typical definition of the Latin word 'natura' would be something like this, almost exclusively qualitative: (1) 'natura naturans' being the spirit of God as father and creator (master builder) of all things, (2) the intrinsic essence or meaning of all things, (3) the complete whole of all created things, (4) natural causes, since God and Nature never act without a reason, which excludes vacuum, (5) every spiritual being's temperament, a blend of the four elements, and (6) the becoming of living beings, the literal meaning of birth (Hreinsson, 2018: p. 68).

Later, the concept of 'nature' acquired increasingly objectified and quantitative meaning, especially during the transition from the Renaissance to early modernity. In modern dictionaries, the various meanings are both qualitative and organic, or objectified: That is, the word nature either refers to a condition where no sharp distinction is made between humans and nature, or nature is regarded as a reified object external to humans and thus an object for domination and manipulation (Hreinsson, 2018: pp. 67–68). The quantification of reality in general is a key issue in the development towards modernity (Crosby, 1997).

The medieval and Renaissance worldview was centred around ideas of balance. A key expression of the context of nature was the Great Chain of Being that developed all through the Middle Ages. It was a holistic conception of the world, almost fully mature in Thomas Aquinas' works in the late thirteenth century and his idea of God as the primary cause of all things is poetically expressed in Dante's *Divine Comedy*. It remained through the Renaissance as a model for the hierarchical order of the world. The untouchable God Almighty was at the top and the angels in the spiritual world below him. Man was in the middle, a rational being, torn between the noble spiritual sphere above and his own sinful flesh that pulled him downwards to the lower regions inhabited by animals, plants and stones, resembling the earthly relations in the old myths mentioned above. Satan reigned in the lower depths with his demons, as many as the raindrops of nine days of rain. This was a balanced order, reflecting the creative, organic and dynamic qualities of nature. Inherent relations between things implied that one had to observe the world from a broad perspective or context.

This is an idea of the world as a unified whole, where everything connects, in different contexts. The earth was regarded as a living being, full of holes, tunnels and fissures inside, burping and farting. A basic idea was the balance between the four elements, earth, water, fire and air, and the human body with its fluids was regarded as a microcosm reflecting the global macrocosm, seeking the same balance. All healing of illness thus sought to restore a lost balance between elements and the temperaments which was reflected in science and medicine. Herbs and stones had virtues due to their relations to the whole.

Within this worldview in the Renaissance, diversity was to some extent respected and even revered, at least by formally or self-educated intellectuals. An Icelandic peasant-fisherman, magician, poet, historian, artist and rebel Jón Guðmundsson, nicknamed Jón the Learned struggled to understand the world in the early seventeenth century, devouring all books, handwritten and printed, he could lay his hands upon. He described the world as a kind of a pluralist infinity, and claimed that only God but no earthly or mortal human could know all the great numbers of species and natures of the spirits and hidden things that God originally created in his omnipotent wisdom. Since the time of the creation of the world, no men have been able to investigate the world, its beasts and natures either internally or externally. Jón the Learned wrote:

> Just as no master painter is so skilled at his craft as to be able in one sketch to portray everything that is internal and invisible inside a human being, the secrets of the earth's crafting and its invisible filling and nature will never be explained by observing its external appearance.
>
> (Hreinsson, 2018: pp. 77–78)

This is an epistemological statement – that humans are not able to know everything about nature or reality – but it also implies a certain kind of cultural sustainability: the idea that the balance embedded in culture is essentially sustainable. This assumption was gradually rejected by the increasing arrogance of Western sciences in the subsequent rationalist centuries. The mechanical worldview that began emerging in the seventeenth century leans on the reductionist quantification and technical approach to reality, neglecting the contextual, qualitative relations of things. A transition from the organic to the mechanic frame of mind and from qualitative to quantitative approaches to reality (Merchant, [1980]1989; Crosby, 1997).

Paradise lost and reclaimed?

God reigned over the medieval and Renaissance worlds but the rational and critical mindset of the Enlightenment and the scientific revolution marginalized him to some extent. But it also eliminated other aspects, the holistic view of nature, the search for balance and the reverence for wonder and diversity. Power and domination was always the other side of the coin. The power systems, secular and religious, oppressed many of these aspects, the witch-craze being the bleakest example. New power relations developed (monarchy and state power), dominating the church in protestant countries, and the bourgeoisie emerged with the power of capital. But a new form of domination emerged along with the revolutions mentioned above, that of man over nature.

This transition, being a main precondition for modernity, implied objectifying fragmentation, i.e. attributes of matter and substance were analysed outside of their wider context. As a result, the sense of the whole was lost or rejected, as was the idea of balance, probably best seen in the way thought has been relinquished to the artificial laws of mainstream economics that have more or less taken over Western value systems. Modern rationalism has abused science and technology based on mechanical assumptions, claiming that whatever governments and big industries want to do is harmless. A striking example of this thinking is the overuse of pesticides and Rachel Carson's revolt on behalf of the environment. Her portrayal of soil is a beautiful description of holistic balance:

> The thin layer of soil that forms a patchy covering over the continents controls our own existence and that of every other animal of the land. Without soil, land plants as we know them could not grow, and without plants no animals could survive.
>
> Yet if our agriculture-based life depends on the soil, it is equally true that soil depends on life, its very origins and the maintenance of its true nature being intimately related to living plants and animals. For soil is in part a creation of life, born of a marvelous interaction of life and nonlife long eons ago.
>
> (Carson, [1962]2002: p. 53)

There has been an ongoing re-evaluation in progressive human and natural sciences, re-emphasizing biological and cultural diversity, in order to regain contexts and recognize the connectedness of everything alive. Ideas that reject dualism, reconnect humans and nature and rediscover the value of diversity in dialogues between cultures and with the past. Recognition of diversity helps regain the balance that the mechanical nature-domination destroyed. Sustainability can only be achieved through the combined recognition of cultural and biological diversity.

Ultimate knowledge will never be reached. The mapping of all genes will never be completed and all species on Earth will never be found, counted and analysed. The limits of human knowledge must be admitted and respected. From that point the relations between humans and nature can be redefined as well as the contexts and implications of the knowledge of nature and culture in non-dualistic terms. It is possible to reject the dominating, mechanistic, instrumentalist approach to nature (Plumwood, 2002: p. 109) in order to reunite humans and nature.

Diversity is a keyword, the idea of qualitative, cultural diversity corresponds to biodiversity in semiotic varieties; revolt against the homogenizing effects of capitalism and production, recognition of the myriad of individuals who should be able to join forces and reach common solutions to urgent issues. It is also important to rethink science in terms of diversity and question all claims on absolute truths. Ideas of biocultural diversity (Blanc, 2015) can be developed in a resistance against the myth of progress. That kind of resistance must deal with power relations.

The British literary critic Jonathan Bate, who introduced the concept of eco-poetics in his wonderful book, *The Song of the Earth* (2000), said, in an essay on the value of the humanities, that 'a merely economic understanding of value makes the service – the instrumentality – greater than the thing served, the real value. The value of humanities research is to identify the nature of the god' (Bate, 2011: p. 4). God is long dead, and the romantic notion of Mother Earth does not really work either but, while God was still alive and kicking, he was, despite all his institutional representatives on Earth, a kind of a dialogical Other for humans. That is, God was an external power, out of reach of humans, setting limits for human capacity and actions. God passed away with the emergence of anthropocentrism. But some kind of a replacement is needed, to set the limits for human knowledge and actions and the only possible replacement is nature. Human limitations can be recognized through pursuing a respectful dialogue with nature, not an arrogant, instrumental domination of nature in the pursuit of ultimate knowledge. Mikhail Bakhtin's dialogism includes a sophisticated idea of answerability – responsibility exactly in this sense – that can be applied to both nature and the past (Bakhtin, 1993).

Perhaps a paradigm-shift is approaching in the twenty-first century, as Carolyn Merchant argues (2016), in the emergence of new sciences of chaos and complexity. That would allow responsible dialogues that acknowledge diversity instead of the static, conceptual violence that has been dominating. Ideas of correspondence between the microcosm and the macrocosm of the whole world are of interest since they reflect a much-needed balance, contrary to the objectifying domination of nature. Sense of the whole and the diversity, as formulated for instance in Tim Ingold's idea of 'meshwork' and the 'texture of the life-world' that can help perceiving organisms (2011: pp. 69–70), can for instance help understand harmony as well as chaos in nature. God is nature in Spinoza's radical philosophy (2002: pp. 217–243; Nadler, 2013a, 2013b), 'not an anthropomorphizing figure with plans and purposes' (Hreinsson, 2018: p. 81) but essentially resisting the objectivization of nature.

Alexander von Humboldt found Spinoza's God and was the great hero of science in the nineteenth century, the period when the dominant powers of modernity consolidated in the shape of corporations, politics and technological know-how, that has fragmented and exploited nature. His name has been memorized in uncountable place-names and toponyms but his ideas have largely been forgotten or repressed by these powers, the ideas of the interconnectedness of all things in nature, although they inspired Darwin's theory of evolution, George

Perkins Marsh's conservationist ideas and Ernst Haeckel's notion of ecology (Wulf, 2015). These nineteenth century ideas are still inspiring, but now, in a similar vein, transdisciplinary ideas of complexity can inspire hope, or in the words of Jennifer Wells: 'The principles of unknowability, uncertainty, and complexification open up the promise of learning once again the qualities of reverence, wonder, and responsibility' (Wells, 2013: p. 308).

Cartesian dualism between flesh and spirit, between humans and nature, developed from the seventeenth century onwards, along with the still dominant mechanical rationalism. That dualism can be replaced with ideas of diversity, complexity and a quest for balance, in the past and present, embedded in culture, in order to break the deadlock of nature-domination and enhance cultural sustainability.

Note

1 From *Playing the Black Piano* by Bill Holm (Milkweed Editions, 2004). Copyright © 2004 by Bill Holm. Reprinted with permission from Milkweed Editions (Milkweed.org).

References

Arendt, H. ([1958]1998) *The Human Condition.* (Second edition). University of Chicago Press, Chicago and London.

Asworth Jr., W. B. (2003) The revolution in natural history. In: M. Hellyer (ed.) *The Scientific Revolution: The Essential Readings.* John Wiley and Sons Ltd., Oxford, United Kingdom: 132–156.

Bakhtin, M. (1993) *Towards a Philosophy of the Act (tr. V. Liapunov, ed. M. Holquist).* University of Texas Press, Texas, United States.

Bate, J. (2000) *The Song of the Earth.* Picador, London.

Bate, J. (2011) Introduction. In: *The Public Value of the Humanities.* Bloomsbury, London.

Blanc, N. (2015) On bio-cultural diversity. In: J. Dessein, K. Soini, G. Fairclough and L. Horlings (eds) *Culture in, for and as Sustainable Development.* University of Jyväskilä, Jyväskilä, Finland.

Bourdieu, P. (1986) The forms of capital. In: J. E. Richardson (ed.) *Handbook of Theory of Research for the Sociology of Education.* Greenwood Press, New York: 241–258.

Carson, R. ([1962]2002) *Silent Spring.* Mariner Books, New York.

Crosby, A. W. (1997) *The Measure of Reality. Quantification and Western Society, 1250–1600.* Cambridge University Press, New York.

Crutzen, P. and Stoermer, E. (2000) The anthropocene. *Global Change Newsletter* 41(1):17–18.

Geertz, C. (1973) *The Interpretation of Culture: Selected Essays by Clifford Geertz.* Basic Books, Inc., New York.

Holm, B. (2004) *Playing the Black Piano.* Milkweed Editions, Minneapolis, United States.

Hreinsson, V. (1999) Ofbeldi, klám og kóngafólk. Goðsagnir í Völsunga sögu. In B. Hafstað and H. Bessason (eds) *Heiðin minni. Greinar um fornar bókmenntir.* Heimskringla, Reykjavík, Iceland: 103–124.

Hreinsson, V. (2014) Cultural amnesia and sustainable development. *Култура/Culture* 7:27–36.
Hreinsson, V. (2018) Ghosts, power and the natures of nature. Reconstructing the world of Jón Guðmundsson the Learned. In: H. Bergthaller and P. Mortensen (eds) *Framing the Environmental Humanities*. Brill, Leiden, The Netherlands: 67–85.
Ingold, T. (2011) *Being Alive. Essays on Movement, Knowledge and Description*. Routledge, London and New York.
Isidore of Seville. (2006) *The Etymologies of Isidore of Seville (tr. with introduction and notes, by S. A. Barney, W. J. Lewis, J. A. Beach, O. Berghoff)*. Cambridge University Press, Cambridge, United Kingdom.
Kieckhefer, R. ([1989]2000) *Magic in the Middle Ages*. Cambridge University Press, Cambridge, United Kingdom.
Löwy, M. (2010) Advertising is a 'serious health threat' to the environment. *Monthly Review: An Independent Socialist Magazine* 61(08).
Martin, W. (2016) Nobel Prize-winning economist Stiglitz tells us why 'neoliberalism is dead'. *Business Insider UK* 19 August 2016. http://uk.businessinsider.com/joseph-stiglitz-says-neoliberalism-is-dead-2016-8?r=UK&IR=T (Accessed 2 December 2017).
McInerny, R. and O'Callaghan, J. (2014) Saint Thomas Aquinas. In: E. N. Zalta (ed.) *The Stanford Encyclopedia of Philosophy (Summer 2014 Edition)*. Standford University, Standford, United States.
Merchant, C. ([1980]1989) *The Death of Nature*. Harper Collins, New York.
Merchant, C. (2016) *Autonomous Nature: Problems of Prediction and Control from Ancient Times to the Scientific Revolution*. Routledge, New York and London.
Miglio, V. G. (2015) Basque whalers in Iceland in the 17th Century: historical background. In: V. G. Miglio and X. Irujo. *Basque Whaling in Iceland in the XVII Century. Legal Organization, Cultural Exchange and Conflicts of the Basque Fisheries in the North Atlantic*. Barandarian Chair of Basque Studies and Strandagaldur ses, Santa Barbara, United States: 21–52.
Nadasdy, P. (2005) Transcending the debate over the ecologically noble Indian: indigenous peoples and environmentalism. *Ethnohistory* 52(2):291–331.
Nadler, S. (2013a) Spinoza. In: E. N. Zalta (ed.) *The Stanford Encyclopedia of Philosophy*. (Fall 2013 Edition). http://plato.stanford.edu/ archives/fall2013/entries/spinoza/ (Accessed 4 April 2016).
Nadler, S. (2013b). Why Spinoza was excommunicated. *Humanities* 34(5).
Palsson, G., Szerszynski, B., Sörlin, S., Marks, J., Avril, B., Crumley, C., Hackmann, H., Holm, P., Ingram, J., Kirman, A., Pardo Buendía, M., Weehuizen, R. (2013) Reconceptualizing the 'anthropos' in the anthropocene: integrating the social sciences and humanities in global environmental change research. *Environmental Science & Policy* 28:3–13.
Plumwood, V. (2002) *Environmental Culture: The Ecological Crisis of Reason*. Routledge, London and New York.
Russell, J. B. and Brooks, A. (2007) *A New History of Witchcraft. Sorcerers, Heretics and Pagans*. New edition. Thames and Hudson, London.
Siewers, A. K. (2009) *Strange Beauty. Ecocritical Approaches to Early Medieval Landscape*. Palgrave Macmillan, New York.
Spinoza, B. (2002) *SPINOZA. Complete Works (tr. Samuel Shirley; ed. with Introduction and Notes by Michael L. Morgan)*. Hacket Publishing Company Inc., Indianapolis, United States and Cambridge, United Kingdom.
Wells, J. (2013) *Complexity and Sustainability*. Routledge, London and New York.

Wulf, A. (2015) *The Invention of Nature: The Adventures of Alexander von Humboldt, the Lost Hero of Science*. John Murray, London.

von Wright, G. H. (2003) *Framfaragoðsögnin (tr. by Þorleifur Hauksson. Introduction by Sigríður Þorgeirsdóttir)*. Hið íslenska bókmenntafélag, Reykjavík, Iceland.

6 Roots and wings

Creativity and the nature–culture interface

Annalisa Cicerchia

Introduction

Cultural models dictate resource use, production and consumption. In our societies, an instrumental view of nature, deeply rooted in anthropocentrism, has led to critical levels of unsustainability on a global scale. The economic crisis, while contributing to a worsening ecological crisis, also represents an opportunity for a profound renewal of our cultural paradigms. From a multidisciplinary perspective, drawing from economic anthropology and cultural economics, this chapter explores the role played in this process by a small but growing number of cultural and creative enterprises that challenge unsustainable production and consumption patterns. Instead, their activity is based on innovative and sustainable redefinition and redesign of the relationship between nature and culture in their processes and products. Up-cycling of waste, design and production of environment-friendly food, and re-discovery of sustainable use of natural resources are discussed with reference to ongoing Italian experiences – but with lessons that are internationally applicable.

Cultural models are mental representations shared by members of a culture that function both to make sense of and interpret sensory inputs and to produce and shape purposive and communicative behaviors. They facilitate our engagement with the world, allowing us to conduct our daily business while on 'autopilot', thus expending little cognitive energy; 'There may even be a prescribed quality to cultural models used in everyday life' (Bennardo and de Munck, 2014: p. 4). Many aspects of our everyday lives, from marriage to etiquette, from hygiene to health, wellbeing and comfort and our daily relationship with nature are defined by cultural models.

Cultural models also direct the way we employ natural resources, produce and consume goods and services, and both generate and dispose of waste. The needs we feel, the ways we satisfy them and the means we avail of them are all culture-laden. Consumption is driven not only by function, but also by symbolic value (Levy, 1959) – a component that is increasingly relevant in our relationships with the things we buy, handle and throw away. Economists define culturalization as the process by which the post-industrial economy has gradually moved from consuming commodities for their function to appreciating the experience of the goods for their symbolic and social dimension (Pine and Gilmore, 1998). This shift towards the intangible value of the things we use notwithstanding, production and consumption have reached critical levels of unsustainability. The work of the environmental sociologists Catton and Dunlap (1978) criticizes the damage inflected upon the planet by what they call the 'Human Exceptionalism Paradigm', i.e. the self-declared exceptional nature of our species, supposedly stemming from our cultural heritage, including language, social organization and technology, historically used to justify the exemption of the humans from ecological constraints (Giddens and Sutton 2010). These elements are crucial when we evaluate human-nature interfaces and potential for cultural sustainability. The analysis of cultural models in relation to the economy gives us possibilities to evaluate the impact of everyday and corporate culture on environmental sustainability.

Challenges in the nature–culture interface

It is a shared opinion that, although with exceptions, the dominant cultural model of wellbeing and comfort, which is basically a cultural expression of the affluent Western societies of the 1960s, remains built upon possession and conspicuous consumption (Veblen [1899]1973) of energy and resource-intense, disposable rather than reusable, polluting and waste-generating material objects: from cars to food, from clothes to packaging and – of recent – to an unprecedented amount of digital devices. Since the 1970s, along with cultural change and globalization processes, and despite repeated claims for cultural diversity, the core of that model of wellbeing and comfort has been adopted, obviously with local variants, by many developing countries, some of which currently boast fast-growing economies, such as India, China and South Korea.

If the Neo-Malthusians tried to show that the planet's survival was incompatible with the current trends of economic and demographic growth (Meadows *et al.*, 1972), 15 years later the World Commission on Environment and Development (1987) searched to formulate the terms of a possible balanced relationship between the two with the notion of Sustainable Development. The Ecological Footprint (Wackernagel and Rees, 1996) provided a tool to assess the different environmental weights of the diverse lifestyles and ways of living on our planet. The dialectic between economic growth and environmental quality is still lively and feeds theoretical developments in many directions, like the Environmental Kuznets curve (Grossman and Krueger, 1995), or the Decoupling theory (Fischer-Kowalski and Swilling, 2011). The question remains: how can we combine the right to wellbeing of today's generations with future generations' right to wellbeing? It seems likely that wellbeing does entail some increased consumption of goods and services over time.

Doubtless, since the early 1970s, products and production processes have changed dramatically, benefitting from substantial de-materialization and, more recently, digitization. Innovation has been enormous, and in many instances it has also been oriented to reducing the demand for resources and minimizing the generation of waste. Aware of the huge amount of academic research on the subject of innovation, and the lack of a shared definition since the concept is contingent and context-dependent (Pavitt, 2006: p. 86), we refer here to a simple notion: 'ideas, successfully applied' (Dodgson *et al.*, 2010: p. 13).

After the publication of the European Commission Report on the Economy of culture in 2006, and the international economic crisis started in 2008, the Cultural and Creative Industries (CCIs) that represent roughly 3 per cent of the world's gross domestic product (GDP) have been increasingly regarded as laboratories for the creation of sustainable technological innovations (KEA, 2006; UNEP and UNESCO, 2013). Processes and products of the CCIs are intensely digital (e.g. music, films, e-books, design, etc.) and often intangible, i.e. less demanding in terms of material and energy inputs. In addition, due to their symbolic, social and communicative content, the CCIs also have a potential to influence behaviours and inspire new sustainable lifestyles.

Culture, cultures, cultural sector

The concept of culture has generated an overly abundant literature in the social sciences of anthropology and sociology. Over 60 years ago, Kroeber *et al.* (1952) listed 164 definitions, only in the domain of cultural anthropology. Some 20 years later, a painstaking review focusing on the semantic content of hundreds of concepts of culture led Bauman (1973) to propose a threefold distinction of the main definitions and to group them accordingly.

In the first group, culture is understood as a hierarchical concept: one that is acquired, cultivated and value-saturated, so that some people have more culture than others, and, in theory at least, it is possible for some to have no culture at all. The second group of definitions, many of which were influenced by cultural relativism (Boas, 1887), point to a differential understanding of culture: the countless different lifestyles one encounters in the world. Culture(s), in this paradigm (the plural form here is significant), are co-extant and comparable and justify the variety of customs, mores and conventions – with the equal dignity of each set of customs being the basis of the notion of cultural diversity. The third category groups all those definitions of culture that indicate a generic understanding – one that appreciates that relationships engaging people and places with plants, animals and larger eco-political systems are both actual and performative (culture as praxis, in Bauman's terms).

We will refer in some instances to the differential concept of culture, which involves both tangible and intangible contents, and in other instances to the pragmatic one, which is particularly appropriate to establish epistemological links with economics, since economic activities and their products represent some of the many praxes through which a culture reveals and expresses itself and interacts with its natural or man-made milieu.

Different cultures determine different models of needs and uses of resources, and design their lifecycle. The idea of disposable, for instance, rests on the assumption of unlimited matter for producing new things to replace those that have been disposed of, and of unlimited capability of disposal by the planet. The comparatively cheaper price of many unsustainable things versus their sustainable version, including food, is a powerful cultural signal and a tool of induced behaviour (Ackermana and Tellis, 2001). Berger and Ward (2010) have reviewed cultural determinants and functions of consumption in social theory. People consume to classify themselves as well as to communicate with others (Douglas and Isherwood, 1978; Holt 1995), and they use consumption to form inferences about others' social identities, preferences and social class (Belk *et al.*, 1982; Fussell, 1983; Holt, 1995). Consequently, consumption can act as a fence or bridge (Douglas and Isherwood, 1978), helping to construct and maintain symbolic borders between groups (Weber 1968/1978; Bourdieu, 1984) and to provide access to social networks and organizations (Kanter, 1977).

Finally, the operational concept also includes the statistical definition of the cultural sector. With the growing economic relevance of cultural products and practices and their social and political implications, the sector has been the subject of continued policy-oriented statistical research since the mid-1980s, from the UNESCO Framework (1986) to the Green Paper by the European Commission (2010). In 2012, a comprehensive revision was published by the European Statistical Systems Net Culture (ESSnet Culture Project, 2012).

Is a creative economy a sustainable economy?

It was during the 1980s that, also due to a sharp reduction of public funding almost everywhere in Europe, the cultural sector was forced to come to terms with earned income and accountability to the marketplace. That went together with a recognition of the economic significance of the commercial cultural industries, and the adoption of managerial practices and rhetoric by cultural institutions and policy-makers (Bilton, 2010). Chris Bilton (cited p. 3) argues that:

> 'Creativity' was relocated at the intersection between these commercial-managerial and cultural-aesthetic worldviews. The convergence of these two worlds is based partly on a redefinition of creativity in managerial terms, as a business commodity and as a management competence, within a global creative economy.
>
> (Caves, 2000)

CCIs are activities, connected with cultural inputs or outputs, that are characterized by the ability to devise and invent new solutions in ways that keep a recognizable track of the cultural heritage they draw from – be it in form of art, symbols, material, functions, operational modes, etc. CCIs' definitions are far from being universally shared: Roodhouse speaks of a 'contorted and torturous definitional historical discourse' (2006: p. 2). Thus, national and international institutions urge the academic world to explore, map, define and analyse this promising sector.

Ignited by the Department of Culture, Media and Sports' first mapping (DCMS, 1998) of the creative industries, research and debate keep growing and going deeper. Recently, Hartley *et al.* (2015) have even hypothesized that the Era of Creativity will soon replace the Era of Information.

No matter how fascinating, a discussion of the concepts of creativity and innovation is much beyond the scope of this chapter. Instead, the chapter confines itself to the recognition of the existence of a separate, specific sector, stemming from a cultural core (DCMS, 1998; Florida, 2002; KEA, 2006; Throsby, 2008; Santagata, 2009), small maybe, but resilient to the 2008 crisis (UNEP, 2011) and able to dynamize the entire economy (NESTA, 2013). For the purpose of the present exercise, therefore, the CCIs are

> knowledge based creative activities that link producers, consumers and places by utilising technology, talent or skill to generate meaningful intangible cultural products, creative content and experiences. The core sectors of the creative industries include advertising, animation, architecture, design, film, gaming, gastronomy, music, performing arts, software and interactive games and television and radio.
>
> (OECD, 2014: p. 14)

In addition, it has been stressed that the CCIs 'constitute a specific cluster of knowledge-based activities that usually combine creative talent with advanced technology (…). The potential of these industries goes beyond the generation of income as creative industries are also a fundamental means of communication and socialisation' (Greffe, 2006: p. 8). In the last few decades, international organizations expressed hope for the potential contribution of the CCIs to a general greening of the economy. Important contributions are, for example, the outcome document of the 2002 United Nations Conference on Sustainable Development (Rio+20), and, more recently, the 2013 United Nations ECOSOC Annual Ministerial Review. Both acknowledge the importance of culture and cultural diversity for sustainable development and argue that investments in identity, innovation and creativity can help to build new development pathways for individuals, local communities and countries.

More with less

Of the many sustainability goals, the reflections in this chapter focus on two imperative reductions: the amount of waste and the demand for resources, both as material inputs and as energy.

Small dimensions and micro-components do not prevent e-waste – the specific new category of waste that derives from the digital world – from having a significant impact. A total of 20 to 50 million tons of e-waste are generated worldwide every year. The world produced 41.8 million metric tons of e-waste in 2014 – an amount that would fill 1.15 million 18-wheel trucks. Lined up, those trucks would stretch from New York to Tokyo and back (Causes International, 2015).

Plastic is still in great demand: with continuous growth in demand for more than 50 years, global production in 2013 rose to 299 million tons – a 3.9 per cent increase in production in a single year. Two-thirds of plastic demand in Europe (46.3 million tons in 2013) was concentrated in five countries: Germany (25.4 per cent), Italy (14.3 per cent), France (9.7 per cent), the United Kingdom (7.6 per cent) and Spain (7.5 per cent). Approximately 40 per cent of that consumption was packaging, 22 per cent consumer and household appliances, furniture, sport, health and safety and 20 per cent building and construction (PlasticsEurope, 2015). Over 80 per cent of the demand for plastics is related to cultural habits and lifestyles concerning purchase and conservation of food and perishables, home furniture and decoration, leisure time and personal care.

According to a recent report, in 2012 '25.2 million tons of post-consumer plastic waste ended up in the waste upstream in the EU countries' (PlasticsEurope, 2015: p. 20). About 62 per cent was recovered through recycling and energy recovery processes while 38 per cent went to landfill (9.6 million tons every year). Patches of plastic waste in the form of micro debris are afloat in both the Pacific and the Atlantic Oceans, causing the death of wildlife. Estimates of their size range from 700,000 km^2 (about the size of Texas) to more than 15,000,000 km^2, or, in some media reports, up to twice the size of the continent of the United States (Moore, 2003; Marks, 2008).

In 2014, the amount of materials extracted, harvested and consumed worldwide was double the 1980 figure and is projected to grow to 100 Gt in 2030. One-fifth of the raw materials extracted worldwide ends up as waste and OECD countries account for about one-third of global waste generation (OECD, 2015).

Resource productivity, expressed in Euro per kilogram (EUR/kg) using current price data for GDP, quantifies the relation between economic growth and the depletion of natural resources, and sheds light on whether they go hand-in-hand or the extent to which they are decoupled. Despite an overall increase in resource productivity, from 1.53 EUR/kg in 2002 to 1.95 EUR/kg in 2014 (26.9 per cent) and a decrease in material consumption, from 15.4 tons per capita in 2002 to 13.3 tons per capita by 2014, the EU-28's material consumption remains above the world average (Eurostat, 2015).

Creative responses: upstream and end-of-pipe

Creativity draws from the intangible and intangible cultural heritage inspiration, orientation and feasibility of alternative sustainable needs, goods and practices. Santagata speaks of creativity and cultural production as an 'input of social quality':

> Some important factors of progress in social quality include growth of the content industries (film, radio and TV, publishing, software, and advertising) and use and development of the cultural heritage (archives, libraries, museums, monuments, art, music and the performing arts).
>
> (Santagata, 2009: p. 22)

He also observes that the cultural heritage accumulated over the centuries, an inexhaustible resource for new creativity and culture, and education/training of human capital or the selection of artists and creatives are basic prerequisites for the existence and development of the creative and cultural industries. In the specific area of our concern here, upstream (e.g. eco-design) and end-of-pipe (e.g. recycling) measures and solutions are at the same time subject to cultural constraints and made possible by cultural repositories of knowledge, techniques, and skills.

Sustainable Product Development or Ecodesign are business strategies that base their competitive advantage on considering all of the environmental issues across a product's life cycle, including carbon footprint, energy efficiency, opportunities for recycling and reuse and toxicity (Nejati *et al.*, 2010; Wimmer *et al.*, 2010). Ecodesign can be seen as a deliberate assumption of constraints, some of which may not be present or evident yet, from the initial design stage of a product. Those constraints refer to each and any step of the product lifecycle – production, transportation, storage, distribution, use, reuse, recycle and final disposal – and to the assessment of their environmental interventions, their impacts and possible damages to human health, resources and ecosystem quality (Valdivia and Sonnemann, 2011).

Regarding end-of-pipe measures, the preferred choices about waste management rank prevention and reduction on top of the scale, followed by recycling, recovery and finally disposal (UNEP, 2011).

Recycling is defined in the technical research literature as converting used materials into new products, resulting in less waste of potentially useful materials, less consumption of fresh raw materials, less energy usage and less water and air pollution (Clay, 2011).

The concept of recycling is used for products that undergo a transformation process aimed at making them suitable for similar purposes (e.g. recycled paper, recycled glass, etc.) (Chini, 2007; Calkins, 2009). Upcycling refers instead to 'the process of converting an industrial nutrient (material) into something of similar or greater value, in its second life' (McDonough and Braungart, 2002: p. 110) and means using waste materials or old products to make new materials or products of better quality. With this specific property of quality improvement, upcycling is characterized by a discontinuity, a leap, the ability to introduce a different perspective and to think out of the box. It is the quality that represents one of the most significant differences between recycling and upcycling, and involves a relevant amount of creativity.

Creative upcycling: three Italian stories

In this section, three short stories of successful creative upcycling will be presented, focusing on the relationship between the original material input and the final product; the creative content and its location within the production process; and the relationship between the creative innovation and elements of the local tradition. The three examples are food scraps upcycled into gourmet food, food waste upcycled into luxury textiles and organic waste upcycled to energy. Even though the examples are from Italy, the insights and qualities are easy to recognize and transfer to other parts of the world.

From food to food: Ecocucina

Ecocucina is a blog by Lisa Casali (nickname: Lisca, Italian for fishbone) that defines itself as a lab and testing ground for a low-cost cuisine that has (almost) no environmental impact. The key idea is to rediscover food saving and upcycling practices of traditional Italian regional cuisine, and combine them with other traditions and recipes. The aim is to reduce the overall environmental impact in the kitchen. It shows how each and every one of us makes decisions about food that have consequences in terms of energy consumption, waste products and emissions and that pollute our atmosphere, our soil and our waters. The blog stresses that it is not necessary to make a radical lifestyle change in order to reduce our ecological footprint. Starting as an independent blog in 2009, in 2015 Ecocucina became part of the online edition of one of the top selling Italian newspapers, with over 1,600,000 visits per day.

Ecocucina shows its followers how to upcycle food scraps into new, delicious and even fashionable food. The project, originally only Italian, has now spread across Europe. Ecocucina is inspired by traditional Italian 'hard-times' recipes and contemporary world cuisine. It enlarges the edible part of our daily food and suggests creative ways to process, cook and serve, not only leftovers, but also skins, peelings and cores, the discarded parts of vegetables etc. into mouth-watering new food, drinks or seasonings. It employs high quality images and tutorial videos that are captivating and useful to provide step-by-step explanations. Time-saving low-impact last generation technology, such as food dryers, are recommended along with hand-operated traditional tools, such as grain grinders, or homemade ingredients, like yeast or vinegar. The most significant areas of impact of the project are waste minimization and reduced pressure on food resources. Ecocucina also aims to raise awareness of the natural aspects of food, the benefits of seasonal produce, locally grown organic and unprocessed food and the association between food consumption and biodiversity – as well as enhancing both the range of edible vegetables and fruits (including wild ones) and the parts of the plants considered edible.

Ecocucina aims at disseminating sustainable practices in the kitchen through creative upcycling of leftovers and discarded parts of food and the presentation of energy saving methods of cooking (e.g. steam cooking in the dishwasher).

From food to fashion: Orange Fiber

The key objective of Orange Fiber is to transform citrus waste – currently some 1,000,000 tons per year just in Italy – into sustainable, vitamin-enriched yarns. It is a startup company run by two young Sicilian women, Adriana Santonocito and Enrica Arena, who wanted to transform citrus byproducts into a sustainable textile that followed the Italian tradition of producing high quality textiles and fashion garments. Adriana developed a sustainable textile from citrus byproducts for her thesis in fashion design. The idea was further developed with Politecnico di Milano, leading to an Italian patent of the innovation in 2013 and an international patent in 2014. In 2014, Orange Fiber was established as an innovative Italian startup and opened two headquarters in Sicily and Trentino. In 2014, the first prototypes of the textile were presented in Milan: two samples of Orange Fiber blended with silk and two Orange Fiber yarns. In December 2015, thanks to funding by Invitalia, the first pilot plant for the extraction of citrus pulp was opened. In 2015, Orange Fiber won the Global Change Award from the H&M Conscious Foundation. Their 100 per cent citrus textile was selected by an international expert jury from among more than 2,700 innovators from 112 different countries and won a grant of €150,000 and a one year innovation accelerator – i.e. an intensive business programme which includes mentorship, educational components, networking and aims at growing business rapidly (Miller and Bound, 2011) provided by H&M Conscious Foundation in collaboration with Accenture and the KTH Royal Institute of Technology in Stockholm. The innovation accelerator will also provide exclusive fashion industry access and offer possibilities to build networks and try out ideas within the fashion value chain.

The project entered its operational phase in 2016. The first textile production run has been completed and some top fashion brand proposals have been evaluated for market application. By 2019, Orange Fiber will fully absorb the leftover production of their host citrus transformation plant to produce 7,000,000 m of sustainably procured fabric for 50 top brands as part of the Greenpeace Detox Campaign. Italy produces just 4 per cent of world's citrus juice: therefore, the opportunity to replicate the process abroad is relevant and will increase Orange Fiber's social and environmental impact. Orange Fiber has quickly moved to a European level: the first textiles were produced in Spain, where the traditional mechanical looms needed for the prototypes were available.

While it clearly addresses the issue of agricultural waste upcycling, Orange Fiber also has a very important role as a demonstration model for how to address the growing world demand for sustainable cellulose fibre alternatives. The two founders note on their website that man-made cellulosic fabrics, like acetate, viscose, rayon and others are a direct product of trees cut down exclusively to feed dissolving pulp mills. Around 70 million to 100 million trees are logged annually for fabrics – approximately one-third of which are from ancient and endangered forests.

Orange Fiber offers an opportunity for more environmentally sustainable production methods than other contemporary methods of yarn production. Cotton production involves high use of water resources, intensive use of land and large quantities of fertilizer, while mineral oil for textiles is both non-renewable and comes with a high environmental impact. Sustainable cellulose fibre from citrus waste can contribute to the creation of a new market for the citrus sector, currently in a severe crisis: each year more than 25 per cent of Italy's oranges are not even harvested because the cost of collection exceeds the sale price.

From organic waste to energy and more: Museo della Merda

Quite provocative in its name, Museo della Merda ('The Shit Museum'), brings together biomechanics and environmental art, the agricultural landscape, and the digesters that turn manure into energy.

Founded in 2015 in Castelbosco, in the province of Piacenza, The Shit Museum creates exhibitions, objects and projects. It brings together the agricultural landscape, biomechanics, environmental art, a new approach to museology and the most advanced forms of ecology applied to research into design and handicrafts. The museum aims to transform natural substances, redressing the balance in the relationship between man and nature.

The museum was founded by the agricultural entrepreneur Gianantonio Locatelli and a group of associates: Luca Cipelletti, who manages its projects and products, Gaspare Luigi Marcone and Massimo Valsecchi. The idea came into being in Castelbosco, on a farm supplying milk for Grana Padano cheese. Here every day 3,500 selected cows produce around 50,000 litres of milk and 150,000 kilos of dung. This huge quantity of excreta is now transformed into a futuristic ecological, productive and cultural project. In addition to fertilizers, up to 3 megawatts per hour of electricity are produced from the manure – which is then used to provide heating for the farm buildings and offices. Artists like David Tremlett and Anne and Patrick Poirier have created site-specific works, and from there, the idea of a proper museum took shape, emerging from manure to deal with the broader theme of transformation. According to their website, the museum is 'an agent of change that dismantles cultural norms and prejudices'. Through educational and research activities, the museum engages audiences on the production of objects of everyday use and the gathering of artefacts and stories concerning excrement in the modern world and throughout history. From the dung beetle, considered divine by the ancient Egyptians and the symbol of the museum itself, to the use of dung in architecture, from ancient Italian to African civilizations, up to the latest scientific research and works of art drawing on the use and reuse of waste and discarded materials, the museum concept evolves around the science and art of transformation.

Being an active lab for creativity and innovation, Museo della Merda boasts a whole catalogue of products made in 'merdacotta' – MERDACOTTA® – for sale. Merdacotta can be crystallized in order to produce objects suitable for contact with food and drink, like any other object in terracotta or porcelain, and a non-lead transparent glaze is applied which is then fired at 1000°C. With their classic 'farmhouse' design, the edges are thick and the insides are capacious. Products in merdacotta are impermeable and stain proof, smooth and waxed, and entirely handmade. They include benches, tables, small and large building cubes and tiles, flower vases, flower pots, tableware, and, obviously, toilets. These are objects that redesign the cycle of nature in a virtuous circle, constituting essential elements of contemporary living.

Final discussion: roots and wings

CCIs capitalize US$2,250 billion and nearly 30 million jobs worldwide (EY, 2015). Their size varies greatly, from one-person enterprise to large companies with thousands of workers, and their products and turnover vary accordingly. The three cases presented here represent small and very small businesses.

Each of the examples is built upon a profound awareness of the specific nature–culture interface involved in their own field: edibles, oranges and dung. The changemakers who have created Ecocucina, Orange Fiber and Museo della Merda are well aware of the complexity of both sides: the natural one, in its multifaceted aspects as source, resource, input, setting, landscape and sink; and the cultural one, in its many dimensions as heritage, tradition, art, language, techniques and taste. Their creativity generates a successful interplay of natural and cultural elements with the effect of bringing new, sustainable solutions to light. All three stories also include a deliberate educational and awareness-raising component, reinforced by a substantial inclusion of aesthetic and artistic inputs.

As David Throsby puts it, 'The essential concern of sustainability is with the maintenance of capital stocks' (Throsby, 2005: p. 5). Hence, cultural sustainability has much to do with handing down to future generations the cultural capital and reviving it through new cultural creations. In this very sense, creative upcycling, as in the proposed examples, is a way of protecting elements of the traditional, received, cultural heritage by reinventing their purpose, use and meaning, while abiding to the present time cultural norms and values. With its characteristic dynamism, ability to acknowledge complexity and work with it, and a higher degree of ecocentrism, creative upcycling is a practical example of the approach to culture-sustainability relations that Soini and Dessein call 'culture *as* sustainability' (2016: p. 4). The creative upcycling cases presented here show precisely the ability to create innovative, culturally appropriate meaning for wasted things and *wasted planet, wasted words and wasted people* are the three key cultural challenges of sustainability described by Hartley *et al.* (2015: chapter 13).

Ecocucina, Orange Fiber and Museo della Merda are soundly rooted in their local traditional knowledge and contribute to make it durable over time. They turn waste into something new, culturally recognized as meaningful, useful, and beautiful. They offer alternatives to unsustainable cultural habits by creating new ones, largely based upon cultural heritage. In this sense, creativity lends wings to traditional culture, to fly towards a sustainable future.

References

Ackermana, D. and Tellis, G. (2001) Can culture affect prices? A cross-cultural study of shopping and retail prices. *Journal of Retailing* 77:57–82.

Bauman, Z. (1973) *Culture as Praxis.* Routledge & K. Paul, London.

Belk, R. W., Bahn, K. D. and Mayer, R. N. (1982) Developmental recognition of consumption symbolism. *Journal of Consumer Research* 9:4–17.

Bennardo, G. and de Munck, V. C. (2014) *Cultural Models: Genesis, Methods, and Experiences.* Oxford University Press, New York.
Berger, J. and Ward, M. (2010) Subtle signals of inconspicuous consumption. *Journal of Consumer Research* 37.
Bilton, C. (2010) Manageable creativity. *International Journal of Cultural Policy.* 16(3):255–269.
Boas, F. (1887) Museums of ethnology and their classification. *Science* 9:589.
Bourdieu, P. (1984) *Distinction: A Social Critique of the Judgment of Taste.* Routledge, London.
Calkins, M. (2009) *Materials for Sustainable Sites: A Complete Guide to the Evaluation, Selection, and Use of Sustainable Construction Materials.* Wiley, New Jersey, United States.
Casali, L. (ongoing) *Ecocucina.* https://ecocucinaen.wordpress.com/ and http://ecocucina-d.blogautore.repubblica.it/ (Accessed 29 November 2017).
Catton, W. R. and Dunlap, R. E. (1978) Environmental sociology: a new paradigm. *The American Sociologist* 13:41–49.
Causes International. (2015) *e-Waste Facts.* www.causesinternational.com/ewaste/e-waste-facts (Accessed 27 December 2015).
Caves, R. E (2000) *Creative Industries: Contracts Between Art and Commerce.* Harvard University Press, Cambridge, United States and London.
Chini, A. R. (2007) *General Issues of Construction Materials Recycling in USA.* IOS Press, Amsterdam.
Clay, M. (2011) *The Green Cycles: Recycling, Freecycling, Precycling, Upcycling, Downcycling and E-cycling.* www.ways2gogreenblog.com/2011/04/14/the-green-cycles-recycling-freecycling-precycling-upcycling-downcycling-and-e-cycling/ (Accessed 8 January 2016).
DCMS. (1998) *Creative Industries Mapping Document.* DCMS, London.
Dodgson, M., Gann, D. M. and Phillips, N. (eds) (2013) *The Oxford Handbook of Innovation Management.* Oxford University Press, Oxford, United States.
Douglas, M. and Isherwood, B. (1978) *The World of Goods: Towards an Anthropology of Consumption.* Norton, New York.
ESSnet Culture Project. (2012) *ESSnet Culture Final Report.* Eurostat, Luxembourg.
European Commission. (2010) *Green paper. Unlocking the potential of cultural and creative industries.* www.hhs.se/contentassets/3776a2d6d61c4058ad564713cc554992/greenpaper_creative_industries_en.pdf (Accessed 25 August 2016).
Eurostat. (2015) *Material flow accounts and resource productivity.* http://ec.europa.eu/eurostat/statistics-explained/index.php/Material_flow_accounts_and_resource_productivity (Accessed 28 December 2015).
EY. (2015) *Cultural times. The first global map of cultural and creative industries.* www.unesco.org/new/fileadmin/MULTIMEDIA/HQ/ERI/pdf/EY-Cultural-Times2015_Low-res.pdf (Accessed 28 August 2016).
Fischer-Kowalski, M. and Swilling, M. (2011) *Decoupling Natural Resource Use and Environmental Impacts from Economic Growth.* www.unep.org/resourcepanel/decoupling/files/pdf/decoupling_report_english.pdf (Accessed 23 July 2016).
Florida, R. (2002) *The Rise of the Creative Class: and how it's Transforming Work, Leisure, Community and Everyday Life.* Basic Books, New York.
Fussell, P. (1983) *Class: A Guide through the American Status System.* Summit, New York.
Giddens, A. and Sutton, P. (2010) *Sociology: Introductory Readings.* Polity Press, Cambridge, United Kingdom.

Greffe, X. (2006) *Managing Creative Enterprises. Creative Industries Booklet No. 3. World Intellectual Property Organization.* www.wipo.int/edocs/pubdocs/en/copyright/938/wipo_pub_938.pdf (Accessed 22 August 2016).

Grossman, G. and Krueger, A. (1995) Economic growth and the environment. *Quarterly Journal of Economics* 110(2):353–377.

Hartley, J. Wen, W. and Siling Li, H. (2009) *Creative Economy and Culture*. Sage, London.

Holt, D. B. (1995) How Consumers consume: a typology of consumption practices. *Journal of Consumer Research* 22(1):1–16.

Kanter, R. (1977) *Men and Women of the Corporation.* Harper, New York.

KEA. (2006) *The Economy of Culture in Europe. Study prepared for the European Commission (Directorate-General for Education and Culture).* http://ec.europa.eu/culture/library/studies/cultural-economy_en.pdf (Accessed 21 August 2016).

Kroeber, A., Kluckhon, C. and Untereiner, W. (1952) *Culture: A Critical Review of Concepts and Definitions.* Vintage Books, New York.

Levy, S. J. (1959) Symbols for sale. *Harvard Business Review* 37:117–124.

Pine II, B. and Gilmore, J. H. (1998) Welcome to the experience economy. *Harvard Business Review* 76(4):97–105.

McDonough, W. and Braungart, M. (2002) *Cradle to Cradle: Remaking the Way We Make Things.* North Point Press, New York.

Marks, K. (2008) The world's rubbish dump. *The Independent* 05 February 2008.

Meadows, D. H., Meadows, D. L., Randers, J. and Behrens III, W. W. (1972) *Limits to Growth: A Report for the Club of Rome's Project on the Predicament of Mankind.* Universe Books, New York.

Miller, P. and Bound, L. (2011) *The Startup Factories. The Rise of Accelerator Programmes to Support New Technology Ventures*. NESTA, London.

Moore, C. (2003) Trashed across the Pacific Ocean, plastics, plastics, everywhere. *Natural History* 112(9).

Nejati, M., Shah Bin, A. and Bin Amran, A. (2010) Sustainable development: a competitive advantage or a threat? *Business Strategy Series* 11(2):84–89.

NESTA. (2013) *A manifesto for the Creative Economy.* www.nesta.org.uk/publications/manifesto-creative-economy (Accessed 9 December 2016).

OECD. (2014) *Tourism and the Creative Economy, OECD Studies on Tourism*. OECD Publishing, Paris.

OECD. (2015) *Material Resources, Productivity and the Environment OECD Green Growth Studies.* OECD Publishing, Paris.

Pavitt, K. (2006) Innovation processes. In: J. Fagerberg and D. C. Mowery (eds) *The Oxford Handbook of Innovation.* Oxford University Press, Oxford, United Kingdom.

PlasticsEurope. (2015) *Plastics – the Facts 2014/2015. An analysis of European plastics production, demand and waste data.* www.plasticseurope.org/documents/document/20150227150049-final_plastics_the_facts_2014_2015_260215.pdf (Accessed 27 December 2015).

Roodhouse, S. (2006) The creative industries: definitions, quantification and practice. In: C. Eisenberg, R. Gerlach and C. Handke (eds) *Cultural Industries: The British Experience in International Perspective.* Humboldt University Berlin, Berlin.

Santagata, W. (ed.) (2009) *Libro Bianco sulla Creatività. Per un modello italiano di sviluppo*. Università Bocconi Editore, Milan, Italy.

Santonocito, A. and Arena, E. (ongoing) *Orange Fiber*. www.orangefiber.it/en/ (Accessed 29 November 2017).

Soini, K. and Dessein, J. (2016) Culture-sustainability relation: towards a conceptual framework. *Sustainability* 8(167):1–12.

The Shit Museum. (2016) *The Shit Museum*. www.theshitmuseum.org/ (Accessed 29 November 2017).

Throsby, D. (2005) On the Sustainability of Cultural Capital. *Research Papers from Macquarie University, Department of Economics* 510.

Throsby, D. (2008) The concentric circles model of the cultural industries. *Cultural Trends* 17(3):147–164.

UNESCO. (1986) *UNESCO Framework for Cultural Statistics*. www.uis.unesco.org/culture/Documents/unesco-fcs-1986-en.pdf (Accessed 26 August 2016).

United Nations. (2002) *The future we want*. http://rio20.net/en/iniciativas/the-future-we-want-final-document-of-the-rio20-conference (Accessed 26 August 2016).

United Nations Economic and Social Council. (2013) *Ministerial declaration of the 2013 'Science, technology and innovation, and the potential of culture, for promoting sustainable development and achieving the Millennium Development Goals'*. www.unesco.org/new/fileadmin/MULTIMEDIA/HQ/CLT/pdf/2_ECOSOC_Ministerial_Declaration_EN.pdf (Accessed 25 August 2016).

UNEP. (2011) *Towards a Life Cycle Sustainability Assessment. Making Informed Choices on Products*. UNEP, Paris.

UNEP and UNESCO. (2013) *Creative Economy Report 2013 Special Edition: Widening Local Development Pathways*. UNESCO, Paris.

Valdivia, S. and Sonnemann, G. (eds) (2011) *Towards a Life Cycle Sustainability Assessment. Making Informed Choices on Products*. www.unep.org/pdf/UNEP_LifecycleInit_Dec_FINAL.pdf (Accessed 4 January 2016).

Veblen, T. ([1899]1973) *The Theory of the Leisure Class: An Economic Study of Institutions. Introduction John Kenneth Galbraith MA*. Houghton Mifflin, Boston, United States.

Wackernagel, M. and Rees, W. (1996) *Our Ecological Footprint: Reducing Human Impact on the Earth*. New Society Publishers, Gabriola Island, Canada.

Weber, M. (1968/1978) *Economy and Society*. University of California Press, Berkeley, United States.

Wimmer, W., Lee, K. M., Polak, J. and Quella, F. (2010) *Ecodesign: The Competitive Advantage*. Springer, Dordrecht, The Netherlands.

World Commission on Environment and Development. (1987) *Report of the World Commission on Environment and Development: Our Common Future*. www.un-documents.net/our-common-future.pdf (Accessed 15 June 2016).

Part II

Planning and policies for cultural sustainability

7 Landscape co-management practices and power structures at the UNESCO World Heritage site of Wachau, Austria

Katharina Gugerell, Marianne Penker and Pia Kieninger

Introduction

Landscapes are vernacular topographies of tangible and intangible cultural heritage (ISCCL, 2016). Though they are often perceived as physical places of accumulated cultural and historic stock, they remain dynamic, responding to and interacting with socio-cultural, economic and environmental driving forces (Bürgi *et al.*, 2012). This is also the case for United Nations Educational, Scientific and Cultural Organization (UNESCO) cultural landscapes in the category 'continuing landscapes' (UNESCO, 2008). Protecting and sharing accumulated historic stock and cultural capital (Soini and Birkeland, 2014) is one possible gateway for the co-management of cultural landscapes and can contribute to their cultural sustainability.

Landscape, nature and cultural heritage have been crucial features of Austria's cultural identity and collective memory since the beginning of the twentieth century (Halbwachs, 1985; Assmann and Czaplicka, 1995; Brix *et al.*, 2004). Rich in history and bio-cultural diversity, the UNESCO World Heritage cultural landscape of Wachau represents an important 'lieux de memoire' (Nora, 1998). Historic landscapes reflect the cultural capital inherited from previous generations (Throsby, 2008), amalgamate it with current socio-cultural practices, and create a diverse system of meandering narrations of land-use (Cosgrove, 1984; Bruckmüller, 1998).

We understand co-management practices as multi-level collaborative efforts between state authorities and local communities, i.e. a broad set of social and institutional practices to negotiate landscape related action, meaning, norms, resource allocations and responsibilities. These practices shape the values and ethical choices related to landscape development and thus the cultural lenses through which different stakeholders understand sustainable landscape development (Soini and Birkeland, 2014).

While the European Landscape Convention or the UNESCO World Heritage Convention promote the involvement of local communities, power dynamics and struggles are often ignored, even though they can have a substantial impact on co-management practices. Hence, local dimensions of power in landscape co-management forms the focus of our chapter. Here we analyse co-management practices, and more specifically (a) the main objectives for landscape co-management in the case study landscape of Wachau; (b) the organizations, actors and public authorities involved in co-management; and (c) the power relations among them. The overall objective of this chapter is to scrutinize the role of co-management and power at the Wachau for the cultural sustainability of landscapes.

Adaptive co-management

Sustainable landscape development is not solely the government's responsibility. Concerned societal actors and businesses are also partners and get involved in the long-term governance of cultural landscapes (Klöpfer, 2016). This shared cultural capital management requires context sensitive, area-based approaches (de Boer and Zuidema, 2015) to develop sustainable management plans, which are mandatory for UNESCO sites. Co-management practices are also defined as collaborative decision-making (Armitage *et al.*, 2009; Berkes, 2009). Therefore, co-management arrangements should also be seen as power-sharing arrangements between state authorities and local communities. Co-management approaches are considered beneficial for cultural sustainability because they are expected to increase local engagement and participation, consider diverse perceptions and values, evoke sharing of higher-level and local resources, enhance legitimacy and increase the quality and equity of decision-making (e.g. Innes, 1995; Soini and Birkeland, 2014; Horlings, 2016). They are expected to support the formation of a pluralistic discourse that addresses society's and the local community's cultural diversity. Thus, adaptive co-management is a dynamic conceptual framework, inevitably incorporating components such as learning, experimentation, adaptation and innovation to address socio-ecological transformations (e.g. Berkes, 2009; Cumming *et al.*, 2012; Porter and Davoudi, 2012). Co-management approaches combine mechanisms of top-down state control, market-based mechanisms and bottom-up civil society activities (Figure 7.1).

Co-management arrangements provide platforms for local citizens and non-governmental organizations to influence societal issues beyond their own private sphere. However, these practices are culturally and institutionally structured into formatted spaces of participation (Giddens, 1986; Muller, 2009). In these pre-defined structures, citizens and other non-governmental actors find limited scope for action or for challenging the governmental domain and their structuring power (Lai and Forester, 1990). An analysis of the shift from top-down to co-management arrangements in the implementation of European Union (EU) nature conservation directives (Rauschmayer *et al.*, 2009) identified a gap between the rhetoric and practice of participatory co-management arrangements. In other cases, however, powerful non-governmental actors have also been observed to have a strong impact on the results of policy-making (Krott *et al.*, 2014).

Communicative approaches, such as landscape co-management face immanent challenges including social conflicts, power asymmetries and inequalities among

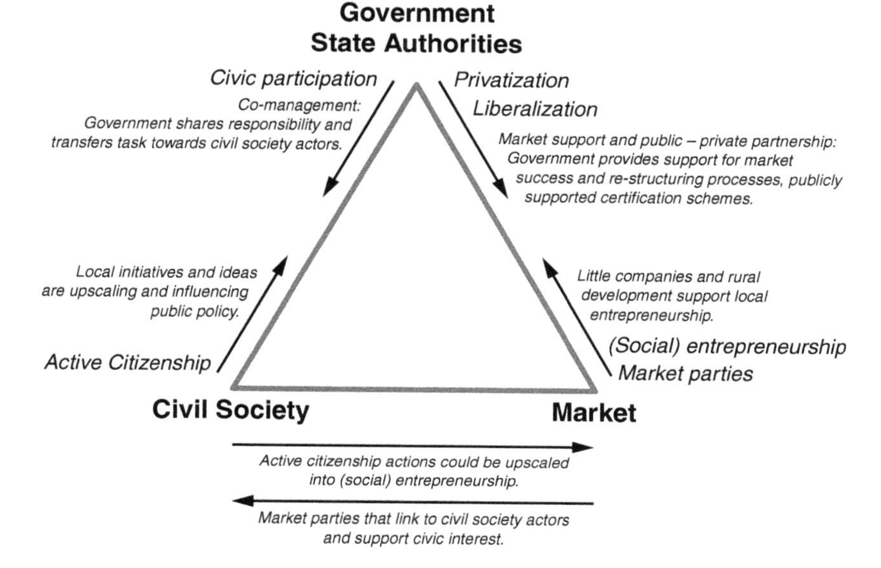

Figure 7.1 Conceptual model of hybrid co-management network, based on van der Steen *et al.*, 2013 and Kieninger *et al.*, 2016.

actors, power mongering and (re-)distribution of power and the domination of powerful groups within policy arrangements (Fainstein, 2000; Suleiman, 2013). Thus, cultural landscapes have always been places of co-management depicting power relations in a wider sense (Olwig and Mitchell, 2007; Kühne, 2013). These are power relations associated with data and definitions (e.g. Red List Species, endangered habitats, heritage), knowledge, resources, meaning (e.g. the definition of valuable, historic or traditional landscapes), zoning of protected areas, restrictions of land use or access to and enforcement of power.[1]

Cultural landscape: Wachau

The Wachau is located along the river Danube in the Eastern part of Austria and shows a distinctive interrelation between natural and cultural features of a basically medieval landscape (Figure 7.2). Its rich bio-cultural diversity and long-term, organic development over centuries resulted in an outstanding landscape, which has been recognized as a UNESCO World Heritage site (UNESCO, 2014). Wine-related management practices were already mentioned in the first century AD and institutional arrangements date back to the High Middle Ages (Weber, 1999). The legacy of this historic landscape is rooted in a continuum of historical land tenure structures, management practices, spatial structures, landscape elements and architectural artefacts. The institutional arrangements and social practices, paired with the natural prerequisites have resulted in an iconic cultural landscape.

Figure 7.2 The UNESCO World Heritage Site cultural landscape of Wachau (Austria), famous for the terraced landscape.

Source: authors.

Tourism has substantially complemented the traditional income source of viticulture and agriculture since the 1950s. Currently 502 viticultural enterprises are cultivating 1344 hectares vineyards – mostly of various varieties of white wine. More than 90 per cent of the winegrowers are members of the regional wine co-operative Domäne Wachau and are delivering at least parts of their harvest to the co-operative; some of them are also selling their grapes to bigger vintners (Feigl and Payerl, 2011). Diverse combinations of on- and off-farm income are common. However, several municipalities in the region struggle with a general shortage of off-farm workplaces: the local population to workplace ratio is as high as 5:1 (LAG, 2015).

Though the management practices in the vineyards have changed remarkably in the twentieth century, they remain embedded in the historic, small-scale spatial structure, located mainly on rock terraces. Abandonment exists, but the booming wine market and public payments for the re-cultivating of terraced vineyards has even resulted in some extensions, despite significantly higher production costs on terraces. Overall, terraced vineyards cover 360 ha with a total length of 722 km stonewalls (AK Wachau, unknown). Apart from being places of wine production, the rock terraces elevate the landscape form and create vernacular beauty (Brady, 2006).

Landscape co-management practices in the Wachau

Landscape, as a nature–culture amalgam, works as a canvas for diverse governance actions of different actors and organizations.

Cultural landscapes, their maintenance and preservation, play an important role in Austrian policy and receive considerable political attention. However, landscapes are rarely congruent with administrative units, which leads to overlaps and gaps between administrative bodies and competing interests between administrative levels and legislations. As a cross-cutting issue, landscapes are addressed in various policies and deconstructed in habitats, Red List Species (nature conservation), farm-level landscape services (agriculture), zoning types (spatial planning) or architectural artefacts (monument protection). Policies, instruments and actions are nested in a multiscale network consisting of: (a) precautionary planning tools (parts of the Wachau are designated as Natura 2000 sites, Nature Parks, Landscape Protection Areas, European Diploma of Protected Areas); (b) regulations, such as the wine law; (c) incentive policies, collaborative and voluntary tools, such as agri-environmental payments or funds for local development; and (d) information tools.

Formal protection of cultural heritage is mainly provided by the Austrian Monument Protection Act (2017), which focuses on architectural ensembles and the built environment, whereas other cultural artefacts – such as the characteristic primary rock terraces – are addressed by a mix of policy instruments, including agri-environmental funding schemes and the Nature Protection Act. These various policies share common perceptions of landscapes as having a positive meaning, as common heritage and a source of identity and as multifunctional environments. The Nature Protection Act refers to regions, indicating a general understanding of different cultural regions and their corresponding characteristic landscapes, establishing a link between conservation and spatial planning that requires the consideration of cultural regions and landscapes in regional development plans and sectorial policies. From investigating different landscape related policies from the municipal to the national scale, we derived the following two main landscape quality goals for the Wachau:

1 preservation of the primary rock terraces as core cultural landscape elements;
2 conservation and further development of the open cultural landscape.

The role of stone walls and rock terraces in Europe's cultural landscapes has been emphasized in many studies (Brady, 2006; Tarolli *et al.*, 2015). Historically, farmers built the retention walls of the Wachau as dry-stone masonry utilizing local building stone. They have become the tangible basis for wine production and important for the region's cultural identity. The Common Agricultural Policy subsidizes the re-cultivation of vineyards, re-building and mending of the stonewalls. Between 1997 and 2003, and between 2008 and 2013, around 20,000 m^3 and 41,879 m^3, respectively of stonewalls were funded, costing around €3.5 million (BMLFUW, 2015; Schmid, 2016). Additionally, landholders are eligible for compensation payments through the agri-environmental programme ÖPUL for environmentally-friendly management practices to improve the environmental quality of the vineyards.

The second goal is the conservation and further development of the open cultural landscape. In the twentieth century, the management and cultivation practices changed significantly in the Wachau. Animal husbandry declined, which resulted in the loss of grassland and arable land. For example, in the village of Spitz an der Donau and the tributary valley Spitzer Graben the number of meadows and pastures decreased from 391 to 86 and arable fields from 118 ha to 9 ha between 1823 and 2010 (Gugerell, 2012). In favourable locations, vineyards and orchards have replaced them. New cultivation practices such as deep ploughing and intensive use of fertilizers, pesticides and herbicides for chemical weed and pest control have resulted in altered vegetation types in vineyards, loss of biodiversity and lower environmental quality (Kieninger and Winter, 2014). Nature conservation contracts focus on landscape maintenance and managing valuable habitats such as (semi-)dry grasslands or abandoned vineyards on Natura 2000 sites. Despite possible subsidies such as less-favoured area payments for hilly grassland, where agricultural production is difficult because of natural disadvantages, the share of grassland is still decreasing.

Civil society-government hybrids

Civic engagement has a longstanding local history. Local people have self-organized in registered, non-profit oriented associations. In 1908, the first Beautification Association Spitz an der Donau was founded and many other municipalities in the region followed. Later, tourism associations replaced them. Their joint goal was to improve the scenery of the villages and surrounding landscapes and to support tourism activities. In the 1940s, local farmers established municipal Local Viticulture Associations, which organized joint procurement, marketing and training to support the vintners' literacy in new management practices and vinification technologies. This collective action increased the quality, price level and reputation of the Wachau wines. Recently new associations of volunteers have formed, e.g. for mowing abandoned vineyards, old pastures or arid grasslands or for supporting refugees and migrants.

In 1972, the citizens' initiative AK Wachau (Working Group Wachau) was established, marking a turning point in the civic domain. The citizens self-organized to protest against and to prevent the construction of a hydropower plant. In the early 1990s, the initiative was a major driver for the designation of the area as a World Heritage site. Since then the goals shifted towards conservation and regional development objectives: conservation of the Wachau in its historic, traditional form; maintenance of the landscape scenery and built environment; and improving and strengthening the local population's awareness of cultural values and practices, tradition and history (AK Wachau, unknown). The AK Wachau, the EU co-financed Liaison entre actions de développement de l'économie rurale (LEADER) Local Action Group (LAG) and the AK Wachau-Dunkelsteinerwald Regionalentwicklung are closely connected by several members who bridge these three co-management organizations by membership in two or three of these boards.

In spring 2016 newspapers reported regional turmoil, ignited by civic resistance against different building projects (AK Welterbe Wachau 2016). The new civic initiative AK Welterbe Wachau emerged, which advocated a restrictive, shape-retentive interpretation of built heritage. The goal of this new World Heritage Wachau group is to prevent building projects that are not following a historic or historicizing design. While emerging from the old AK Wachau, the new group criticizes the strong development orientation of the old working group and the loss of its original ideals and values (Schopf, 2016). Apart from power struggles over the definition of cultural heritage goals, members of the new AK perceived power asymmetries between the members and non-members of the old AK. They disapproved of the top-down communication by an exclusive club and mentioned the power concentration in the hands of a few locals holding multiple mandates as another reason for initiating the new AK.

The LEADER region Wachau-Dunkelsteinerwald with 51,250 inhabitants, 17 municipalities, three abbeys and a budget of €3 million for the period 2014–2020 is part of the EU co-financed Rural Development Policy and fosters area- and community-based innovation. Three general goals are guiding the programme: creating added value; stabilization and sustainable development of natural resources and cultural heritage; and improvement of public welfare. Everybody is eligible to submit project proposals, which are selected by the LAG, i.e. a multi-actor selection committee with 50 per cent civic actors as members.

Civic-market hybrids

In the Wachau, two voluntary, registered associations are managing Protected Denominations of Origin (PDO): Vinea Wachau Nobilis Districtus (200 members) and the association for the Wachau apricot Verein zum Schutz der Wachauer Marille. An EU-registered PDO is an intellectual property right that provides producers with legal protection against imitation or misuse of the geographical product name and is a useful marketing tool. Through the PDO logo, consumers can easily recognize traditional quality products and can rely on their authenticity in terms of regional origin or traditional production (Gugerell *et al.*, 2017). They are also widely considered as club goods with entry barriers along a spatial-cultural boundary. Initially, only members meeting the terroir characteristics defined in the local code of practice Codex Wachau could use the label. This was non-compliant with the EU idea of PDOs (Torre and Traversac, 2013) and was subsequently subject to a lawsuit (Vinea Wachau, 2010). As a result, the PDO has become accessible for all producers from the delineated geographical area who followed the code of practice. However, the association introduced another entry barrier under trademark law.

Actor constellations in the Wachau

Many actors and stakeholders are involved in co-management practices both to implement landscape conservation objectives and to advocate and achieve individual or sectorial interests. As local authorities, they are legally responsible and accountable for the implementation of higher-level laws and regulations. Mayors and elected representatives of the local governments are important players in the local and regional co-management platforms, such as the LAG or AK Wachau, where they hold majorities in the leadership boards. Though LAGs decision boards are formally required to involve 50 per cent civil society representatives to ensure the community-based approach; a fact check shows that governmental representatives (including former local politicians) were enlisted as civic society representatives with their civilian profession. (Vice-) mayors play a core role in the actor constellation bridging different organizations. They are focal points in the tightly woven network. Self-governed civil society organizations are active in the fields of conservation, agriculture or tourism. Economically strong representatives from viticulture and tourism also play important roles in these organizations; often they are elected members of local governments and professional organizations. There seems to be some overlap between those having economic and political power.

Landscapes and cultural sustainability

In this sub-section, we will discuss three interlinked tensions emerging from the case study. These are cultural diversity and tensions between heritage preservation and landscape development, shift and tensions in the constellation of actors and power relations.

Cultural diversity, heritage preservation and landscape

The UNESCO nomination stresses the combination of settlements, agricultural use and rich material evidence of heritage as being important for the outstanding universal value and the authenticity of the site. The new AK aims to perpetuate a traditional design vocabulary. Others prioritize landscape and settlement developments that provide jobs and housing for the young population to prevent them from leaving the Wachau. Vintners, who adapt building or cultivation techniques to today's agricultural practices, feel obliged to follow the historic image. Farmers and house owners also mimic the historic image to please the tourists' eyes. In the policies and guidelines analysed, landscapes are positively connoted and linked to conceptual ideas like home, endangerment or protection. The analysis, however, shows that it might need a stronger recognition of the diversity of values, perceptions and attitudes as well as their material cultural manifestations (Soini and Birkeland, 2014). Cultural homogeneity or an objective truth about the compromise between landscape development and heritage protection does not exist. The societal valorization of cultural landscapes inherits a normative layer and intrinsic trigger that enhances their protection and preservation (Kühne, 2013).

Rock terraces and stonewalls are material historical-cultural witnesses. Their historical construction technique – dry stone masonry – is based on the layering of the stones, and they provide rich biotopes for plant communities and animals. Nowadays farmers also use mortar or faced brickwork to (re)build or repair stonewalls, thus different techniques co-exist. Vintners who receive Common Agricultural Policy restoration funding are restricted to dry stone or mortar techniques. However, mortar and brick-face walls do not have the same qualities as historic building techniques but are merely imitating their visual appearance. The historical building technique is part of the intangible cultural heritage, the material evidence of its long historical evolution and the tacit building and cultivation knowledge reproduced within the actual social practices.

Different perceptions of landscape change co-exist. From a transformative perspective, walls built with new building technologies create a new historic layer expressing the current practices and management systems, which are embedded in a globalized agricultural system. From this viewpoint, a strict preservation of historical cultural heritage would not reflect the changing societal, economic and technological context. (This raises the issue of cultural sustainability and change, a topic that is raised in many chapters in this volume.) Change could manifest itself in the landscape in a way that is not in line with today's socio-cultural practices and thus not authentic.

From a more static conservative perspective, conserving historic stock is essential to sustain the authenticity and integrity of cultural landscapes. The local debate illustrates only limited awareness of the cultural value of the walls and terraces as historical elements, instead focusing on their erosion-combating and marketing function and as 'scenery décor' for the tourism industry. Furthermore, dry-stone walls aid ecological quality and biodiversity in vineyards, which is also of value to many people in the Wachau. Several local farmers perceive themselves as providers of landscape or ecosystem services compensated by tax-financed policies. For many of them, building or maintaining traditional stones is a service delivered to and remunerated by society in the same way that providing clean water, biodiversity or other landscape amenities is a paid service. With this discourse and the associated payments, heritage-related activities have become objects of payment. The global debate on CO_2 certificates illustrated that the definition of prices also manifested a right to pollute and created a contested market around emission trading (Gilbertsen and Reyes, 2009). Similarly, landscape-related payments can support a redefinition of rights, e.g. to remove landscape elements such as rock terraces.

Nature conservation, agriculture and built heritage are contested and politicized. However, official programmes rarely refer to cultural diversity. Local co-management platforms have to find their own procedures and principles to deal with associated tensions between landscape preservation and development. This can also involve – as in the Wachau – the foundation of a new competing organization, which contests entrenched norms, perceptions and practices established in co-management platforms.

Shifts and tensions in the constellation of actors

Adaptive co-management approaches aim towards multi-scale and multi-level partnerships (Pahl-Wostl, 2009; Nagendra and Ostrom, 2012). A glance at the history of civic initiatives in the region illustrates that agricultural and tourism associations have been active for many decades. The local viticulture associations constitute early forms of governance hybrids where civic associations are active in market-based activities and interact with public authorities. They are early co-management arrangements, where public authorities such as the Chamber of Agriculture share power with and delegate tasks to local associations while providing financial support and guidance. Initiatives have evolved over time, developing nuanced institutional designs and organizational structures to professionalize their practices, i.e. by hiring professionals (Edelenbos and Meerkerk, 2011). Associations such as AK Wachau or Vinea, developed from loose initiatives to professionally organized and institutionalized regional stakeholder organizations. Nonetheless, while the constellation and interaction of actors in the Wachau is communicated as smooth and harmonious externally, the initiatives represent the conflicting interests of a diverse community. The individual actors' power and their ability to use new co-management platforms such as LEADER and Natura 2000 shape the discourse and the results of policy-making (Krott *et al.*, 2014).

Power 1: legitimacy and the role of governmental actors

At first glance, the actor-network appears to be a diversified network built by different civic-society hybrids representing the local diversity of values and perceptions. One layer deeper, however, the stakeholder analysis shows that the municipalities and especially the mayors are taking core positions in the network. Occupying management and decision-making positions, they can also broker information and resources through the network. As focal nodes, they act as gatekeepers and shape the local discourse through their ability to push or inhibit certain topics (Arts *et al.*, 2006; Klijn and Edelenbos, 2013). They have the formal power to control rights, allocate resources and draft and decide on local policies or regulations – as local government authority qua office. Thus, they are producing and reproducing formatted spaces of participation (Muller, 2009).

Consequently, it is important to keep a differentiated, critical perspective towards co-management constellation and to question the actual political agency of citizens in such communicative and deliberative approaches. The case study shows there are critical voices who question if co-management approaches actually go beyond rhetoric or showcase participation (Uitermark and Duyvendak, 2008; Rauschmayer *et al.*, 2009). A broad variety of different actors can support a culturally diverse discourse and can also support the integration of different meanings and interests to provide a common ground for long-term sustainable landscape development. Though this new initiative emerged from a protest-response towards the previous actor constellation and organizational gridlocks, they are also fully aware of the opportunities that elected government positions offer. The protagonists of the new initiative might even use it as a stepping stone for the next election. One participant of the focus group openly considered entering the political arena at the next municipal elections. The professionalization and institutionalization of regional stakeholder groups seems to lead to a certain power concentration and pragmatic narrowing down to more homogenous perceptions. Therefore, new initiatives fulfil an important role of opening up narrow clubs to broader pluralistic perceptions, values and priorities.

Power 2: conflictual actor constellations and narratives

New co-management arrangements, such as LAG, Natura 2000 or the World Heritage working groups intervene in pre-existing power relations and create new narratives about social realities. Inclusion and sensitivity towards power sharing are critical elements for integrative co-management arrangements. The common heritage of the Cultural Landscape Wachau is the dominant narrative launched in the 1970s and established in 2000 with the UNESCO World Heritage designation. The treaty obliges the member state to implement and protect the enlisted cultural heritage. The current discourse between the new and the old AK Welterbe illustrates the cultural diversity and the cracks between different narratives. It publicly negotiates whether the old AK Wachau abandoned its original ideals and values. The gist of the matter is a tough debate on design language and local 'Baukultur' (Zech *et al.*, 2006), illustrating that voluntary guidelines are providing guidance, but are relying on the locals' willingness to comply with those shared standards.

Actor constellations and different discourses either align along shared narratives or they can turn into competing and conflictual ones, creating diverging realities, interpretations and re-interpretations, which support some realities and make alternative ones less evident. On the one hand, public policies and local associations were not able to come up with a broadly shared narrative on 'Baukultur' and cultural heritage. On the other, agriculture and nature conservation policies share the strong narrative of compensating famers for providing landscape services to society. Well-endowed funding schemes support landscape-related activities on farmland. Co-management processes are conflictual by nature because they are cultural arenas in which to balance different interests within a field of power inequality, conflicting meanings and diverse values. While the emergence of the AK Wachau was triggered by local opposition towards a big infrastructure project, the new association AK Welterbe Wachau might be illustrating recent local power struggles and conflictual pathways surfacing around the topic of local Baukultur.

Power 3: the power of place

Geographical indications such as PDOs on the European level or the French AOC system are based on territorial exclusion. Inclusion or exclusion from the delimitated geographical area of the Wachau, which is defined differently by different organizations and actors, can make a vital difference. It can result in higher price margins than for equivalent products without a geographic indication (Bowen and de Master, 2011; Dentoni *et al.*, 2012). The relevance of territorial exclusion is vividly illustrated by a 50-year enduring lawsuit, pursued by the French municipality Fontaine-sur-Ay to become a part of the Champagne appellation (Deluze, 2010). The contested geographical definition of the Wachau is expressed in the diverse delimitations of the region and represents the struggle over the power of place.

Concluding remarks

Co-management approaches, where the government shares power with local communities, are expected to support landscape sustainability by generating better and more effective management plans benefiting from diverse perspectives, values and resources. Co-management should also increase democratic legitimacy (Klijn and Edelenbos, 2013; Lai and Forester, 1990). The case study shows that active citizenship and a strong bond between people and their landscape (McCreary and Milligan, 2014) can actually drive landscape governance. This bond crystalizes in communities' collective memory and shared narratives which create a possible basis for the sustainable development and governance of cultural landscapes. However, co-management practices are by no means platforms of idyllic and harmonious social interaction. They are cultural arenas, where actors with different interests, power and perceptions meet, negotiate and fight. New co-management platforms can create opportunities for more pluralistic perspectives, power-sharing and improved decision-making, but they may also just provide new platforms for old powerful actors and networks who have access to information, legitimacy, status and economic power. The example discussed in this chapter sheds light on different administrative processes, both bottom-up and top-down, from the perspective of cultural sustainability. The processes are contradictory, containing different values and knowledge, and it is in some sense impossible to avoid contradictions and particular power dynamics. It is necessary to understand their co-existence.

Note

1 The case study design is based on a mixed methods approach, as the triangulation of results from diverse sources promise more robust insights into a complex local context. The analysis methods involved qualitative content and stakeholder analysis of legal texts and policy programmes dating back to the 1940s, transcripts of interviews with local and regional actors (Gugerell, 2012), and a focus group with five members of a 'new' civil society group in summer 2016.

References

AK Wachau. (unknown) *Der Arbeitskreis Wachau*. www.arbeitskreis-wachau.at (Accessed 15 August 2016).

AK Welterbe Wachau. (2016) Bausünde Weissenkirchen. *Stellungnahme zum Kurier* 10 May 2016.

Armitage, D. R., Plummer, R, Berkes, F., Arthur, R. I., Charles, A. T., Davidson-Hunt, I. J., Diduck, A. P., Doubleday, N. C., Johnson, D. S., Marschke, M., McConney, P., Pinkerton, E. W. and Wollenberg, E. K. (2009) Adaptive co-management for social-ecological complexity. *Frontiers in Ecology and the Environment* 7(2):95–102.

Arts, B., Leory, P. and Tatenhove, J. v. (2006) Political modernisation and policy arrangements. *Public Organisation Review* 6:93–106.

Assmann, J. and Czaplicka, J. (1995) Collective memory and cultural identity. *New German Critique* 65:125–133.

Berkes, F. (2009) Evolution of co-management: role of knowledge generation, bridging organizations and social learning. *Journal of Environmental Management* 90(5): 1692–1702.

BMLFUW. (2015) *Merkblatt Umstellung und Umstrukturierung im Weinbau*. www.bmlfuw.gv.at (Accessed 29 November 2017).

Bowen, S. and de Master, K. (2011) New rural livelihoods or museums of production? Quality food initiatives in practice. *Journal of Rural Studies* 27:73–82.

Brady, E. (2006) The aesthetics of agricultural landscapes and the relationship between humans and nature. *Ethics, Place and Environment* 9(1):1–19.

Brix, E., Bruckmüller, E. and Sterkl, H. (2004) Das kulturelle Gedächtnis Österreichs. Ein Einführung. In: E. Brix and E. Bruckmüller (eds) *Memoria Austriae I. Menschen, Mythen, Zeiten*. Verlag für Geschichte und Politik, Vienna:9–25.

Bruckmüller, E. (1998) Demokratiezentrum Wien Die Entwicklung des Österreichbewusstseins Demokratiezentrum Wien. In: R. Kriechbaumer (ed.) *Österreichische Nationalgeschichte nach 1945. Die Spiegel der Erinnerung: Die Sicht von innen*. Böhlau, Vienna: 369–396.

Bürgi, M., Kienast, F. and Hersperger, A. (2012) In search of resilient behaviour: using the driving forces framework to study cultural landscapes. In: T. Plieninger and C. Bieling (eds) *Resilience and the Cultural Landscape*. Cambridge University Press, Cambridge, United Kingdom: 113–125.

Cosgrove, D. (1984) *Social Formation and Symbolic Landscape*. Univ of Wisconsin Press, Wisconsin, United States.

Cumming, G. S., Olsson, P., Chapin III, F. S. and Holling, C. S. (2012) Resilience, experimentation, and scale mismatches in social-ecological landscapes. *Landscape Ecology* 28(6):1139–1150.

de Boer, J. and Zuidema, C. (2015) Towards an integrated energy landscape. *Urban Design and Planning* July: 1–16.

Deluze, A. (2010) *What Future for the Champagne Industry?* American Association of Wine Economists, Reims, France.

Dentoni, D., Menozzi, D. and Capelli, M. G. (2012) Group heterogeneity and cooperation on the geographical indication regulation: the case of the 'Prosciutto di Parma' Consortium. *Food Policy* 37(3):207–216.

Edelenbos, J. and Van Meerkerk, I. (2011) Institutional Evolution within local democracy – local self-governance meets local government. In: J. Torfing and P. Triantafillou (eds) *Interactive Policymaking, Metagovernance and Democracy*. ECPR Press, Essex, United Kingdom: 169–186.

Fainstein, S. S. (2000) New directions in planning theory. *Urban Affairs Review* 35(4): 451–478.

Feigl, E. and Payerl, H. (2011) *Die Sicherung der Traubenlieferung an die Winzergenossenschaft 'Domäne Wachau'* (presented at 21: OEGA Jahrestagung, EURAC, Bolzano, Italy): 73–74.

Giddens, A. (1986) *The Constitution of Society Outline of the Theory of Structuration*. Polity Press, Cambridge, United Kingdom.

Gilbertsen, T. and Reyes, O. (2009) *Carbon Trading. How it Works and Why it Fails*. Dag Hammarskjöld Foundation, Uppsala, Sweden.

Gugerell, K. (2012) *Das UNESCO Welterbe 'Kulturlandschaft Wachau' im Spannungsfeld von Erhaltung und Dynamik. Zum Verhältnis von Landschaft, Farming Styles und Politisch Rechtlicher Steuerung*. University of Natural Resources and Life Sciences, Vienna.

Gugerell, K., Uchiyama, Y., Kieninger, P., Penker, M., Kajima, S. and Kosaka, R. (2017) Do historical production practises and food heritages really matter? Food with Protected geographical indications in Japan and Austria. *Journal of Ethnic Foods* 4(2): 118–125.

Halbwachs, M. (1985) *Das Gedächtnis und seine sozialen Bedingungen*. 4th ed. Suhrkamp, Berlin.

Horlings, L. (2016) The worldview and symbolic dimension in territorialisation: how human values play a role in Dutch neighbourhood. In: J. Dessein, E. Battaglini, L. Horlings (eds) *Cultural Sustainability and Regional Development. Theories and Practises of Territorialisation*. Routledge, London and New York: 43–58.

Innes, J. E. (1995) Planning theory 's emerging paradigm: communicative action and interactive practice. *Journal of Planning Education and Research* 14(3):183–189.

ISCCL. (2016) *Rural Landscapes Principles-Final Draft*. http://landscapes.icomos.org (Accessed 29 November 2017).

Kieninger, P. and Winter, S. (2014) *Phytodiversität im Weinbau – naturschutzfachliche Analyse von Bewirtschaftungsmaßnahmen und Weiterentwicklung von ÖPUL Massnahmen*. Grünen Berichtes, Vienna.

Kieninger, P. R., Gugerell, K. and Penker, M. (2016) Governance-mix for resilient socio-ecological production landscapes in Austria – an example of the terraced riverine landscape Wachau. In: UNU-IAS and IGES (eds) *Mainstreaming Concepts and Approaches of Socio-ecological Production Landscapes and Seascapes into Policy and Decision-making*. (Satoyama Initiative Thematic Review vol. 2). United Nations University Institute for the Advanced Study of Sustainability, Tokyo.

Klijn, E. H. and Edelenbos, J. (2013) The influence of democratic legitimacy on outcomes in governance networks. *Administration & Society* 45(6):627–650.

Klöpfer, M. (2016) *Umweltrecht*. C.H.BECK, Munich, Germany.

Krott, M., Bader, A., Schusser, C., Devkota, R., Maryudi, A., Giessen, L. and Aurenhammer, H. (2014) Actor-centred power: the driving force in decentralised community based forest governance. *Forest Policy and Economics* 49:34–42.

Kühne, O. (2013) *Landschaftstheorie und Landschaftspraxis: Eine Einführung aus sozialkonstruktivistischer Perspektive*. Springer, Wiesbaden, Germany.

LAG. (2015) *LAG Wachau-Dunkelsteinerwald Lokale Entwicklungsstrategie 2014–2020*. LEADER, Spitz/Donau.

Lai, O.-K. and Forester, J. (1990) Planning in the face of power. *Contemporary Sociology* 19:540.

McCreary, T. A. and Milligan, R. A. (2014) Pipelines, permits, and protests: carrier Sekani encounters with the Enbridge Northern Gateway Project. *Cultural Geographies* 21(1):115–129.

Monument Protection Act. (2017) *Bundesgesetz betreffend den Schutz von Denkmalen wegen ihrer geschichtlichen, künstlerischen oder sonstigen kulturellen Bedeutung (Denkmalschutzgesetz – DMSG), BGBl. Nr. 533/1923.* www.ris.bka.gv.at/Dokumente/Erv/ERV_1923_533/ERV_1923_533.pdf (Accessed 13 December 2017).

Muller, E. (2009) Formatted spaces of participation: interactive television and the changing relationship between production and consumption. In: M. v. Bommen S. Lammes, A-S. Lehmann, J. Raessens and M. T. Schäfer (eds) *Digital Material – Tracing New Media in Everyday Life and Technology*. Amsterdam University Press, Amsterdam: 49–63.

Nagendra, H. and Ostrom, E. (2012) Polycentric governance of multifunctional forested landscapes. *International Journal of the Commons* 6(2):104–133.

Nora, P. (1998) *Zwischen Geschichte und Gedächtnis*. Fischer-Taschenbuch-Verlag, Frankfurt, Germany.

Olwig, K. R. and Mitchell, D. (2007) Justice, power and the political landscape: from American space to the European Landscape Convention. *Landscape Research* 32(5):525–531.

Pahl-Wostl, C. (2009) A conceptual framework for analysing adaptive capacity and multi-level learning processes in resource governance regimes. *Global Environmental Change* 19(3):354–365.

Porter, L. and Davoudi, S. (2012) The politics of resilience for planning. A cautionary note. *Planning Theory & Practice* 13(2):299–333.

Rauschmayer, F., Berghöfer, A., Omann, I. and Zikos, D. (2009) Examining processes or/and outcomes? Evaluation concepts in European governance of natural resources. *Environmental Policy and Governance* 19(3):159–173.

Schmid, R. (2016) *E-Mail Communication. Wachau Umstellungsförderung gem VO (EU) Nr. 479/2008, 19 August 2016*. BMLFUW, Vienna.

Schopf, G. (2016) *Neuer Arbeitskreis als 'offenes Forum'*. www.noen.at/krems/neuer-arbeitskreis-als-offenes-forum/11.368.999 (Accessed 01 September 2016).

Soini, K. and Birkeland, I. (2014) Exploring the scientific discourse on cultural sustainability. *Geoforum* 51:213–223.

Suleiman, L. (2013) The NGOs and the grand illusions of development and democracy. *Voluntas* 24(1):241–261.

Tarolli, P., Sofia, G., Calligaro, S., Prosdocimi, M., Preti, F. and Dalla Fontana, G. (2015) Vineyards in terraced landscapes: new opportunities from Lidar data. *Land Degradation and Development* 26(1):92–102.

Throsby, D. (2008) Linking Cultural and Ecological Sustainability. *International Journal of Diversity in Organisations* 18(1):15–20.

Torre, A. and Traversac, J.-B. (2013) *Territorial Governance. Local Development, Rura l Areas and Agrofood Systems*. Springer Verlag, Berlin.

Uitermark, J. and Duyvendak, J. W. (2008) Citizen participation in a mediated age: neighbourhood governance in the Netherlands. *International Journal of Urban and Regional Research* 32(1):114–134.

UNESCO. (2008) *Operational Guidelines for the Implementation of the World Heritage Convention. Paris.* http://whc.unesco.org/archive/opguide08-en.pdf#annex3 (Accessed 13 December 2017).

UNESCO. (2014) *Wachau Cultural Landscape*. http://whc.unesco.org/en/list/970 (Accessed 29 November 2017).

van der Steen, M., van Twist, M., Chin-A-Fat, N. and Kwakkelstein, T. (2013) *Pop-up publieke waarde. Overheidssturing in the context van maatschappelijke zelforganisatie.* NSOB (Nederlandse School Voor Openbar Bestuur), Den Haag, The Netherlands.

Vinea Wachau. (2010) *Wir kämpfen für die hohe Qualität und den Schutz der Marken Steinfeder, Federspiel und Smaragd.* www.vinea-wachau.at/fileadmin/Bibliothek/images/Presse/Pressetexte/pt_vinea_wachau_zeigt_staerke.pdf (Accessed 1 September 2016).

Weber, A. O. (1999) *Studien zum Weinbau der altbayrischen Klöster im Mittelalter. Altbayern – Österreichischer Donauraum – Südtirol.* Franz Stei., Wiesbaden, Germany.

Zech, S., Dorfstetter, G. and Bork, H. (2006) *Generelle Untersuchung der landschaftlichen Verträglichkeit von Siedlungserweiterungen in der Wachau, St. Pölten, Austria. Amt der Niederösterreichischen Landesregierung - Abteilung Raumordung und Regionalpolitik.* www.raumordnung-noe.at/fileadmin/root_raumordnung/infostand/oertliche_raumordnung/siedlungserweiterung_wachau/wachau.pdf (Accessed 3 December 2017).

8 Adaptation and cultural sustainability of the winter-seining community in the Southwest Finland Archipelago

Kirsi Sonck-Rautio

Introduction

Global change, including climate change, is affecting local communities everywhere. Today the world is a rapidly changing place. While these events occur at the global level, the outcomes are often experienced most strongly at a local level. For example, climate change leads to local flooding. These constant, rapid and sometimes unexpected changes have raised concerns for the future of local communities who are often faced with an urgent need to adapt. This places increasing emphasis on the importance of studying the local adaptation processes, capacity to adapt and community resilience at the local level in order to enhance the sustainability of communities in the face of global change.

To advance this task, adaptive capacity indicators have been developed by researchers (e.g. Smit and Pilifosova, 2001). With these indicators researchers are able to identify the vulnerabilities of a given community and, as a result, develop and apply better adaptation processes. However, identifying whether an adaptation has succeeded or not is a difficult task. One possible indicator of success could be that the adaptation promotes the overall sustainability of the community. For this task, it is argued here that in addition to economic, social and environmental sustainability (which have been well studied) we need to have a greater understanding of the nature and character of cultural sustainability – in order to develop indicators to identify whether outcomes are culturally sustainable.

This chapter examines the role of culture within adaptive capacity indicators in the context of a former winter-seining community in Rymättylä, southwestern Finland. The winter-seining community of Rymättylä is useful for examining this issue because of the historical development of the industry, where adaptation and community resilience have played a critical role after the long-established winter-seining sector experienced a rapid decline in the 1990s. Winter-seining is a form of fishing which is conducted under ice cover with a large 'seine' and requires a large amount of man power. In Rymättylä, winter-seining was used to harvest Baltic Herring during freezing winter months when the Archipelago Sea was frozen. The adaptation process, adaptive capacity and resilience of the community is analysed here in retrospect, and the identified indicators of adaptive capacity are examined in the context of cultural factors and cultural sustainability. The study is based on the author's ongoing research among the fishermen in the Southwest Finland Archipelago, and on fieldwork conducted in the area in 2006–2007 and 2015–2016.

Important concepts and theoretical framework

The key concept of this chapter is adaptation. In a cultural ecological sense, adaptation refers to adjustment that happens when a local community (however it is defined) reacts to changes in its environment, and, in order to overcome these obstacles, takes advantage of the resources available to ensure its own survival (Cohen, 1968; Bennett, 1976; Sonck, 2011). This concept is very useful for examining the effects of global changes on a specific community. Very often within this research context, local communities are treated as systems. This is also the case in this study. Each social system is connected to wider networks and does not function within itself, as if it were immune to external factors. Social systems are also connected to the physical environment and therefore the community and its environment are seen in this chapter as an open 'socio-ecological system' that is closely connected to global networks and subject to global changes, such as climate change. This approach is familiar to political ecologists but also to researchers studying adaptation to global changes and the social impacts of climate change (e.g. Noble *et al.*, 2014).

One relevant concept is resilience, which was introduced to the field of ecology by ecologist Crawford Holling (1973) in his paper 'Resilience and stability of ecological systems'. The term describes the degree to which a system is able to rebound and recover from a stimulus or stimuli and still maintain its state variables (Holling, 1973). Although originally an ecological term, resilience can also be applied in social sense. Adger (2000) tries to determine the parallels between social and ecological resilience and argues that a common ground can be found in social stability and resource dependency. He argues, as with Smit and Pilifosova (2001), that resource dependency – or in other words, specialization – increases the risks for communities (i.e. decreasing adaptive capacity). Social and ecological resilience are closely related, even integrated in the sense that together they are more than a sum of the social and ecological systems (Berkes and Ross, 2013). In this chapter, it is contended that this close relationship also extends to culture, in the sense that there is a clear interdependency between nature and culture (also see Svane-Mikkelsen, this volume: p. 225). It problematizes the notion of resilience from the perspective of cultural sustainability and asks: how are they related and do resilient communities promote cultural sustainability or the other way around?

In order to assess both the possibilities and threats that a community faces and its capability to adapt successfully, the concept of 'adaptive capacity' is useful. Adaptive capacity is often regarded as a synonym for adaptability (Gallopín, 2006; Smit and Wandel, 2006). Those systems that have a high capacity to adapt are capable of responding to change easily and rapidly (Smit and

Wandel, 2006) and by enhancing adaptive capacity can increase their potential to cope with changes and uncertainties related to global changes. For a researcher, adaptive capacity determinants can be used as a tool for analysis.

The adaptive capacity framework used in this study is that developed by Smit and Pilifosova (2001). These authors pointed out that the scholarship on adaptive capacity is very much limited in the climate change field, but in the fields of hazards, resource management and sustainable development, the indicators and determinants of adaptability of societies are seen in similar ways. From the literature and co-operation with the disciplines mentioned above, adaptive capacity determinants were identified as economic wealth, technology, information and skills, infrastructure, institutions and equity. Quite often high adaptive capacity and high resilience seem to indicate successful adaptation. But how does successful adaptation relate to sustainable development and specifically culturally sustainable development?

'Sustainable development' research has gone through several changes since the introduction of the notion in 1987 by the Brundtland Commission. Sustainable development is most often seen as standing on three pillars, which represent ecological, economic and social dimensions of development. Later on, the role of culture in sustainable development has been debated and the addition of culture as an aspect of sustainable development has been initiated by some institutions, for example, United Cities and Local Governments (Soini and Birkeland, 2014). However, defining cultural sustainability is not an easy task, since it is also connected to the question of how culture is defined. Quite often cultural sustainability is seen as embedded within the pillar of social sustainability. Dessein *et al.* (2015: p. 8) add two other ways of dealing with culture in the context of sustainable development. Culture can be seen as 'framing contextualizing and mediating mode – one that can balance all three of the existing pillars and guide sustainable development between economic, social and ecological pressured and needs'. The third way of treating culture would be seeing culture as a fundamental coordinator of all sustainable actions (Dessein *et al.*, 2015: p. 8).

Social scientists Katriina Soini and Inger Birkeland (2014) analyse cultural sustainability in the context of scientific research and find seven different storylines that frame the discourse of cultural sustainability. These storylines are cultural heritage, cultural vitality, economic viability, cultural diversity, locality, eco-cultural resilience and eco-cultural civilization. This study fits best into the storyline of eco-cultural resilience, since it is described as a systemic way of thinking and emphasizes the need of both natural and social knowledge as well as the importance of indigenous knowledge and tradition.

Winter-seining and Rymättylä as a socio-ecological system

At the beginning of the twentieth century Rymättylä was a small municipality in the Southwest Finland Archipelago, with around 2000 inhabitants. It is surrounded by the Archipelago Sea which is part of the Baltic Sea. The community relied mainly on agriculture and fishing for its subsistence. Winter-seining was developed in order to catch fish (Baltic Herring) hiding underneath the ice cover and has been practiced in Rymättylä for at least five centuries (Anttila, 1968). This form of fishing requires a large work force and ice that is thick enough to carry dozens of men and women, horses and later tractors. Rymättylä fishermen possessed extensive knowledge of not only the fish but of the weather conditions and the currents of the sea. Close to 100 holes would be dug on ice in a set pattern, covering an area as long as 1 km and several 100 m wide. Then a large seine (net) with a circumference of approximately 400 m was laid under ice cover with the help of wooden sticks (or aluminium) 30 m long. The seine was then moved through the patterned area up to the exit hole – a process that was repeated all the way from the entry hole to the exit hole. The seine would catch the herring on the way.

For decades winter-seining was crucial for the survival of the community. Between 1941–1950 winter-seining was the main subsistence method for 71 families in the area (Matinolli, 2000: p. 316; Sonck, 2011: p. 24). Up until the 1930s winter-seining also worked as an informal social security system for the less fortunate, since everyone who was willing to participate and get paid (with fish) was welcome on the ice (Sonck, 2011). Each co-operative had approximately eight shareholders, each of them owning their share of the net and other equipment. Between 1880 and 1930 co-operatives generally employed 50 to 100 people. This number decreased significantly after the 1960s due to demand for more effective forms of fishing and the motorization which followed. By the 1990s only five to ten people per co-operative were employed.

Anthropologist Jukka Pennanen (1986) conducted fieldwork in Rymättylä and noted that winter-seining was still a flourishing sector of the fishing industry, but voiced concern for the future of winter-seining with the ever-increasing forces on international markets. Pennanen was right to be worried, since it took only ten years for the livelihood to diminish to the point that it was merely a curiosity (Sonck, 2011).

This type of livelihood and social system required certain attributes from the environment. First of all, the Archipelago Sea and its ecosystem provided the community with the herring. Many factors, such as salinity, ice cover, appropriate algae and the occurrence of salt water copepods affect the amount and size of the herring, thus having a considerable influence on the local human system, while the people living close to the Archipelago Sea and using its resources had an effect on the conditions of the herring as well. Environmental factors are not the only ones affecting the local system. Social change, such as urbanization has a major impact on the human community. Most of the changes, however, are the result of global changes, and not the actions of the local communities.

Gradual changes influenced the system in such a way that during the 1990s the Rymättylä socio-ecological system, which was based on the winter-seining livelihoods, transformed dramatically, as demonstrated in Table 8.1.

External factors changed the functions of the system so profoundly, that it could not hold its original structure. The last straw for winter-seining was the

Table 8.1 Local effects of external factors

Component of a system	*External factors*	*Local effects*
Ecological	Climate change, global warming, eutrophication	Mild winters – loss of ice, decrease in salinity of water, decrease of saltwater copepods (nutrition)
Technological	General motorization of livelihood	More efficiency – less need for workforce, own innovations and diffusion of outside innovations, dependency on tractors, snowmobiles and echosounders – gradual loss of local knowledge and skills
Economic	Globalization of markets, increasing competition	Increasing competition, changes in local trade systems, changes in local and national consuming habits
Social	Legislation, regulations, urbanization, changes in demographic and vocational structures	Younger generations moving to bigger cities, new regulations, etc., complicating fishermen's ways of practising livelihood, changes in institutions and infrastructure
Cultural	Changes in values, forms of decision-making, changes in forms of knowledge	Decrease of the value of local traditions, decrease of local ecological knowledge, loss of skills and expertise, changes in interests and consuming habits

mild winters from the mid-1990s onwards, which meant there was practically no ice to walk on. Winter–seining as a livelihood ceased to exist, although many of the local people would have been willing to continue practicing it.

The adaptive capacity, resilience and vulnerability of Rymättylä

Smit and Pilifosova (2001) determined the key adaptive capacity determinants to be economic resources, technology, information and skill, infrastructure, institutions and equity. As an adaptive capacity determinant, economic resources include capital resources, financial means, wealth and poverty or any economic condition of nations or specific groups. Since adaptive capacity research more often takes place in developing areas, poverty is usually a strong indicator of vulnerability. This, however, as Keskitalo *et al.* (2011) point out, is rarely the case in developed industrial regions. In Nordic regions access to economic resources seems to be closely connected with access to wage employment.

Also, as Keskitalo *et al.* (2011) argue, Nordic industry scales are often large and very closely linked with global market-based systems. Small-scale entrepreneurs cannot compete with large-scale industry and are therefore subjected to the markets they have created. Still, a large-scale actor may employ the majority of the community and thereby ensure its ability to inhabit otherwise remote environments. The downside of this arrangement is, however, that markets fluctuate markedly, and being dependent on one large-scale actor makes communities vulnerable. Smit and Pilifosova (2001) also note that economic resources often closely interact with access to resources, which in market-based systems is determined by economic assets.

This is certainly also true in Rymättylä. As long as the fisheries in Rymättylä were self-subsistent, the livelihood was fairly profitable. Once the fisheries adopted a wage labour system and started to work together with the fish dealers from the nearest city, Turku, they were unknowingly (supposedly) connected with the larger-scale industry and were vulnerable to increasing competition, as the arrival of the trawlers later in the 1960s would prove. The trawlers would also travel further out to the open sea and disturb the natural migration routes of Baltic Herring by harvesting the herring before it reached its spawning beds in the coastal areas, where the winter-seiners usually worked. Of course, trawlers were also accused of over fishing, but the validity of the allegation is hard to prove (Sonck, 2011).

Technological resources determine the ways societies can respond to stresses and harness their resources (Smit and Pilifosova, 2001). Keskitalo *et al.* (2011) highlight the importance of technology as an adaptive capacity determinant, since having access to technology means having a chance to compete within the market; '(T)echnological development and application in turn further increases the need for economic competitiveness and rationality within the sector' (p. 585). According to Keskitalo *et al.* (2011) this is especially true of the fishing industry; and so it was in Rymättylä as well. The increasing competition forces the fishermen to invest a lot of capital into motorized equipment, such as snowmobiles and tractors. The whole system was subjected to the scheme of Western rationalization, where the efficiency of primary production increased the amount of income, but at the same time increased the capital the production demands, while also lowering the value of the product. Put simply, while the expenses were rising, the consumer prices were decreasing, thus adding to the pressure for more efficient productivity (Heikkinen *et al.*, 2007). Sometimes technological innovation also rises within the community and becomes part of professional identity and traditions. Innovation and diffusion are cultural phenomena, and should also be regarded as such. Innovations often arise within the community to meet the community's needs, whereas diffusion of innovations can be a voluntary and practical adaptation of new ways of dealing with problems or to enhance productivity. One example of this type of adaptation was a particular kind of barrel, a sort of pulling device, which came to Rymättylä with immigrants from Karelia during the Second World War (Sonck, 2011). In Rymättylä, local innovations separated Rymättylä winter-seining culture from others in the area and made them special and unique. The nature of technology defines the ways it affects the community culturally and socially.

Information and skills are also important determinants of adaptive capacity, since 'successful adaptation requires a recognition of the necessity to adapt, knowledge about available options, the capacity to assess them and ability to implement the most suitable ones' (Fankhauser and Tol, 1997, quoted in Smit and Pilifosova, 2001: section 18.5.2.). This type of information could be regarded as Traditional Ecological Knowledge (TEK) or Local Ecological Knowledge (LEK). TEK has been defined as tacit knowledge learned by observing and by reproducing this knowledge in everyday life with behaviour and speech (Cruikshank, 2005). Anthropologist Conrad Kottak (2006) argues that one significant task of ecological anthropology – which also includes LEK – is to 'assess the extent and nature of ecological awareness and activity in various groups and to harness parts of native ethnoecological models to enhance environmental preservations and amelioration' (Kottak, 2006: p. 45).

Keskitalo *et al.* (2011) divide information and skills into two categories. First, scientific knowledge – which in Nordic societies is usually created in research institutes and higher research and education institutions. This type of scientific knowledge does not always agree or communicate with the other type of knowledge, which Keskitalo *et al.* (2011) consider to be technological/local knowledge. This is the knowledge I regard as TEK. Keskitalo *et al.* (2011) note that in peripheral regions the transfer of knowledge is usually disturbed when the population is starting to age and the new generation no longer has the experience-based traditional knowledge that is needed to practice the specific type of trade. Although Rymättylä is not so peripheral, this still applies. Most of the winter-seining fishermen were ageing and could not practise winter-seining anymore. Younger generations moved off the island or just decided to take on something easier and more profitable for a living (Sonck, 2011). This indicator considers cultural factors, but does not really articulate them as cultural.

Good infrastructure is usually seen as an advantage to adaptive capacity. However, in some cases infrastructure also disturbs the natural state of the environment and/or prevents – for some – access to resources, or helps the competing actors to access the limited resources (Keskitalo *et al.*, 2011). In these cases infrastructure may, indeed, enhance vulnerability. In Rymättylä's case the bridge that was built in 1972, which connected the island with the mainland, and provided the fish traders with easier access to trading spots, enabled the transition from a relatively self-subsistent community into a market-based one. On the other hand, decent roads and the bridge did increase the amount of commuting opportunities, as well as attracting tourists and other visitors. Good infrastructure also allows local people to interact with different communities in a more active and profound way, which of course has cultural and social consequences, positive and negative, depending on the point of view. It certainly enables economic diversification. Smit and Pilifosova (2001) write that an efficient way to enhance adaptive capacity is to diversify economically, if possible, and develop more diverse combinations of livelihood, which good infrastructure enables. From a cultural point of view, one can ask the question, if economic diversification is involuntary, is it still culturally sustainable? This was the direction of the development in Rymättylä as well, since many of the former fishermen started to specialize in crops like potatoes and cucumbers, or focused on aquaculture.

Well organized social institutions and management capacities, such as consistent policies and tenure arrangements enhance adaptive capacity (Smit and Pilifosova, 2001). Considering management, it is rather usual for ongoing legislation or reform to have a negative impact on adaptive capacity. This category may also include cultural factors, such as changing values within the community itself. In Rymättylä, the change of values could be seen most clearly in the attitudes of the new generation towards winter-seining, and its physical and economic difficulties. With this came a generation that also lacked the proper skills and equipment for winter-seining (Sonck, 2011). This indicator also does take cultural factors into consideration. Seeing legislation and reform having a negative impact to adaptive capacity does imply that while making decisions, local cultural factors – and therefore the perspective of cultural sustainability – has not been considered. Changing values, however, does not necessarily mean that the cultural sustainability is endangered, since change is inevitable. Sustainability should not be confused with stability in the sense that nothing should change. Change can be culturally sustainable within certain circumstances, which most often include local empowerment and independency to make their own change.

The sixth determinant of the adaptive capacity, equity, is highly relevant to the fisheries in Rymättylä today. Equity refers to allocation of power and access to resources, whether the attention is on the community, nation or global actors. From the perspective of cultural sustainability being also about local communities' empowerment, and the possibility for them to influence their own surroundings, the notion of equity is crucial. From a Nordic perspective, unequal distribution is not present in an obvious way, but in the form of legislation and restrictions (see Daugstad and Fageraas, this volume: p. 181). These institutionalized rules ensure that some groups gain better access to certain resources and some are excluded from them. These rules also determine who gets to be part of the decision-making and 'create formalized interactions within which actors act under conditions of economic rationalization' (Keskitalo *et al.*, 2011: p. 588). Rymättylä inhabitants did have equal access to resources, although being able to be one of the members of the co-operative required some capital (a horse or later a tractor or a snow mobile). But everyone willing to participate in winter-seining was allowed on ice, and each man or woman was appointed a task according to their physicality or skills. This was during the time when winter-seining was still a self-subsistent mode of livelihood. From the 1960s wages had to be paid with money instead of fish, the fishing quotas forced the co-operatives to take their seines further to the sea and increasing competition and motorization decreased the need for labour. By the 1980s the co-operatives employed only their members and those who could not afford to buy their share, had to seek work elsewhere. Cultural factors are also present here, since the allocation of power is a cultural character – a notion which is rarely recognized.

Reflections

Rymättylä today hardly resembles the community it was 50, or even 30 years ago. As many other communities around the world affected by globalization and global environmental changes, Rymättylä has a new and more modern way of life. It is community that recognizes the value of traditions but that has little means to keep the traditions alive. Fortunately, Rymättylä has a very active local village association that aims to sustain, gather and exhibit old fishing traditions.

Rymättylä is now part of city of Naantali (due to a merger in 2009), and its demographics and vocational structure have changed drastically. Only a few fishermen still exist, and most inhabitants are now farmers, blue-collar or white-collar workers commuting to the nearest cities, artisans and/or entrepreneurs. Tourism employs a growing number of people, and Rymättylä has a status currently as one of the most popular summer-house locations. From an economic perspective, the changes to the system were not negative in general; in 2000 the town of Rymättylä was practically debt free (Town of Rymättylä, 2002). But, when considering the winter-seining based socio-ecological system, the adaptation was not so successful – it ceased to exist, changing its structure so drastically that it is not the same socio-ecological system it was before. The dependency on the ecosystem has changed its form, thereby changing the function of the whole system. Every other change in the system had affected its functions so profoundly, it could no longer hold its ground once the milder winters came. This means that people had to give up something that was important to them and to their identity – an old traditional way of life. Many of the inhabitants gave up winter-seining involuntarily and even those not directly involved with it saw the decline of it as an unfortunate course of development. I would therefore argue that however economically and seemingly successful this adaptation of Rymättylä was, it was not culturally sustainable. This argument leads to a question with much wider relevance: if adaptation is not culturally or socially sustainable, can it be regarded as successful?

One could make the assumption that the liberalization and the invasion of the principles of economic rationalization in Rymättylä have reduced the ecosystems as well as the social resilience, therefore covering the whole of the socio-ecological system. Neil Adger (2000) writes that 'This loss of resilience is associated with negative impacts on livelihoods and, in the context of the institutions of common property management, collective institutional resilience is also undermined (p. 348). This could be the case for Rymättylä as well, and quite certainly applies in similar conditions.

Social vulnerability refers to 'the exposure of groups of people or individuals to stress as a result of the impacts of environmental change. Stress, in the social sense, encompasses distribution to group's or individuals' livelihoods and forced adaptation to the changing physical environment' (Adger, 2000: p. 348). From this argument, I can conclude that the social vulnerability of Rymättylä's winter-seining community in 1990s was high, and the system failed to rebound from the results of environmental change, i.e. the mild winters in the late 1990s. Since resilience as a concept describes the degree to which a system is able to recover from disturbance, I would be inclined to argue that the resilience of the socio-ecological system of winter-seining community of Rymättylä was low.

Quite often the concepts of adaptive capacity and adaptation seem to assume that adaptation is a positive thing. But how do we define successful adaptation and whose perspectives do we value? Who can define the difference between adaptation and maladaptation in local context? Kirsten Magis (2010) points out that socio-ecological systems may respond to disruption by maintaining, adapting or transforming. Resilience is perceived as absorbing disturbances in order to preserve their structures, to adapt and to change. Sometimes systems undergo major transformations. However, these transformations are considered to be necessary for the survival of the system. Transformability by definition refers to the capacity of the system to create a new system once the social, ecological and economic conditions have changed too much for the system to exist (Walker *et al.*, 2004). In the case of Rymättylä's winter-seining, the transformation cannot be regarded as necessary for the survival of the socio-ecological system. On the contrary, from the perspective of the community, the development was heading in the wrong direction and the idea of cultural sustainability was endangered. Transformability of the Rymättylä winter-seining socio-ecological system was high, whereas the resilience in general was not. In seeking cultural and social resilience (and sustainability), it is easy to start seeking stability instead. In reality, cultural sustainability in this context is more related to the community's ability and opportunities to have agency and guide the direction of their development in a way that includes the cultural heritage important to them, and as ethnologist Katriina Siivonen put it: '(C)ommon cultural heritage should be selected, formulated, and used in co-operation between those people who are in any way involved' (2007: p. 17). Here traditional ecological knowledge and local ecological knowledge can play a very important role in binding together cultural, social, ecological and economic sustainability. Many studies have shown that analysing the human-nature interface by facilitating socio-ecological system thinking has created more successful nature management plans. Also including local ecological knowledge in conservation and management planning has become more popular (see Huntington, 2000; Gadgil *et al.*, 2008; MacClanahan *et al.*, 2009; Zykowski *et al.*, 2011).

Change is constant, so having a stable socio-ecological system does not mean it is prone to staying intact. Having a resilient socio-ecological system, on the other hand, means it is capable of reacting, creating new and making good of the changes it must face. In her article, Kirsten Hagis (2010) explores the connection between social sustainability and community resilience and concludes that: 'Members of resilient communities intentionally develop personal and collective capacity that they engage to respond to and influence change, to sustain and renew the community, and to develop new trajectories for the communities' future' (Magis, 2010: p. 402). Community resilience might – in addition to social sustainability – also indicate cultural sustainability.

Most studies focusing on community-level adaption highlight the question of economic sustainability and adaptation. But since communities are also formed around lifestyles, traditions and identities, which are very often closely connected to the physical environment the community is living in, and which are extremely important to the wellbeing of the people in the community, these factors should be more included more often when examining adaptive capacity and resilience. But as shown with this analysis, the underlying assumption of cultural sustainability is embedded within the adaptive capacity indicators, but they are yet to be articulated and taken into more careful consideration. Since adaptive capacity research has influenced international and national adaptation strategies (it creates the knowledge that is applied when decision-makers set out legislation and regulations to promote adaptive capacity), these points of view should be taken into account.

References

Adger, W. N. (2000) Social and ecological resilience: are they related? *Progress in Human Geography* 24(3):347–364.

Anttila, V. (1968) *Rymättylän talvinuottakalastus muuttuvana elinkeinona 1885–1967*. University of Turku, Department of Ethnology, Turku, Finland.

Bennett, J. W. (1976) *The Ecological Transition: Cultural Anthropology and Human Adaption*. Pergamon Press Inc, New York.

Berkes, F. and Ross, H. (2013) Community resilience: toward an integrated approach. *Society and Natural Resources* 26(1):5–20.

Cohen, Y. A. (1968) *Man in Adaptation: The Cultural Present*. Transactions Publishers, Chicago, United States.

Cruikshank, J. (2005) *Do Glaciers listen? Local Knowledge, Colonial Encounters and Social Imagination*. UBC Press, Vancouver, Canada.

Dessein, J. K., Soini, K., Fairclough, G. and Horlings, L. (eds) (2015) *Culture in, for and as Sustainable Development. Conclusions from the COST Action IS1007 Investigating Cultural Sustainability*. University of Jyväskylä, Jyväskylä, Finland.

Fankhauser, S. and Tol, R. S. J. (1997) The social costs of climate change: the IPCC second assessment report and beyond. *Mitigation and Adaptation Strategies for Global Change* 1:385–403.

Gadgil, M., Olsson, P., Fikret Berkes, F. and Folke, C. (2003) Exploring the role of local ecological knowledge in ecosystem management: three case studies. In F. Berkes, J. Colding and C. Folke (eds) *Navigating Socio-ecological systems: Building Resilience for Complexity and Change*. Cambridge University Press, Cambridge, United Kingdom: 189–208.

Gallopín, G. C. (2006) Linkages between vulnerability, resilience, and adaptive capacity. *Global Environmental Change* 16:293–303.

Heikkinen, H. I., Lakomäki, S. and Baldridge, J. (2007) The dimensions of sustainability and the neo-entrepreneurial adaptation strategies in reindeer herding in Finland. *The Journal of Ecological Anthropology* 11:25–42.

Holling, C. S. (1973) Resilience and stability of ecological systems. *Annu. Rev. Ecol. Syst.* 4:1–23.

Huntington, H. P. (2000) Using traditional ecological knowledge in science: methods and Applications. *Ecological Applications* 10:1270–1274.

Keskitalo, E. C. H., Dannevig, H., Hovelsrud, G. K., West, J. J. and Swartling, Å. G. (2011) Adaptive capacity determinants in developed states: examples from Nordic countires and Russia. *Regional Environmental Change* 11:579–592.

Kottak, C. (2006) The New ecological Anthropology. In: N. Haenn and R. R. Wilk (eds) *The Environment in Anthropology: A Reader in Ecology, Culture, and Sustainable Living.* New York University Press, New York.

Magis, K. (2010) Community resilience: an indicator of social sustainability. *Society & Natural Resources* 23:401–416.

Matinolli, E. (2000) *Rymättylän Historia II.I – Luonto, 1800- ja 1900-luvut, murre.* Rymättylän kunta ja seurakunta, Turku, Finland.

Noble, I. R. Huq, S., Anokhin, Y.A., Carmin, J., Goudou, D., Lansigan, F. P., Osman-Elasha, B. and Villamizar, A. (2014) Adaptation needs and options. In: C. B. Field, V. R. Barros, D. J. Dokken, K. J. Mach, M. D. Mastrandrea, T. E. Bilir, M. Chatterjee, K. L. Ebi, Y. O. Estrada, R. C. Genova, B. Girma, E. S. Kissel, A. N. Levy, S. MacCracken, P. R. Mastrandrea and L. L. White (eds) *Climate Change 2014: Impacts, Adaptation, and Vulnerability. Part A: Global and Sectoral Aspects. Contribution of Working Group II to the Fifth Assessment Report of the Intergovernmental Panel on Climate Change.* Cambridge University Press, Cambridge, United Kingdom: 833–868.

Pennanen, J. (1986) *Talviapajilla – Ammattimaisen talvikalastuksen sata vuotta.* Finnish Literature Society (SKS), Helsinki.

Siivonen, K. (2007) The right to stand outside of cultural heritage. A condition for sustainable cultural development. *Ethnologia Fennica* 34:6–20.

Smit, B. and Pilifosova, O. (2001) Adaptation to climate change in the context of sustainable development and equity. In: J. M. McCarthy, N. Canziani, A. Leary, D. J. Dokken and K. S. White (eds) *Climate Change 2001: Impacts, Adaptation, and Vulnerability, Contribution of Working group !! to the Third Assessment Report of the Intergovernmental Panel on Climate Change, Publishes for the Intergovernmental Panel on Climate Change.* Cambridge University Press, Cambridge, United Kingdom.

Smit, B. and Wandel, J. (2006) Adaptation, adaptive capacity and vulnerability. *Global Environmental Change* 16:282–292.

Soini, K. and Birkeland, I. (2014) Exploring the scientific discourse on cultural sustainability. *Geoforum* 51:213–223.

Sonck, K. (2011) Se on Rymättylän niin vanha perinnehomma toi ammatti – Ympäristön, yhteiskunnan ja paikallisyhteisön vuorovaikutus Rymättylän talvonuottauksen muutoksessa 1880-luvulta 1980-luvulle. Unpublished Master's thesis, Faculty of Humanitis, University of Oulu, Finland.

Town of Rymättylä. (2002) *Rymättylä Strategia 2010.* http://roola.fi/Roola/2015_Tapahtumat_files/Rymattyla%202010%20strategia.pdf (Accessed 1 September 2016).

Walker, B. H., Holling, C. S., Carpenter, S. R. and Kinzig, A. P. (2004) Resilience, adaptability and transformability in socio-ecological systems. *Ecology and Society* 9:5.

Zykowski, S., Curtis, A. and Watts, R. J. (2011) Using fisher local ecological knowledge to improve management: the Murray crayfish in Australia. *Fisheries Research* 110:120–127.

9 Preserving cultural landscapes

A cultural sustainability perspective

Rob Burton

Introduction

The importance of farmed cultural landscapes as sites of economic, ecological and cultural sustainability is well recognised both in Europe and globally. They are created through generations of farmers working the land – often in relatively poor environmental conditions – using local materials, local building styles and management practices often unique to their communities. Regions such as the Alps in Europe, the upland moors of Great Britain or the island landscapes of Vega in Norway (see Daugstad and Fageraas, this volume: p. 181) have inspired generations of poets, novelists and painters, who have etched the landscape into the national identity through poetry, art, painting and other cultural pursuits. Governments are well aware of the importance of these landscapes. As result, these areas receive some of the highest agricultural and cultural landscape subsidies for the maintenance of traditional practices and buildings and, at the same time, have been lavished with national and international protection and recognition.

Despite this, some of the most prized cultural landscapes are under threat from changes in the population structure of rural communities. The Pyrenees National Park in France/Spain (Marín-Yaseli and Martínez, 2003; Mottet *et al.*, 2006), the Burren in Ireland (O'Rourke, 2005), the Lake District National Park in the United Kingdom (Burton *et al.*, 2005; Harvey *et al.*, 2013) and the Massif Central in France (André, 1998; O'Rourke, 2006), are all experiencing the same problem – the number of farming families managing the landscape is declining. If unchecked, this demographic change risks undoing longstanding relationships between humans and nature that are responsible for maintaining the nature–culture interface.

One of these regions, the Lake District National Park in Cumbria, United Kingdom, was at the centre of a study in the mid-2000s investigating how farmers' social capital was supporting agricultural production (Burton *et al.*, 2005, 2009). The report suggested, on the basis of interviews with upland farmers, that if the farming communities continued to decline, the cultural landscape was at risk as traditional practices would cease to be followed. This chapter returns to this study to address an issue not tackled in the original report, namely, how changes in the everyday practices of farmers are influencing the development and transmission of the traditional farming culture and, therefore, the long-term future of the cultural landscape. To augment this information, it both reanalyses some of the original interview transcripts and updates the analysis through a review of recent literature and online documents.

The chapter follows Kroeber and Kluckhohn's (1952: p. 181) widely used definition of culture, namely:

> Culture consists of patterns, explicit and implicit, of and for behaviour acquired and transmitted by symbols, constituting the distinctive achievement of human groups, including their embodiments in artefacts; the essential core of culture consists of traditional (i.e., historically derived and selected) ideas and especially their attached values; culture systems may, on the one hand, be considered as products of action, on the other as conditioning elements of further action.

For this chapter therefore, 'cultural sustainability' is defined as the maintenance of cultural systems required for preserving the cultural landscape. This does not simply mean keeping farmers on the land – which can lead to a countryside that looks similar, but lacks authenticity (an important component for both cultural heritage preservation and tourism, see Daugstad and Kirchengast, 2013). Rather, it is about the need to ensure continuity of the living culture, i.e. the sustainable transmission of cultural beliefs and practices from one generation to the next. In addressing the issue of the breakdown of these cultural systems, the chapter examines how changes to agriculture is disrupting the traditional culture and suggests why government measures aimed at preserving the appearance and function of the cultural landscape are unable to prevent the decline of the culture itself.

The character of farming in the Lake District National Park

Agriculture has played a critical role in the development of the distinctive landscape of the Lake District. According to documents submitted for United Nations Educational, Scientific and Cultural Organization (UNESCO) World Heritage status in 2011 (LDNPA, 2011a) the current appearance of the Lake District region can be attributed to a single historical period – the so-called 'great rebuilding' that took place between 1660 and 1740. Driven by the legal establishment of the rights of yeoman farmers in the early 1600s, this period saw the widespread renewal of farm houses, agricultural buildings and structures in a manner that reflected the technologies, materials and management approaches of the period. These same rights preserved the region through the extensive landscape changes that occurred in other parts of Europe during eighteenth and nineteenth centuries while, more recently, the unsuitability of the region to intensive agriculture has protected it from any significant change.

The legacy of this unique development has been the continued existence of functional agricultural structures that reflect traditional management practices, namely farmhouses and out-buildings surrounded by 'in-bye' fields in the valley bottoms, 'intakes' of semi-improved land bordered by a wall that separates improved land from the open fells (mountains) and common grazing at altitudes above the fell wall (LDNPA, 2008) (see Figure 9.1). It is the continued practice of traditional farm management within a traditional landscape that provides the Lake District area with its distinctiveness. The LDNPA (2013) considers farming to be:

> … the most critical economic, social, environmental and cultural activity in the Lake District. It is the key human activity that gives the Lake District its sense of place and its distinctive and iconic landscape character, and it is central to the identity of many Lake District communities. It plays a critical underpinning role for both tourism and the food and drink sector.

Today's Lake District landscape continues to reflect traditional agricultural practices. A particular feature of the region is the continued use of 'hefting' as a means of managing sheep. Hefting uses the territorial instincts of sheep to manage individual flocks in areas of common grazing without the need for fencing or intensive management (see Short, 2000; Mansfield *et al.*, 2006). Hefted sheep become used to particular environments and consequently, over

Figure 9.1 Typical hill farm from the Lake District.

Source: author.

generations, develop resistance to particular parasites, mineral deficiencies and plant toxins (Davies *et al.*, 2008). Most importantly in terms of the environment and landscape, however, hefting enables the even grazing of rough pasture which both maintains the pasture in a better condition and reduces the opportunity for the regrowth of bracken (Short, 2000), maintaining the historical appearance of the landscape. However, maintaining a hefted farm has some specific requirements. In particular, because of the collective management practices required, social capital amongst farmers is essential to maintain the hefts and therefore the integrity of the landscape (Burton *et al.*, 2009).

The decline of local farming communities in the Lake District

Despite the importance of preserving farming communities for the maintenance of the cultural landscape there is evidence that farming communities in the Lake District are in danger. Ten years ago, researchers and community groups alike warned that without addressing the problem of farm succession the traditional practices required to manage the cultural landscape could collapse (Burton *et al.*, 2005; Federation of Cumbria Commoners, 2006). This problem does not yet appear to have been resolved. For example, on 26 March 2011 the Herdwick Sheep Breeders Association (HSBA, 2011) wrote a public letter expressing concern for, amongst other things, the 'worryingly small numbers of young people entering hill farming'. This letter further cites Susan Denyer the United Kingdom's adviser to UNESCO on cultural World Heritage sites as expressing concern for the Lake District:

> This decline in numbers of people living and working on the land means that there is now an inadequate structure to allow communal management of some of the key elements such as walls, hedges, watercourses and grazed common fells. In many valleys the bones of the landscape survive but are hanging on by a thread, as the social and economic systems that supported them are weakening.

Articles in the farming press express similar concerns. For example, in an article in *British Farmer & Grower* the Chairman of the Federation of Cumbrian Commoners is cited as saying 'Looking forward I see the existence of traditional farming systems on commons as remaining very fragile because of economics and changing lifestyle expectations which make it harder to convince upcoming generations of their worth' (No authors listed, 2013: p. 35). Recently the Lake District National Park Authority (LDNPA) have acknowledged that 'an aging workforce, and a lack of young people entering the industry are issues which could impact Lake District's special qualities' (LDNPA, 2011b: p. 52). Finally, a recent report into farming in the Lake District concluded 'only a minority are confident about the succession to their family business' (Harvey *et al.*, 2013: p. i).

Policies to address this problem focus on promoting the economic development of the region through diversification of farm businesses and supporting farmers to produce environmental and cultural goods. Here farmers in the Lake District have a considerable advantage. Cumbria Tourism estimates that in 2014 the Lake District received 16.4 million visitors who bought £1.15 billion to the region's economy (Greenwood, 2015). In addition to this potential income source, fell farmers in the Lake District are also eligible for an 'Uplands Entry Level Stewardship' subsidy which offers higher levels of payment for farming of land within 'Severely Disadvantaged Areas' (Natural England, 2013) along with a 'commons supplement' for managing common grazings (No authors listed, 2013). However, in response to overgrazing in the past decades, a policy of reducing stocking rates on the fells means that agri-environmental payments are generally dependent on a reduction of stocking rates and/or adjustments to grazing regimes (Martin *et al.*, 2013).

Theoretically, given the presence of a £1.15 billion tourism market and some of the highest levels of agri-environmental subsidies in the United Kingdom there ought to be a thriving community of young farmers in the Lake District. Instead, the farming communities of the Lake District are under threat. Here it is proposed that the key problem with contemporary European Union cultural landscape policies is that they focus on preserving landscapes and economic sustainability rather than preserving cultural sustainability. In a policy world where success has to be measurable through indicators there is no measure of cultural sustainability – i.e. whether the meanings and relationships between the local communities and their landscapes can be maintained. Yet, it is this relationship that ensures the continued existence of important cultural landscapes – not the number of buildings restored, number of entrants into agri-environmental schemes or any other measurable structural (material or social) features. The next section suggests a number of ways in which structural change in the Lake District is affecting the cultural connection between the farming communities and the land and, critically, how this influences the transmission of the farming culture from one generation to the next.

Exploring the connections between policy, structural and cultural change

The social impact of decreasing stocking rates on the fells

One of the key policies for preserving traditional agriculture in the Lake District and preserving the environment and cultural landscape is the use of agri-environmental payments. Overgrazing in the uplands has been a problem in recent decades and, consequently, the reduction of grazing pressure to promote the sustainable management of moorland shrubs has become a key component of policy measures in the region (Martin *et al.*, 2013). These agri-environmental requirements have been criticised by farmers groups as having two detrimental social impacts on the farming community.

First, farmers are concerned that the reduction in sheep numbers reduces the total need for labour and, consequently, makes training and attracting young people into the profession increasingly difficult (HSBA, 2011). This impacts on the size of the agricultural community in the region which, in turn, can interfere with the generation of cultural and social capital.

Second, reducing sheep numbers reduces the grazing pressure on the boundaries of the heft meaning that flocks spread out further and farmers consequently have higher labour requirements (Davies *et al.*, 2008). Thus, while the reduction of sheep numbers would normally make management easier, in this case it can make traditional farming more difficult.

If reducing stocking rates makes farming more difficult a paradox occurs whereby measures to restore the 'traditional' environmental condition of the land through paying for physical improvements ends up damaging the sustainability of the community required to deliver the environmental goods. An important consideration here is the social context within which stocking rates have increased. Returning the fells to the lower stocking rates of the past, while potentially environmentally beneficial, ignores the historically lower lifestyle expectations and larger family sizes (Brandth and Overrein, 2013) that increased the likelihood of succession. In addition, farmers observe that much satisfaction from farming comes from the successful management and breeding of livestock (see Burton, 2004; Yarwood and Evans, 2006). While it cannot be imagined that there is a simple relationship between the number of animals and levels of satisfaction, it is possible that any decline in sheep numbers limits the satisfaction farmers receive from farming (as was noted by two farmers' sons in Burton *et al.*, 2005).

Changing socialisation practices

A second change to social processes in the Lake District is the impact of regulatory and structural change on the ability of farmers to socialise (or enculturate) successors. The importance of early childhood socialisation for creating successors has been noted by a number of researchers, with the accompanying of the farmer around the farm being an important first step in the process (e.g. Sachs, 1973; Brandth and Overrein, 2013; Fischer and Burton, 2014). In both Norway (Brandth and Overrein, 2013) and Scotland (Fischer and Burton, 2014) it has also been observed that as the workload on farmers increases, so the amount of time farmers are able to devote to early childhood socialisation declines. Further, mechanisation and increasing specialisation of roles in agriculture mean that a number of jobs children used to be able to participate in (such as moving stones by hand) are not performed by manual labour any more, while other tasks, such as shearing, are performed by contract labour (Brandth and Overrein, 2013).

Another issue raised by both Fischer and Burton (2014) and Brandth and Overrein (2013) is the impact of increasingly strict health and safety requirements on the socialisation process as farmers are often precluded from being accompanied by their children by regulations that were not in place in the past. Similar observations were made in unpublished data from Burton *et al.*'s (2005) study. For example, female farmer 4 observes that when they were children there would be ten to 12 children on the farm at the weekends, while male farmer 4 observes:

> When I was born and bred on my grandfather's farm. I used to have my own wheelbarrow and shovel and brush and I could go and muck my grandfather's ... clean my grandfather's cows out and they wouldn't move or flinch. He used to sort of milk them all by hand in them days ...

Farmer 5 similarly observed a lack of young people in farming and observed that, when he was a child, '(W)e used to jump on the back of the tractor at hay time and things like that'. In both cases the farmers observed that the lack of children working on the farm was in part due to a lack of interest by the new rural generation but was also attributable to fear in the farming community of legal prosecution should something happen to the children. As farmer 5 observed:

> It's all changed isn't it since you and me were lads. It's all health and safety now. You've got to be very careful or you're up shit creek aren't you. If one of them gets injured or falls off a ladder or anything really. Trip over a bale and break your arm you're liable nowadays aren't you.

There is little doubt that increasing health and safety requirements has positive impacts in terms of the safety of children on the farm. However, what is not considered is the impact such measures are having on the socialisation of children into agriculture and how this, in turn, can influence the transfer of the farm (and culture) to the next generation. In a place such as the Lake District and the other high value cultural landscapes where incomes are low and the work difficult, this weakening of the socialisation process may be particularly problematic.

Building the culture into the land

The importance of stone walls and buildings for cultural landscape is noted in many European studies (see, for example, Scharrer *et al.* and Gugerel *et al.*, this volume: p. 151 and p. 109, respectively). What is rarely explored, however, is the importance of the walls and buildings to the culture of the farming communities. Khalil (2000: p. 57) observes that to become symbolically significant to a culture an object 'must play an important role in the everyday livelihood of the agents concerned' and that, critically, 'The symbolic message can be effective only if others readily perceive the difficulty of acquiring the said products'. Stone walls not only represent considerable invested labour but also have what Brady (2006: p. 14) describes as 'an unintended beauty in the patterns that result in the walls themselves from the need to place stones in such a way as to achieve a good fit to produce a solid, strong form'. In the Lake District farmers are losing their cultural connections to this important symbol. Burton *et al.* (2005) observed how the significance of stone walls on farmers' property is greatly enhanced by the investment of their personal labour during construction – in particular as children. As farmer 16 noted:

> You should see the wall I first put up when I was 13 in Ambleside, it's a right scrap but it's still up. So you see, you get lots of pleasure out of that, you know, you actually see what your endeavours are doing.

Much of the stone-walling is now done by contractors who may, or may not, be associated with the eventual custodianship of the structure. This loss of a connection between the farm family and the material landscape is important. A strong link between the farmer and culturally constructed objects enhances the motivation of the communities to maintain their connection with traditional features. For example, the likelihood of selling land is lessened when the land has been extensively worked by earlier generations of the farm family (Raedeke *et al*., 2003; Burton, 2004) while stone walls built by the farm family in the past are more likely to be preserved (Setten, 2004). The importance of this aspect of social/cultural change relates to the earlier observation that it is not primarily money that keeps farmers working in these regions but rather their attachment to their farms and land. The failure of farm succession in areas of high cultural landscape value may thus be in part attributable to the lack of cultural 'investment' in (or embodiment in) the farm structures.

The impact of limiting the development of housing

Public visits to the Lake District area are based largely around activities enhanced by high public goods provision in the cultural landscape. Examples of such activities are hill walking, scenic driving and wildlife watching, with emphasis placed on the historical stone-walled farm landscapes and the cultural working of the land (Burton *et al.*, 2005). Researchers and local government organisations believe it is this demand that drives the housing economy in the region. For example, the LDNPA stated that quality of life and landscape are the main forces behind the very high level of demand for housing in the Lake District (LDNPA, 2006). Similar connections between rapidly rising house prices and rugged mountain landscapes delivering scenic and recreational public goods have also been observed in national parks in the United States (Smaldone *et al.*, 2005). In United Kingdom national parks in general, Silcock *et al.* (2013) contend that house prices are significantly higher. Of the national parks they looked at, housing in the Lake District was the most unaffordable with the value of property within the park boundary receiving a 90 per cent premium over the regional average.

This pressure has led to strict planning restrictions on new developments in order to preserve the cultural character of the region (LDNPA, 2013). In particular, while efforts have been made to provide affordable housing for locals, since April 2006 no new housing has been provided to meet the demand for second homes, holiday homes or holiday lets. By preventing new building but allowing existing farms to be split up into land, out-buildings and farm house and sold (with a higher total value than a complete working farm), the LDNPA has unwittingly created a strong economic incentive for retiring farmers to break up the farm. Thus, paradoxically, the working farms required to maintain traditional hefted land management are under pressure from policies intended to preserve the traditional nature of the cultural landscape (Burton *et al.*, 2009).

A further issue is that cultural expectations have changed since the development of the landscape in the seventeenth and eighteenth centuries. Current structures reflect a time when living with older generations in one farm building was perceived as the acceptable or normal cultural practice (as was the case in Norway, e.g. Villa, 1999). However, changes in social expectations over the decades mean that this is increasingly unacceptable in many places, although economic pressures in former Eastern European countries mean multi-generational households are still common (e.g. Zutinic and Grgic, 2010). Thus, while traditional farms may have functioned with simply one farm house, there is a strong case for contemporary social units to possess two dwelling buildings in order to facilitate the succession process. This issue has been recognised and addressed in areas around the national park. In particular, in noting that many of the regions' successful farms had two unrestricted dwellings associated with the business, the Upper Eden Neighbourhood Development Plan (Woof, 2012) incorporated new building regulations to enable easy transition of farm properties.

New communities, new cultures

A final area where the cultural sustainability of the region is being challenged comes from the invasion of new cultural beliefs and values. Unpublished data from the 2005 interviews suggests the importance of school-based social networks for the socialisation of farmer's children. For example, the successor of farmer 1 noted a high level of co-operation with a neighbouring farmer's son who he was in the same class as throughout his schooling. However, the son also observed that: 'Most of my friends at my school weren't really related to farming because there weren't a huge amount of people my age who were farming'. In noting that most of his son's friends had gone to university and moved out of the area, his father added: 'That's the difference between that generation and ours. My classmates there's a lot of them around. Folk didn't shift far then'. One impact of this changing composition of schools is on the aspirations of farmers' children. In particular, farmer 19 observed:

> In the 30s, when things were really bad, everybody was bad. Nobody had anything. Whereas now, you've got farmers sons and daughters going to school with other people, *and they're seeing what other people have got, and the rest of society racing away basically.*

Not only is there a subconscious aspirational issue with changing rural populations, but as the proportion of non-farming children in local schools increases, social pressure is exerted to conform to a new set of norms as farmer 5 notes, 'It isn't fashionable to say when you go to school that you're working on a farm and things like that. They're not bothered now. They'd rather play on their video games.' In traditional agricultural communities where social capital and collaboration are important (Sutherland and Burton, 2011), this educational change could have important implications for the future sustainability of the region as the close bonds formed by being socialised together in an agricultural community (Fischer and Burton, 2014) are increasingly absent from the region while wider cultural influences are increasing.

Discussion and conclusion: the need for policies focused on cultural sustainability

The case of the Lake District illustrates how important it is for policy-makers to consider culture when trying to promote sustainable cultural landscapes and, critically, how a focus on the structures of the landscape (whether social, economic or environmental) is not sufficient to guarantee policy success. Central to the problem is the inseparable relationship between culture and the human and natural environments. Whether it is the effect of lowering stocking rates on levels of social/cultural capital in the farming community; the effect of health and safety regulations on early childhood socialisation processes; the incompatibility of old farm structures with new cultural aspirations; the infusion of new cultural values from outside the traditional community; or changes in the farming role that break traditional links between the construction of the landscape and the cultural capital (skills/knowledge) of the farming families – all of these factors can contribute to a failure to recruit the next generation of farmers and thus the loss of cultural continuity. When it is considered that the Lake District region receives some of the highest subsidies for cultural landscape in the United Kingdom as well as attracting significant numbers of tourists there is clearly a major policy failure here.

It would not be fair to suggest that the issue of farm continuity is not being addressed at all. Training schemes such as the Fell Farming Trainee Project or Fell Futures Apprenticeship Scheme have been established in the Lake District to try to help younger people to enter into fell farming. However, these schemes make the assumption that farming (supported by environmental and cultural landscape payments) will remain profitable enough to provide for recruits in the future. On past experience, this seems unlikely. A recent report for the Lake District National Park suggested that over the previous ten years the majority of farmers had financially only just broken even and noted that greater profitability was required to enable future investment (Harvey *et al.*, 2013). To the authors of this report the continuation of the current generation of fell farmers in agriculture seemed puzzling as they note: 'these farmers appear to be content to live as paupers in the interests of sustaining their businesses and livelihoods' (p. iv). However, reliance on a willingness of famers to live as paupers is not sustainable. The current generation of farmers may be prepared to live as paupers but it appears this does not extend to the next generation of farmers who represent the future of both the culture and the cultural landscape.

Preserving culture is not an easy task. The physical character of the Lake District has remained relatively unchanged since the period of the 'great rebuilding' and current policies aim to keep it so. However, the landscape features that are so highly valued were made to meet the needs of a culture with social structures, values and practices very different to those of today. Policies that enforce strict environmental or structural requirements – no matter how well intentioned – effectively turn a landscape based on a living culture to one based on a prescribed historical cliché that may, or may not, fit with contemporary values and lifestyles. In the meantime, the current generation of farmers continue to farm as economic 'paupers' simply because they are so culturally embedded in the landscape and local community that the value of their social and cultural capital more than compensates for the poor economy, i.e. they are paupers economically, but not culturally (see Burton, 2004, 2012; Sutherland and Burton, 2011). Their children, however, have other experiences, connections, expectations and options.

An important question here is why do policy-makers fail to recognise the importance of maintaining the farming culture in the region? Widespread warnings that the farming community is in decline in the Lake District have been around since at least the mid-2000s – yet the response seems to be have been limited. In part, it is because of the measures of policy success employed. Standard measures such as area of land entered into agri-environmental agreements, number of stone walls repaired, or even the amount of money distributed to farmers all suggest that policies are succeeding in their objective to preserve cultural landscape. However, while economic (e.g. income), social (e.g. unemployment) and environmental (e.g. metres of stone wall restored) indicators are relatively easy to measure, they tell us nothing about the effect of policy on the likely continuation of culture, i.e. the extent to which cultural beliefs, values, meanings and practices are being passed on from one generation to the next. In a world where capital is becoming more important than people (see Hreinsson, this volume: p. 79), the overuse (and misuse) of quantifiable indicators and statistics increasingly renders people and cultures invisible as focus falls on maintaining the physical manifestations of culture.

Although this chapter has focused on an area of cultural landscape in the United Kingdom, the findings have implications for all attempts to promote cultural landscape sustainability. In particular, the case study suggests that policies focusing only on the economic, environmental and social pillars of sustainability are unlikely to be effective in the long term. Cultural sustainability as it is defined in this chapter (i.e. the preservation of cultural systems required for maintaining the cultural landscape) is needed to maintain the economic, environmental and social value of cultural landscape. Without cultural sustainability, the other pillars will be greatly diminished or lost entirely. Policy-makers therefore need to think beyond the 'three' pillars of sustainability to a fourth pillar – that of the cultural sustainability. The status quo may lead to the creation of landscapes that are historical but not cultural and, while 'sustainable' in a physical sense represent part of globalised 'Disneyfication', i.e. they become a non-place operated by non-persons dealing in non-things (Matusitz and Palermo, 2014). Resolving this involves understanding the need to maintain cultures in their living, changing form rather than tying them to historical clichés of past cultures, while at the same time ensuring that important intergenerational aspects of culture are able to continue to develop and be transferred in the face of rapidly changing social and economic environments.

Acknowledgements

This chapter was written with the assistance of the Norwegian Research Council's project STRUCTURES (project number: 199349).

References

André, M-F. (1998) Depopulation, land-use change and landscape transformation in the French Massif Central. *Ambio* 27(4):351–353.

Brady, E. (2006) The aesthetics of agricultural landscapes and the relationship between humans and nature. *Ethics, Place & Environment* 9(1):1–19.

Brandth, B. and Overrein, G. (2013) Resourcing children in a changing rural context: fathering and farm succession in two generations of farmers. *Sociologia Ruralis* 53(1):95–111.

Burton, R. J. F. (2004) Seeing through the 'good farmer's' eyes: towards developing an understanding of the social symbolic value of 'productivist' behaviour. *Sociologia Ruralis* 44(2):195–216.

Burton, R. J. F. (2012) Understanding farmers' aesthetic preference for tidy agricultural landscapes: a bourdieusian perspective. *Landscape Research* 37(1):51–71.

Burton, R. J. F., Mansfield, L., Schwarz, G., Brown, K. M. and Convery, I. T. (2005) *Social Capital in Hill Farming: Report for the International Centre for the Uplands*. Macaulay Institute, Aberdeen, United Kingdom.

Burton, R. J. F., Schwarz, G., Brown, K. M., Convery, I. T. and Mansfield, L. (2009) The future of hefted upland commons in areas of high public goods provision: learning from the Lake District experience. In: A. Bonn, K. Hubacek, J. Stewart and T. Allott (eds) *Drivers of Change in Upland Environments*. Routledge, London: 309–323.

Daugstad, K. and Kirchengast, C. (2013) Authenticity and the pseudobackstage of agri-tourism. *Annals of Tourism Research* 43:170–191.

Davies, O., Morgan, M. and Werrett, M. (2008) *Assessment of the impact of hefting (heafing or learing). ADAS report BD1242*. ADAS Pwllpeiran, Aberystwyth, United Kingdom.

Federation of Cumbria Commoners. (2006) *Common Interests: A Cumbrian Perspective on Common Land and Life (promotional DVD)*. Federation of Cumbria Commoners, Newmarket, United Kingdom.

Fischer, H. and Burton, R. J. F. (2014) Understanding farm succession as a socially constructed endogenous cycle. *Sociologia Ruralis* 54(4):417–438.

Greenwood, R. (2015) *STEAM Tourism Data*. LDNP Partnership Agenda, Item 5, Annex 1. 12th June. Cumbria Tourism, UK. www.lakedistrict.gov.uk/__data/assets/pdf_file/0005/ 582953/5b.-STEAM-data.pdf (Accessed 26 December 2016).

Harvey, D., Thompson, N., Scott, C. and Hubbard, C. (2013) *Farming & Farm Forestry in the Lake District: A Report for the Lake District National Park Partnership, Farming & Forestry Task Force*. Newcastle University, Newcastle, United Kingdom.

HSBA. (2011) *Open letter*. 26th March 2011. www.cumbriacommoners.org.uk/files/hsba_letter_of_concern.pdf (Accessed 26 December 2016).

Kahlil, E. (2000) Symbolic products: prestige, pride and identity goods. *Theory and Decision* 49(1):53–77.

Kroeber, A. L. and Kluckhohn, C. (1952) *Culture: A Critical Review of Concepts and Definitions*. The Museum, Cambridge, Unites States.

LDNPA. (2006) *Annual Monitoring Report April 2005–March 2006*. Lake District National Park Authority, Kendal, United Kingdom.

LDNPA. (2008) *Annual Monitoring Report April 2007–March 2008*. Lake District National Park Authority, Kendal, United Kingdom.

LDNPA. (2011a) *Lake District World Heritage Project: Draft Nomination Document*. LDNPA, Kendal, United Kingdom.

LDNPA. (2011b) *Annual Monitoring Report April 2010–March 2011*. Lake District National Park Authority, Kendal, United Kingdom.

LDNPA. (2013) *Annual Monitoring Report April 2012–March 2013*. Lake District National Park Authority, Kendal, United Kingdom.

Mansfield, L., Burton, R. J. F., Schwarz, G., Brown, K. and Convery, I. T. (2006) The heft: a multifunctional management tool. *The International Journal of Biodiversity Science, Ecosystem Services and Management* 2(3):238–241.

Marín-Yaseli, M. L. and Martínez, T. L. (2003) Competing for meadows. *Mountain Research and Development* 23(2):169–176.

Martin, D., Fraser, M. D., Pakeman, R. J. and Moffat, A. M. (2013) Natural England Review of Upland Evidence 2012 – Impact of moorland grazing and stocking rates. *Natural England Evidence Review* 006.

Matusitz, J. and Palermo, L. (2014) The Disneyfication of the world: a grobalisation perspective. *Journal of Organisational Transformation & Social Change* 11(2):91–107.

Mottet, A., Ladet, S., Coque, N. and Gibon, A. (2006) Agricultural land-use change and its drivers in mountain landscapes: a case study in the Pyrenees. *Agriculture, Ecosystems and Environment* 114(2–4): 296–310.

Natural England. (2013) *Environmental Stewardship Handbook*. (Fourth Edition). Natural England, York, United Kingdom.

No authors listed. (2013) Maintaining and improving viability of commons in the hills. *British Farmer and Grower* April:34–35.

O'Rourke, E. (2005) Socio-natural interaction and landscape dynamics in the Burren, Ireland. *Landscape and Urban Planning* 70(1–2):69–83.

O'Rourke, E. (2006) Changes in agriculture and the environment in an upland region of the Massif Central, France. *Environmental Science and Policy* 9(4):370–375.

Raedeke, A., Green, J., Hodge, S. and Valdivia, C. (2003) Farmers, the practice of farming and the future of agroforestry: an application of Bourdieu's concepts of field and habitus. *Rural Sociology* 68(1):64–86.

Sachs, R. E. (1973) The farmer: an entrepreneur personality? *Sociologia Ruralis* 13(2):194–211.

Setten, G. (2004) The habitus, the rule and the moral landscape. *Cultural Geographies* 11(4) 389–415

Short, C. (2000) Common Land and ELMS: a need for policy innovation in England and Wales. *Land Use Policy* 17(2):121–133.

Silcock, P., Rayment, M., Kieboom, E., White, A. and Brunyee, J. (2013) *Valuing England's National Parks. Final report for National Parks England. Cumulus Consultants Ltd and ICF GHK*. National Parks England, London.

Smaldone, D., Harris, C. and Sanyal, N. (2005) An exploration of place as a process: the case of Jackson Hole, WY. *Journal of Environmental Psychology* 25(4):397–414.

Sutherland, L-A. and Burton, R. J. F. (2011) Good Farmers, good neighbours?: The role of cultural capital in social capital development a Scottish farming community. *Sociologia Ruralis* 51(3):238–255.

Villa, M. (1999) Born to be farmers? Changing expectations in Norwegian farmers' life courses. *Sociologia Ruralis* 39(3):328–342.

Woof, T. (2012) *Upper Eden Neighbourhood Development Plan*. Cerberus Printing, UK. www.eden.gov.uk/EasySiteWeb/GatewayLink.aspx?alId=30285 (Accessed 22 December 2016).

Yarwood, R. and Evans, N. (2006) A Lleyn sweep for local sheep? Breed societies and the geographies of Welsh livestock. *Environment and Planning A* 38(7):1307–1326.

Zutinic, D. and Grigic, I. (2010) Family farm inheritance in Slavonia region, Croatia. *Agricultural Economics – Czech* 56(11):522–531.

10 Terraced landscapes

The significance of a living agricultural heritage for sustainable regional development

Bettina Scharrer, Thomas Hammer and Marion Leng

Introduction

Terraced landscapes and terraced cultivation are part of the universal cultural heritage of humanity. They represent an agricultural practice that for hundreds of years has allowed land to be used for cultivation even in topographically, hydrologically or climatically difficult terrain. Terracing is found all over the world, and in Europe continues to be widely practiced particularly around the Mediterranean, in the north-west and in parts of Central Europe. This type of cultivation may appear rather marginal when considered from the perspective of modern, industrialised agriculture. However, in the last two decades both practitioners and academics have become more aware of the multifunctional and cultural significance of terraces and their associated forms of sustainable land use. This is especially true for actors in the Parc Naturel Régional des Monts d'Ardèche (PNRMA), a protected region with many terraced landscapes in south-central France.

This chapter examines the PNRMA case to show the significance of terraced landscapes for a region and its identity. Discussion also focuses on how the inhabitants of the region deal with this cultural heritage in order to make the greatest possible use of its potential, and to preserve, revive and develop knowledge about dry-stone walling and cultivation. The PNRMA is an interesting case for reflecting on the role of culture in sustainable development, given the diversity of actors highlighting culture as an essential factor for the region's sustainable development. In a study examining the PNRMA,[1] nine aspects of culture were identified as relevant to the cultural sustainability of rural regions. Five of the factors are directly perceptible expressions of culture, namely: intangible cultural heritage, tangible cultural heritage, cultural landscapes, contemporary culture and the combination of these aspects, cultural diversity. Mental and social dispositions account for the remaining aspects, namely aesthetic and sensory perception, regional identity, participation and social cohesion. In combination, these aspects can be considered as part of the cultural dimension of sustainable development, but they also act as drivers of sustainable regional development.

Using the example of terraced landscapes in the Monts d'Ardèche and describing the progressive way in which the PNRMA deals with these landscapes, this chapter illustrates the fundamental role that the various aspects of culture play in sustainable development and shows how they interact with each other. Moreover, the terraced landscapes reflect the interface between culture and nature in a very concrete and tangible way – as can also be seen in Gugerell *et al.* (this volume: p. 109).

The first section discusses the general significance of terraced landscapes and dry-stone walls as interfaces between culture and nature from the perspectives of research and the various actors involved in the PNRMA. The second section looks at the role of the PNRMA in regional and landscape development and the third section draws specific attention to challenges connected with the maintenance and further development of terraced landscapes in the PNRMA. The fourth section examines preconditions and selected strategies for dealing sustainably with this unusual agricultural heritage and presents examples of best practice. The chapter concludes with lessons learned on cultural heritage in the PNRMA that can inspire other places with terraced landscapes.

Terraced landscapes symbolising the interface of culture and nature

Terraced landscapes are a specific form of historically evolved cultural landscape and represent a distinct synthesis of topography, land use and building culture (Schegk, 2014: p. 85). They are a direct reflection of the development of human society and its interaction with nature, and a reminder that since the very start of agriculture human beings have not been able simply to use nature but have first needed to work to transform it into arable land. Terraced landscapes and their cultivated plantings show this transformation of nature, which should not be confused with the destruction of nature (Bätzing, 2014: p. 381). Rather, terracing of the original 'wild nature' led to the emergence of landscapes of particularly high ecological and aesthetic value, landscapes that offered people a livelihood even in regions with very difficult terrain.

The transformation of such areas into useable agricultural land is an immense cultural achievement. It represents the application of a large body of knowledge that has evolved over time and through the untiring collective work of farmers who developed the agricultural land by building and maintaining dry-stone walls (Blanc, 2001: p. 15). The cultural distinctiveness of terraced landscapes and their ecological functions is thus reflected by a vernacular architecture (Latin 'vernaculus': indigenous, traditional or local) that is not the product of famous architects but is a collective, anonymous, nameless 'architecture without a pedigree' (Rudofsky, 1989: p. 1). It stands not for the sophisticated architecture of its era in the sense of a narrowly defined concept of culture, but rather for attributes like rustic, rural, regional and elementary. It results from the collective efforts of a society,

> a collaborative art that is not the product of a few intellectuals or specialists but has emerged from the spontaneous and enduring activity of an entire

> people who are carried by a collective heritage and act under the influence of collective experience.
>
> (Belluschi quoted in Schegk, 2014: p. 102)

The terraces created by this vernacular architecture reflect the interface of culture and nature and also correspond with many of the aspects of landscape development that can be termed sustainable from a present-day perspective. The stone terraces are the expression of an elementary cultural practice that was (and in some cases still is) necessary for day-to-day human life and economic activity. The use of local resources, or stones from the immediate vicinity, allows the walls to be harmoniously and aesthetically integrated in the surroundings. This is also the case in the PNRMA:

> If you step back a bit, you see that they [the stone terraces] help to create beautiful, well-balanced landscapes, an integrated whole, where everything is integrated but where nature has its part to play too. [...] There's a balance that needs to be created between the vegetation and the land itself. The same goes for water, the way things flow and circulate. [...] So you have these lines, really wonderful places, that still survive and which are still very, very beautiful. You just have to start maintaining them again, to bring them back into use.
>
> (Delahaye, 2014[2])

Thanks to the stone terraces, particularly readable and distinctive landscapes emerged – 'landscapes with a memory' (Ewald, 2014: p. 397). This comment pertains without doubt particularly to the constructed and modelled terraced landscapes in the PNRMA, where at their height terracing practices accounted for 90 per cent of agricultural produce. Terraces are still found today in at least half of all municipalities (Blanc, 2001: p. 17).

> Chestnut trees and terraces are certainly the most visible elements running through this common culture: they are to be seen throughout the region and they bear witness to the harmony between human activity and a tough but special environment. All of the agriculture practised on the slopes reflects this close relationship: the chestnut trees and the crops grown on the terraces are the result of adaptation to the environment and are still today an example of a landscape heritage site of Europe-wide importance.
>
> (PNRMA, 2001: p. 7)

The PNRMA landscape and its terraces are also a reflection of the history of nutrition. Terraces were not built without reason, but were constructed out of necessity. While today we are facing problems such as food waste and overproduction, the terraced landscapes reflect the achievements and efforts of an agricultural and early industrial society striving to feed a growing population with the means and agricultural practices of the pre-fossil era, and therefore working to make the use of terrain in difficult situations possible in the long term.

Nutritionally speaking, it is now no longer necessary to continue terraced cultivation in Europe. The industrialisation of agriculture has led to increasing yields and thus rendered the labour-intensive building of terraces obsolete. In the last century, this contributed to a massive rural exodus from numerous districts with terraced cultivation, including the PNRMA. However, in many places, terraced landscapes survived agricultural modernisation – which, in some areas, implied the total clearance of much of the landscape – because abandoning the exploitation of steep slopes was more logical than their intensification (similar to the situation in the Lake District in the United Kingdom, see Burton, this volume: p. 109). The locational characteristics of these stony cultural landscapes meant that they offered too little potential for intensive agriculture (Schegk, 2014: pp. 74, 85). The example of the PNRMA illustrates this. Here the terraces have either been abandoned and left to succession, or labour-intensive terracing has continued with high-quality regional and speciality crops such as wine, vegetables, (medicinal) herbs, sweet chestnuts, fruit trees and olives, often grown according to the tenets of organic farming. The terraced areas thus represent a resource that it would still be possible to draw upon.

Problems often arise when terraces are completely abandoned, as they have functions other than food production. They stabilise the slopes, protect against erosion and flooding and regulate water regimes. They provide habitats for specific fauna and flora, some of which are endangered, and thus contribute to biodiversity conservation (see Ammann *et al.*, 2012: pp. 11–15, 203–233; Bätzing, 2014: pp. 381–382; Witschi, 2014: pp. 329–375; Delahaye, 2014). Especially in the Mediterranean region, terracing guarantees protection against potentially catastrophic consequences of extreme weather events, as Martine Guiton showed for the floods in Nimes in 1988 and in Vaison la Romaine in 1992 (Giorgis, 2001: pp. 94–96; Delahaye, 2014). Last but not least, the terraces in the PNRMA shape local and regional identity. Both inhabitants and tourists attribute inherent values (such as beauty) to the terraced landscape which enhance quality of life.

In the last two decades, awareness of the significance of terraced landscapes for sustainable land use has increased throughout the world. This is expressed in the rise in the number of terraced landscapes in Europe that have been recognised as World Heritage sites. Examples of these include the cultural landscapes of Cinque Terre in Italy (1997), the wine terraces of Douro in Portugal (2001), the Wachau in Austria (2002) (see Gugerell *et al.*, this volume: p. 109), the Oberes Mittelrheintal in Germany (2002) and the wine terraces of Lavaux in Switzerland (2007) (Schegk, 2014: p. 86). Selecting such sites for protection raises positive awareness of terraced landscapes and aids the marketing of speciality crops produced there. But this strategy is not a viable solution for all terraced landscapes, as it is neither possible nor useful to award all such landscapes protected status.

Tasks and roles of the PNRMA in landscape development

The terraces in the Ardèche are part of an entire complex of terraced landscapes in south-east France which in places displays pharaonic proportions and which is unique in its density and diversity. In contrast to certain wine regions (e.g. Lavaux in Switzerland), the terraces in this area are not concentrated in a clearly delineated district but are extensively distributed. They influence large areas of the landscape and cannot be maintained as an ensemble by scattered individual initiatives. They can only be preserved by actors who are capable of developing large-scale visions, applying long-term strategies and establishing functioning networks. From the very inception of the PNRMA in the 1990s, it was clear that a major task would be to lead the preservation and further development of this enormous agricultural heritage.

As landscape development concepts and spatial planning measures related to terraced landscapes cannot be developed individually at the municipal level, the French regional nature parks institution (*Parcs naturels regionaux*, PNR) assumes an important role in this respect. PNRs are inter-municipal associations and thus are ideally placed to act as hubs ensuring co-operation between municipalities within the perimeter of the park and with the departments, regions and national level. According to the Fédération des parcs naturels regionaux de France, rural sustainable development is the main goal of PNRs. These parks are 'project areas where development and management policies are being conducted on the basis of respect and enhancement of the heritage, both natural and man-made, in other words, the landscape heritage [...]' (Donadieu and Périgord, 2005: p. 230). PNRs should follow a policy and development plan for their landscape that represents the common interests of regional authorities and inhabitants. How the development of the landscape unfolds should concern everybody and not be confined to the interests of specialists in a top-down manner (Donadieu and Périgord, 2005: p. 231). In the words of a dry-stone wall specialist working closely with the PNRMA:

> [The PNRMA] involves people who by definition think about things and use their heads, and they get others to join in all down the line. So we're talking about participation: local people, politicians. And then I think the park itself is a tool. [...] It provides a key for local people and elected politicians, who often conduct micro-policies, little things that don't last, that perhaps tend to be a bit ad hoc, decisions taken on the hoof, that are purely local. They don't weigh things up so much. But this is a way to arrive at a more global vision, to see things affecting the area as a whole.
>
> (Delahaye, 2014)

This statement also shows that in the Massif Central area regional nature parks and the Parc National des Cévennes play important roles for the sustainable development of terraced landscapes.

Selected problems and challenges

Maintaining and further developing is not conserving

Despite the increased attention given to terraced landscapes and the many positive aspects associated with dry-stone walls, maintaining thousands of kilometres of dry-stone walls represents an immense challenge. There is no point in preserving the terraces merely to satisfy cultural and historical interests (Bätzing, 2014: p. 382); their various benefits – whether social, economic, cultural or ecological – must also be recognised by the inhabitants.

The actors of the PNRMA do not want to place their landscape under a glass dome. Instead, they want to develop the landscape and raise awareness of its distinctive values among inhabitants (PNRMA, 2014: p. 19). This aim matches the PNR's understanding of culture: 'Culture is by definition a living thing. Neither harking back to the past nor forgetting it, cultural activity is evidence of a shared history, of cohesiveness, and enables local people to take possession of their region' (PNRMA, 2001: p. 18).

It is beyond question that, being the most prominent cultural heritage of the region, the PNRMA terraces are extraordinarily important in shaping the region's identity:

> Dry-stone terraces are our greatest heritage. You've got miles and miles of terraces that people have built. They are certainly … well, for me, they are part of our heritage, in the same way that some regions have the Loire châteaux, we have these terraces […] They really are an extraordinary piece of work. There's a skill in them… […] So, well, for me, the terraces are part of our identity.
>
> (Perret, 2014[3])

Having a regional identity encourages the public and cultural engagement of a region's inhabitants and thereby also fosters sustainable development. Feeling at home and having a sense of belonging to a place is also considered part of a 'good life'; in this sense, identity means sharing in the cultural significance of space (Ipsen, 2006).

The actors of the park are aware that individual and collective perceptions affect the expectations projected on the landscapes and their management (see Backhaus *et al.*, 2007: p. 108). The goal of the PNRMA is therefore to use bottom-up processes and involve the inhabitants in debating how development should unfold. By encouraging the population's direct participation in shaping future developments, the PNRMA is implementing an important aspect of cultural sustainability. Participatory decision-making processes give all stakeholder groups the opportunity to express their views, enabling them to reach a consensus in the case of conflicting interests and leading to decisions that are sustainable because they enjoy the population's support (Krainer, 2010: p. 91). The PNRMA's participatory approach is also in line with the goals set in Art. 1a, 5c, 6c of the European Landscape Convention (Council of Europe, 2000).

In concrete terms, this means negotiating which terraces should continue to be used and in what way, which should be renovated and which should no longer be maintained. There is little point in restoring terraces without allocating them a reasonable future function; this would merely create museum-like landscapes devoid of life. This aspect of the debate is also highlighted by Donadieu and Périgord, who criticise the conservation of cultural heritage for its own sake, as it destroys the landscape. A landscape is rather a living organism in a state of continuous transformation (Donadieu and Périgord, 2005: p. 83). The PNRMA shares this view:

> We want to preserve them [the terraces] as part of our heritage, but at the same time there is no point in restoring them if there is no activity to back them up.[...] We have seen that a lot of people are interested in the terraces. Lots of people expect the park to restore the terraces. But that's just it: we don't want to restore them merely for the sake of it, simply to have something that looks pretty.
>
> (Perret, 2014)

The focus should therefore be on the development of approaches for sustainable utilisation, a conclusion that both the park and the representatives of the stone-walling community share. This notion of integrating agricultural heritage in today's world is also reflected in the park's overall goal for cultural heritage: 'The aim is to put life into these heritage sites by developing their ability to adapt to the changes in society and in the land, and by integrating them into the policy of preserving and developing economic activities' (PNRMA, 2014: p. 21).

The PNRMA endorses the dynamic development of these cultural landscapes while simultaneously preserving their authenticity and diversity, which are an important foundation of the region's identity and image and contribute to the quality of life of its inhabitants. A balance needs to be found between preservation and modification, so as to enable use of the landscape in a way that makes sense from a present-day perspective and ensures the landscape's integration in residents' everyday lives.

Maintaining the terraces in the remote, sparsely settled valleys of the park is an immense challenge, particularly in terms of tackling forest expansion and ensuring that the landscape remains open. The terraces can only be used if local inhabitants are prepared to cultivate or use them. Of course, the Ardèche has profited from the French 'neo-rural' movement and the resulting in-migration, which has offset the great rural 'exodus' of the twentieth century, which peaked around 1960. However, newcomers are not evenly distributed throughout the region. In many terraced valleys, like in the Vallée de la Drobie in the southern Cévennes, large-scale out-migration has been halted since the 1970s. But in-migration is still low or inexistent, the population is aging and some residences are only used as second homes.

Furthermore, agricultural production suffers from the locational disadvantage of longer transportation times. It is not automatically easier for high-quality speciality crops such as wine to find a niche on the international market (Höchtl and Bieling, 2013: p. 306). Strategies for improving the prominence and marketing of these quality products are therefore required.

The question of knowledge transfer and current practice

Closely linked to the dry-stone walls is knowledge about the various techniques of construction and vernacular architecture; or, in other words, the know-how and thus the intangible cultural heritage. Whenever inhabitants, landscape architects or public authorities of a region that is particularly characterised by dry-stone wall terraces think about the future development of their landscape and its maintenance or succession, it is essential that they consider knowledge transfer tasks and the promotion and upgrading of the dry-stone walling profession. Without the necessary know-how it will not be possible to maintain the dry-stone walls in the long term. According to stone-walling specialist Yvan Delahaye, the process of knowledge transfer was interrupted about 30 to 40 years ago as a result of agricultural modernisation. The older generations still possess the relevant knowledge, but as it is only transferred by word of mouth, it is at risk of being lost unless it is properly inventoried. A newly discovered interest in know-how among the younger generations is very helpful in this context (Delahaye, 2014).

The tasks of knowledge transfer and renovation can only be successfully carried out in close co-operation with dry-stone walling professionals. Here the park's institution can contribute to the diffusion of knowledge among laypeople and support the creation of networks. This is important because the stone walls can no longer be maintained by the farmers alone, who nowadays make up only 4.6 per cent of the population of the Département Ardèche. Furthermore, many non-farming residents have dry-stone walls inside their properties. In France 44,000 farmers (roughly 8 per cent of all farmers) are already maintaining or erecting dry-stone walls (see Figures 10.1 and 10.2) (Lasica and Naudet, 2015: p. 18). This is a welcome sign that vernacular architecture continues to be lived.

Strategies for dealing with terraced landscapes

Networking and finance strategies

Terraced landscapes are situated in many parks in the Massif Central and south-east France. Since its establishment, the PNRMA has strived to create an interregional and transnational network of parks and actors from the dry-stone walling community to make use of synergies and initiate learning processes. This has led to the emergence of new co-managed projects, most of which are embedded in the European Liaison entre actions de développement de l'économie rurale (LEADER) programme.

At the interregional level, the PNRMA has formed an alliance with nine other parks in the Massif Central, the Parcs Naturel du Massif Central (IMPAC). One of the overall goals of IMPAC is the sustainable development of the Massif

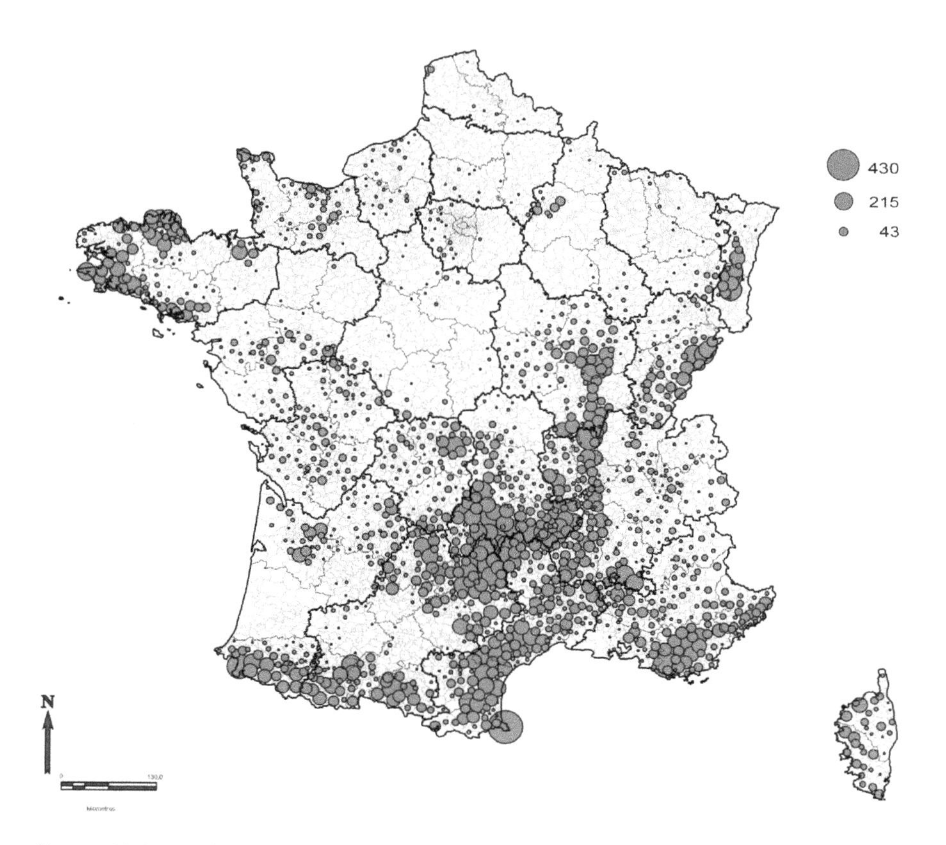

Figure 10.1 Number of farms that maintained terraces in 2010, by canton (smallest administrative district visible on map).

Source: Solagro 2013; reproduced courtesy of Solagro.

Central to create a 'terrain culturel'. This involves upgrading and developing the cultural heritage in the area – an important part of which is the terraces – in an experimental and innovative way based on co-operation and sharing of experiences. Collaboration with the Parc National des Cévennes is particularly relevant, as it is well-known as a pioneer in and major promoter of engagement with vernacular architecture. This interregional association of parks sharing common challenges (due to socio-geographical similarities) is the first of its kind in France.

Networks also play a major role within the park, e.g. between dry-stone wallers and municipalities aiming to analyse and renovate their terraces. The PNRMA often links interested parties, informing dry-stone wallers about requests from municipalities and providing rapid access to professional advice and dry-stone walling specialists.

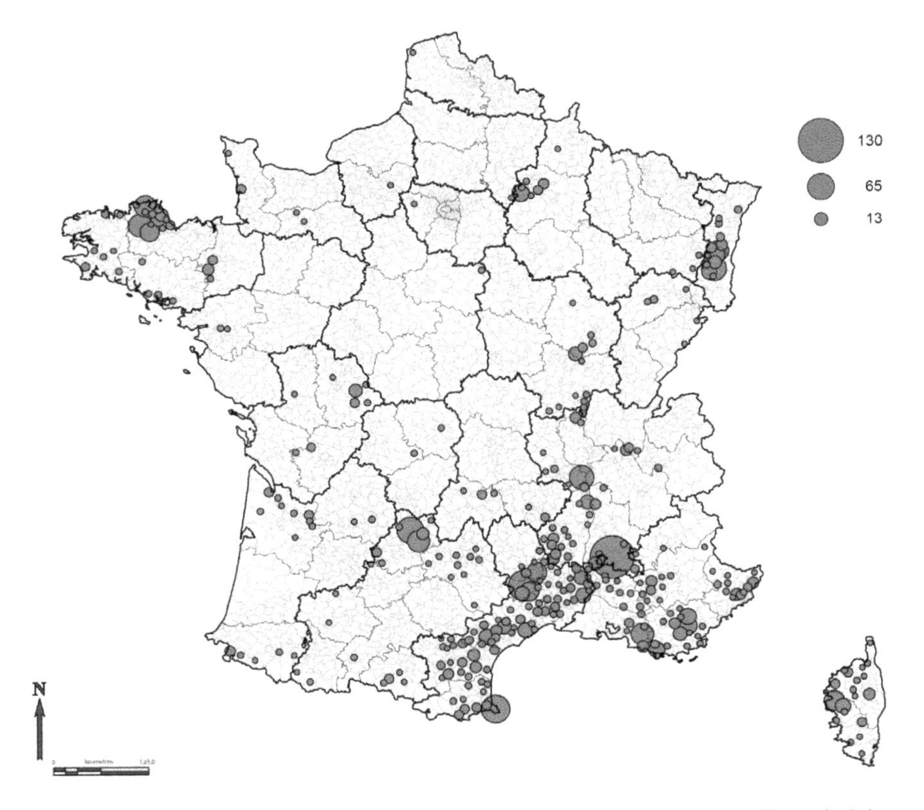

Figure 10.2 Number of farms that created terraces in 2010, by canton (smallest administrative district visible on map).

Source: Solagro 2013; reproduced courtesy of Solagro.

Funding issues are another important aspect in renovation and awareness projects. In addition to the regular support that French PNRs receive from the park municipalities, the department(s), the region(s) and the state, the PNRMA is involved in the Projet Stratégique Agricoles et de Développement Rural of the Région Rhone Alpes and in the European LEADER programmes. This brings extra funding for sustainable rural development, including initiatives to maintain terraced landscapes. In the course of the last three LEADER phases, the park received almost €5.5 million for more than 400 projects.

Furthermore, these programmes often generate valuable, sometimes transnational, partnerships and other networks. For example, the project 'Les paysages de terrasses: des millénaires d'innovation' led to partnerships with the regions of Alta Langa in Italy, Ipiros in Greece and Serra de Tramuntana in Majorca, enabling exchanges of experience, learning and networking that continued after the project itself was completed.

For the latest LEADER period (2014–2020), the PNRMA joined Le Pays de l'Ardèche méridionale and Le Syndicat Mixte Eyrieux Ouvèze Vernoux to form a new Local Action Group (LAG), 'GAL Ardèche3'. The aim is to create regional synergies beyond the perimeters of the park. A new joint programme entitled 'Nos ressources territoriales, un passeport d'avenir' will enable the support of further projects to promote the terraces.

Actors involved in knowledge transfer and professionalisation

In order to enable both the transfer of knowledge and practical renovation work, the PNRMA has set up a network with professionals from the dry-stone walling community. Encouraged by the high density of dry-stone walls and terraces in south-east France, this community has been active in the region for the last 20 years and has assumed a major role in the transfer of knowledge. An important partner from this network is Yvan Delahaye, a professional dry-stone waller, president of the Association des muraillers de Provence and leader of the training centre Elips, situated within the park. There are also links to the umbrella organisation Fédération Française des Professionnels de la Pierre Sèche, which brings together various more longstanding regional associations of professional dry-stone wallers, three research institutes and institutional partners such as the Chambre des Métiers et de l'Artisanat de Vaucluse (CMA84), which is important in the south-east of France, and the Parc National des Cévennes. A significant part of safeguarding knowledge transfer is to compile and write down experience-based knowledge, which is otherwise only transferred by word of mouth. Indeed, this goes hand-in-hand with the use and transmission of the know-how. Training courses, information events and raising awareness help to revive practices and make them known among a broader public. A further important step in safeguarding knowledge transfer was taken with the publication of a handbook for practitioners (CAPEB *et al.*, 2008).

The other main tasks are the renovation or rebuilding of dry-stone walls and the inventorying of terraces. New walls and walls that have been adequately renovated have a (renewed) lifespan of about 200 years. In the PNRMA, the multifunctional use assigned to the terraces is defined before renovation. Terraces can be used for agriculture, as gardens or park landscapes, as places for learning and pedagogic purposes, or as a cultural and historical trail, for cultural events, etc. In cases where nobody can be found to manage the terraces, they are planted as extensively as possible, usually with fruit trees.

The dry-stone wallers are also striving to establish a nationally recognised training programme and a viable market for dry-stone walling. In-depth analyses by the dry-stone walling community have shown that the French market for dry-stone walling has considerable potential for growth, as this form of building is increasingly recognised as forward-looking and sustainable (see Lasica and Naudet, 2015). In order to make the intangible heritage of the vernacular architecture more visible at the international level, the dry-stone walling community in the south-east of France has joined forces with the Société internationale pluridisciplinaire pour l'étude de la Pierre Sèche in a transnational application to the United Nations Educational, Scientific and Cultural Organization for the recognition of dry-stone walling as intangible cultural heritage (see Chambres de Métiers et de l'Artisanat, 2015: p. 3).

Initiatives to promote the terraced landscapes

Since its establishment, the park has continually initiated and supported the renovation of terraces, re-cultivation, academic research, awareness campaigns and terracing courses, among many other cultural events related to the terraces. These projects have often had a multi-functional focus, as seen in the case of the creation of the Désaignes educational trail, where social and cultural activities were included in activities to restore the terraces and replant grape vines. In the interests of raising awareness and transferring know-how, partners such as the Ecomusée des Terrasses in Saint-Michel de Chabrillanoux also receive support.

The PNRMA programme 'Coups de pousse: Rénovez vos terrasses et calades en pierre sèche' has been running for years, encouraging associations and municipalities to initiate projects to maintain stone walls. The PNRMA offers specialist advice and financial support for the projects, which are intended as concrete examples encouraging commitment and involvement in the revival of the terraces. This strategy has thus far been successful:

> Everyone can learn about these dry-stone walls. So that is what's important today. At this particular moment everyone wants to get involved. Everyone realises that this is our heritage, and everyone wants to learn how to restore them. So we hold training courses for people employed by the municipalities or the villages, for farmers, for people like me.
>
> (Perret, 2014)

However, the development of strategies for future utilisation is just as important as renovation. In terms of agriculture, regional and high-quality speciality crops are promising. These include vegetables (potatoes, onions) and herbs for culinary and medicinal purposes. However, wine production is viewed as the most lucrative use of the terraces, given this product's economic viability and progress in terms of quality labels (see DRAAF de la région Auvergne-Rhône-Alpes, 2011: p. 4). The awarding of labels such as A.O.P. (Appellation d'Origine Protégée), A.O.C. (Appellation d'Origine Contrôlée), I.G.P. (Indication Géographique Protégée) and Bio (organic farming) is an important strategy to support sales of products. In the Département Ardèche, 40 per cent of all agricultural products have quality labels and 12 per cent of all farms are run organically (DRAAF de la région Auvergne-Rhône-Alpes, 2011: p. 4).

In order to better differentiate produce that has been cultivated on terraces from other goods, it should be processed locally and the connection with the dry-stone walls should be made clearly visible. Discussions about creating a special label for 'terrace wine' are being held in other regions with wine terraces;

indeed, individual seals already exist, e.g. in Valais in Switzerland (see Höchtl and Bieling, 2013: p. 312). It is helpful in this context that the focus in the Département Ardèche is generally very much on non-interchangeable, regional, seasonal and sustainable goods (e.g. with the label 'D'Ardèche & de Saison') and that the principle of 'circuits courts' is promoted. The comparatively strong presence of organic agriculture and the solidarity economy (the Associations pour le Maintien de l'Agriculture Paysanne) support the labour-intensive and sustainable terracing.

Another development strategy concerns the socio-cultural field. The terraces can become meeting places and be used as venues for concerts, theatre plays and other art performances. The PNRMA encourages and supports these, as showed in the best practice example below.

'Le sentier des Lauzes' in the Vallée du Drobie

The association Sentier des Lauzes was created in the year 2000 by inhabitants of the Vallée du Drobie to discuss development opportunities and challenges for their sparsely populated valleys and to launch local development initiatives. The association gathered contributions from various artists working on development perspectives for the valley, which were exhibited along a track connecting the villages of Dompnac and Saint-Mélany. Artists were invited to live in the locality for several months and develop their works while interacting with the landscape and the local population. This initiative was closely linked to the PNRMA, who guided and financially supported various subprojects.

The subproject 'Regards croisés sur les paysages' was implemented within the framework of the LEADER+ programme together with the PNR du Vercors, PNR du Pilat and PNR de Lorraine and with the involvement of inhabitants, artists and scientists between 2005 and 2007. The basic idea was to explore how artistic performances coupled with question and answer sessions with local officials, representatives of voluntary organisations and academics can help to encourage people to think about land management. The project involved transdisciplinary workshops with residents, functionaries, artists and scientists, and resulted in works of art along the circular track, as well as verse, photo exhibitions, theatre performances and other cultural events.

Furthermore, numerous stone terraces were restored and put to use for wine and herbs. A particular group of terraces arranged in the form of an amphitheatre was given a new function and now serves as an open-air stage for cultural events. Using dry-stone walling techniques, a cabin was built as a retreat for artists-in-residence and scientists. Over the last 15 years, well-known artists from all over the world have joined the project (see sur le sentier des lauzes website).

This project also stimulated a discussion about the aesthetical value of the terraces. Several activities enabled people to appreciate and experience the immaterial values of the landscape, and to perceive the landscape in its aesthetic, sensory and emotional dimensions. Experiencing the landscapes in a contemplative way – in this case, through art projects – supported the inhabitants in reflecting on questions of the landscape's future development.

The project is a great success and a good illustration of the meaning and interaction of many aspects of cultural sustainability. It has contributed to the creation of economic value (tourism) and to social cohesion. Furthermore, it has enabled the renovation of individual terraces and helped inhabitants of the villages and hamlets to develop new development perspectives for the landscape, which in some areas is threatened by forest encroachment. Gilles Clément, an ecological landscape architect involved in the project described this landscape as 'a piece of the global garden, a foretaste of harmonised cohabitation between Nature and mankind' (2007: p. 3).

Conclusion

Terraced landscapes represent a universal agricultural heritage which embodies a particularly sustainable, long-lasting form of co-evolution of nature and culture. Contesting the dominant orientation of industrialised, growth-focused agriculture, terraced landscapes show important potential for sustainable landscape development and agriculture on hillsides and mountains. Terraced landscapes, together with their use and management not only contribute to the ecological dimension of sustainability but also to cultural sustainability.

Terraced landscapes are not just museum-like relicts of bygone times. They enable the application of valuable experience-based knowledge on sustainable ways of shaping the landscape. This is not just about theory, or about archiving and documenting the past in books and pictures, but about a tangible experience that ranges from building to the utilisation and management of land. Terracing, which holds the soil, offers an opportunity to experience agriculture in a direct and grounded way, which is a novelty or an innovation in the context of an agricultural world that is otherwise becoming increasingly less rooted in the soil and more prone to erosion. Precisely because terracing is labour intensive and can thus only find a market niche by cultivating high-quality regional produce, it illustrates alternative development paths – 'less is more', 'local and seasonal' and 'specific and unique' – instead of homogenised and interchangeable. Seen in this light, intact or reactivated terraced landscapes are real-life laboratories and living databases for sustainable production and know-how.

Terraces are particularly relevant for areas in which they still exist, such as the PNRMA. There is support in this regional park for regaining control over and actively using the terraced landscapes, also because terraces, along with chestnut woods, are characteristic elements of the identity of the Ardèche. The park officials and the dry-stone walling community use innovative and integral methods to revive the terraces. In doing so, they highlight the cultural character of the landscape, in some cases with the support of artists.

The example of the PNRMA also shows that preserving a large-scale terraced landscape is only possible when this is desired and supported by the local community, and when the terraces are actually used. Participation – an essential aspect of cultural sustainability – is implemented through social negotiation processes in which a diversity of stakeholders debate and jointly decide on the landscape components that are worth preserving. In addition to involving residents, it is also necessary to engage experts or professionals in the specialised network to promote knowledge sharing and transfer. Furthermore, the ideal scenario also includes an actor who functions as a hub and promotes or initiates projects, leads the creation of networks, facilitates access to funding and raises awareness. This is the role performed by parks such as the PNRMA. As shown in this chapter, French regional parks in general and the PNRMA in particular are central actors within a governance system that takes care of culture and also fosters culture as a basis for sustainable development.

Notes

1 This chapter presents results of the 'The cultural dimension of sustainable regional and landscape development' project, under COST Action IS 1007 'Investigating Cultural Sustainability' (2013–2015) and supported by the Swiss State Secretariat for Research and Innovation.
2 All references to Delahaye, 2014 are from an interview conducted with Delahaye, a stone-walling specialist and expert.
3 All references to Perret, 2014 are from an interview conducted with Perret, who heads the Cultural Heritage and Cultural Activities department of the Parc Naturel Régional des Monts d'Ardèche.

References

Ammann, C., Burri, M., Lutz, M., Meyer C.-A., Nanchen, E., Omlin, S., Payot, C., Meilland, A., Pont, S, Rey, S., Rey, C. and Schmid, A. (2012) *Murs de Pierres, Murs de Vignes*. Éditions du Musée valaisan de la vigne et du vin Infolio, Sierre-Salquenen and Gollion, Switzerland.

Backhaus, N., Reichler, C. and Stremlow, M. (2007) *Alpenlandschaften –Von der Vorstellung zur Handlung. Thematische Synthese zum Forschungsschwerpunkt I 'Prozesse der Wahrnehmung'*. vdf Hochschulverlag AG an der ETH, Zürich, Switzerland.

Bätzing, W. (2014) Leben in den Alpen – mit Zukunft. In: Stiftung Umwelt-Einsatz Schweiz. (ed.) *Trockenmauern: Grundlagen, Bauanleitung, Bedeutung*. Haupt, Bern, Switzerland: 379–383.

Blanc, J.-F. (2001) *Terrasses d'Ardèche. Paysages et Patrimoine*. (Publisher unknown).

CAPEB, ABPS, Muraillers de Provence, CBPS, CMA84 and ENTPE. (2008) *Guide de bonnes pratiques de construction de murs de soutènement en pierre sèche*. école nationale des traveaux publics de l'état, Lyon, France.

Chambres de Métiers et de l'Artisanat. (2015) *Pierre sèche, bilan et perspectives*. www.professionnels-pierre-seche.com/userfiles/files/Web%20Bilans%20%26%20perspectives%20-%20Copie.pdf (Accessed 8 December 2017).

Clément, G. (2007) *Le Belvédère des Lichens*. Parc naturel régional des Monts d'Ardèche. Montpezat sous Bauzon and Jean-Pierre Huguet éditeur, Saint Julien, France.

Council of Europe. (2000) *European Landscape Convention*. www.coe.int/en/web/conventions/full-list/-/conventions/rms/0900001680080621 (Accessed 15 January 2015).

Donadieu, P. and Périgord, M. (2005) *Clés pour le paysage*. Orphrys, Paris.

DRAAF (Direction Régionale de l'Alimentation, de l'Agriculture et de la Forêt de Rhône-Alpes). (2011) *Agreste Rhône – Alpes, coup d'oeil. Recensement agricole 2010.* http://draaf.auvergne-rhone-alpes.agriculture.gouv.fr/IMG/pdf/No_133_RA_2010__ARDECHE_cle8e1197-1.pdf (Accessed 8 December 2017).

Ewald, K. (2014) Landschaft im Wandel – das Gesicht der Schweiz. In: Stiftung Umwelt-Einsatz Schweiz. (ed.) *Trockenmauern: Grundlagen, Bauanleitung, Bedeutung*. Haupt, Bern, Switzerland: 394–400.

Giorgis, S. (2001) Les terrasses de cultures, lieu de l'innovation obligatoire. *Aménagement et Nature* 141: 89–96.

Höchtl, F. and Bieling, C. (2013) Instrumente zur Erhaltung historischer Terrassenweinberge. In: W. Konold and C. Petit (eds) *Historische Terrassenweiberge. Baugeschichte, Wahrnehmung, Erhaltung.* Bristol-Stiftung, Zürich and Haupt, Bern, Switzerland: 301–330.

Ipsen, D. (2006) *Ort und Landschaft*. VS Verlag für Sozialwissenschaften, Wiesbaden, Germany.

Krainer, L. (2010) Auf dem Weg zu einer Kultur nachhaltiger Entscheidungen. In: G. Banse, O. Parodi, A. Schaffer (eds) *Wechselspiele: Kultur und Nachhaltigkeit. Annäherungen an ein Spannungsfeld.* Edition Sigma, Berlin: 79–96.

Lasica, Y. and Naudet, F. (2015) *Etude du Marche National de la Pierre Sèche, Synthèse.* La Fédération Française des Professionnels de la Pierre Sèche, Avignon, France.

No authors listed. (date unknown) *Sur le Sentier des Lauzes*. www.surlesentierdeslauzes.fr (Accessed 30 November 2017).

PNRMA. (2001) *Charte Constitutive du Parc naturel régional des Monts d'Ardèche 2001–2013.* www.parc-monts-ardeche.fr/images/phocadownload/charte_pnrma_2000_2010-3.pdf (Accessed 08 December 2017).

PNRMA. (2014) *Rapport de charte du Parc naturel régional des Monts d'Ardèche 2013–2025.* http://fr.calameo.com/read/00038517522ed3e491091 (Accessed 8 December 2017).

Rudofsky, B. (1989) *Architektur ohne Architekten. Eine Einführung in die anonyme Architektur*. Residenz-Verlag, Salzburg, Austria.

Schegk, I. (2014) Wissen. In: Stiftung Umwelt-Einsatz Schweiz. (ed.) *Trockenmauern: Grundlagen, Bauanleitung, Bedeutung*. Haupt, Bern, Switzerland: 45–159.

Witschi, F. (2014) Flora, Fauna – Lebensraum Trockenmauer. In: Stiftung Umwelt-Einsatz Schweiz. (ed.) *Trockenmauern: Grundlagen, Bauanleitung, Bedeutung*. Haupt, Bern, Switzerland: 329–378.

11 Tourism and sustainable development in rural communities on the Black Sea coastline

Miroslav Taşcu-Stavre

Introduction

This chapter seeks to exemplify how the rural areas of the Black Sea coastline manage to maintain their characteristics while also developing themselves by means of an environment-friendly tourism business, all in spite of the mounting pressure caused by the expansion of mass tourism during the first decade/half of the 1990s. Traditionally, sustainable development is analysed from three perspectives: socially, economically and environmentally. The approach used for this analysis, while not in contradiction to the traditional canon, focuses rather on cultural sustainability and the idea that the key to understanding development patterns can be found within specific institutional contexts as well as in the manner in which local communities handle 'outside' challenges (Ostrom, 1986, 1990). In order to understand the institutional context, which ultimately dictates the path of development, we have studied the way in which the analysed communities have related to the presence of tourists throughout time. These tourist–host relationships are researched by means of semi-structured interviews and by resorting to a micro-history of the area, established with the help of information provided by previous analytic endeavours such as those performed by Miruna Tîrcă (2004), Vintilă Mihăilescu (2005), Simina Guga (2006), Liviu Vasile (2011) and Taşcu-Stavre (2011, 2013, 2015, 2016; Taşcu-Stavre and Bănică, 2014).

The selection process for the two rural communities of the Black Sea coast was not random. Although 2 Mai and Vama Veche are located less than 3 km from each other, they experience very different development paths, to the point of being in contrast with each other. This fact seems all the more peculiar considering that both are subordinate to the same administrative body, namely the Limanu Local Council (Taşcu-Stavre, 2011). Thus, the question that arises is how have these neighbouring communities developed so divergently and what role has tourism played in their development?

Before proceeding with the analysis itself we must first detail some aspects of the notions of sustainable development and sustainable tourism. The Brundtland Commission suggested a proper definition of sustainable development almost 30 years ago, referring to it as a 'development that meets the needs of the present without compromising the ability of future generations to meet their own needs'

(WCED, 1987: p. 39). Unfortunately, sustainable development has always been a flexible concept interpreted in many different ways. As such, no less than 70 definitions of the term 'sustainable development' have been identified (Kirkby *et al.*, 1995 cited in Kambites, 2014: p. 337). We cannot hope to resolve the conceptual issues regarding sustainable development within this endeavour, but we will instead try to illustrate some more profound aspects of the host-tourist relationships and how practices such as hostel-based tourism are good foundations for sustainability. In this regard, we will be mostly focusing on the characteristics of sustainable tourism:

> Sustainable tourism is tourism and associated infrastructures that [...] operate within natural capacities for the regeneration and future productivity of natural resources; recognize the contribution that people and communities, customs and lifestyles, make to the tourism experience; accept that these people must have an equitable share in the economic benefits ...
>
> (Eber cited in Butler, 1999: p. 10)

Tourism is seen, in many parts of the world, as a fundamental component on which development strategies are based upon because it generates jobs, attracts investments and generates benefits for local or national authorities (Smith, 1995; Tisdell, 2000). Whether this will be the case is an empirical question. However, an important challenge that is usually associated with developing tourism consists of understanding exactly how tourism expansion will impact local communities. A large enough flux of tourists during a holiday season may affect local cultures and impact local economies and the environment, thus altering the lifestyles and expectations of local communities. Usually, one could argue that tourism-related research is more concerned with the tourists' experience and the overall tourism industry than with their effect on the local community or hosts (Burns, 2004: p. 7).

However, research into the effects of tourism upon local communities does have a considerable history in its own right. The works of authors such as Greenwood (1972), Smith (1989), Urry ([1990]2002) and Lanfant *et al.* (1995) in the fields of anthropology and sociology paved the way for analysing the manner in which relationships between tourists and host communities develop. While Greenwood's (1972) pioneering study focuses on the socio-economic effects of tourism in Spain's Basque country, particularly from the agricultural standpoint, Smith's (1989) volume, as well as that of Lanfant *et al.* (1995), deal with how the identity of a host community is changed by the interaction with tourists from around the world. The presence of tourists in a certain community is undoubtedly an agent of change. A main concern for researchers is whether the aforementioned presence of tourists favours sustainable development. In turn, the three pillars of development (economic, social and ecological) are dependent on the bonds between tourists and the local community. Where there is a longstanding history of interaction and a culture of co-operation and coexistence, the chance that the tourists' effect on the host community is beneficial increases.

Culture has a role in harmonising various viewpoints: 'This role moves culture into a framing, contextualising and mediating mode that can balance all three of the pillars and guide sustainable development between economic, social, and ecological pressures and needs' (Dessein *et al.*, 2015: p. 28). For the purpose of this analysis, culture could be considered as '[a] driver of sustainability processes' (Soini and Birkeland, 2014). Neither individual nor collective experiences take place in a vacuum; they are moulded by the location in which they take place and by our views and beliefs regarding said location, 'What gives a place its specificity is not some long internalized history but the fact that it is constructed out of a particular constellation of relations, articulated together at a particular locus' (Massey, 1993 cited in Horlings, 2015: p. 259). Indeed, the views of the tourists frequenting the 2 Mai and Vama Veche area played a highly significant role in the shaping and evolution of the area. The fact that this area was viewed as different to most other places on the Black Sea coastline led to it being organised differently, through the consolidation a rural-based form of tourism that can trace its roots to the harmonious interaction between tourists, hosts and the environment. We uphold Birkeland's (2015: p. 165) view that 'culture appears and is understandable through narrative organisation, and cultural sustainability can emerge as a social process created through narratives that connect the past with the future, and the local with the global' and add that whenever the narrative of the hosts meets those of the tourists, as a form of positive confirmation of expectations, the chance of a harmonious development increases.

This chapter focuses on the long-term experience of the host communities in the two selected coastal settlements, based upon the premise that sustainable development implies the simultaneous fulfilment of both the host community's aspirations and the tourist's needs. In this way, the relationship between hosts and guests clearly expresses the nature–culture interface as a meeting-place of different aspirations and interests through the need to protect the natural environment of the coastal area, ultimately responsible for drawing in the constant flux of tourists to the area.

Tourism in 2 Mai and Vama Veche up to 1989

There are few statistical figures for tourism on the Black Sea coast (let alone the 2 Mai/Vama Veche area specifically). However, up to the beginning of the First World War, some of the Black Sea settlements, such as Eforie, Techirghiol or Mangalia, were indeed part of a national system of balneary (spa) resorts (Bubulete, 2010: p. 79). After the First World War, such resorts on the Black Sea coast saw an increase in popularity, a fact that was concurrent with the consolidation of Romanian administration over Dobrudja, an area that had become a part of Romanian territory in 1878 and which had been disputed during the war. The fact that local administrations made plans for the systematisation of existing resorts lead us to believe both that there was a constant tourist presence in the area during holiday seasons and that there was an interest in increasing the number of said tourists (Mănescu, 2010: pp. 68–73).

A key event that led to a shift of the tourist flow towards 2 Mai and Vama Veche was the Ceding of the Cadrilater in 1940. The Cadrilater (Quadrilateral) is an area in southern Dobrudja, north of the Turtucaia-Balcic line. Romania obtained this territory following its participation in the Second Balkan War and administered it between 1913 and 1940, when the signing of the Treaty of Craiova led to its return to Bulgarian rule. This moment is defining because it led to a change in holiday destinations for artists and socialites, who up to that point were almost exclusively travelling to Balcic (Tîrcă, 2004: pp. 16–17). After becoming the site of one of the royal family's residences, Balcic served almost as a pilgrimage site for most of the interwar-era painters (Retegan, 2010: pp. 83–90). The events of 1940, coinciding with an increase in demand for tourist housing, led to the understandable dispersal of tourists towards older resorts (Mangalia, Carmen Sylva, Techirghiol) and to newly-established ones (2 Mai, Vama Veche or Schitu). It is also worth noting that the core of the tourist wave heading for 2 Mai and Vama Veche was rather avant-garde, composed of artists, writers, teachers and architects, among others (Taşcu-Stavre, 2016: p. 112; Tîrcă, 2004). This trend was maintained and even expanded over time, to the point that the social composition of tourists in the 1980s mirrored that of the inter-war period (despite the change in regime). The appeal of rural, guest-house based tourism grew because it fulfilled the expectations of this group of bohemian tourists. This guest-host interaction led to the creation of a mutually beneficial formula, with a pleasant and unassuming experience for the tourist and with benefits (material or otherwise) for the hosts.

The tourist–host relationship in 2 Mai

According to Miruna Tîrcă's (2004: p. 23) research, tourists tended to rent rooms in 2 Mai along the main road, especially on the side of the seashore. The host's offer included housing in one or more of the available rooms of their house and, if requested, up to three meals a day. In time, the relationship between the host and the tourist became tighter, to the point of them considering it to be a symbolic kinship, as is revealed by a series of interviews conducted by Tîrcă (2004: p. 32). The tourists would end up returning to their hosts each year, being welcomed upon their arrival as kindred and causing sadness upon their departure: 'We could barely wait for summer to come, for us to meet up as if we were family (…) we had gotten used to them as if they were family, we would cry for them when they left' (Victoriţa Popescu in Tîrcă, 2004: p. 32). This type of relationship was favoured by the fact that the tourists and hosts shared the same living space, which, as opposed to the impersonal nature of hotel housing, encouraged more profound contacts between people. Niculina Tuţan, one such host, relates: 'we turned from tourists into friends. […], we spend time together, they organize all manner of stuff, I allow them to do as they please, they are united (…)' (Niculina Tuţan in Tîrcă, 2004: p. 33). Such relationships gained a new aspect during the post-war period. In addition to closeness and openness they also began exhibiting reciprocity, as tourists would in turn invite their hosts to visit them. This trend gained momentum during the communist era, as can be seen during further interviews by Miruna Tîrcă: 'I know I was about ten years old in '61 when a family took me to Bucharest, there was this movie director, Hoffmann, who took me in for a few days at their place' (Maura Mihailova in Tîrcă, 2004: p. 33).

As such, this kind of relationship is part of what anthropologists call the logic of the gift (Mauss, 1997). We observe traditional business exchanges based on the 'to give – to receive' dynamic, rather than on the modern method of the contract. This is further substantiated by another local who states that

> I was invited to Bucharest numerous times, there are many whom I did visit, and when I would see their living conditions I would come home and tell my kids: 'we need to do anything to keep him (the tourist) from leaving dissatisfied, to make him feel at least like he were in a hotel, if not at home'
>
> (Maria Gheorghe in Tîrcă, 2004: p. 33)

A partial conclusion that can be reached based on these interviews supports a conclusion that tourism 'strengthens the cultural identity of the host destination and increases community identity and increases understanding of other cultures' (Ap and Crompton, 1998; Easterling, 2004). For all areas, the constant passing of strangers takes a toll on local communities. With regards to 2 Mai, the familial relationship created between the hosts and the guests makes both parties try to resemble the other. So, the tourist tries to be accepted by the local communities and in the meantime the guests try to rise to the cultural and social expectations of the tourist.

The fact that hostels were such popular tourist destinations during the interwar era is not random, but rather caused by a lack of alternatives. This situation started to change in the 1950s, when the transition between regimes in Romania led to the beginning of the nationalisation process, which also engulfed these aforementioned destinations. This only intensified during the decade and on into the 1960s, when a programme designed to build seaside resorts commenced, leading to both a radical change in already existing settlements, such as Mamaia, Eforie or Mangalia, as well as to the appearance of new tourist destinations, like the Olimp, Neptun, Jupiter, Cap Aurora or Venus resorts, among others. What had once been a coast littered with settlements of varying characteristics, from fishermen villages to spas, was largely transformed by the 'Romanian Littoral Systematization Plan' developed by the Central Institute for Urban and Regional Systematization in 1953. That year marks the beginning of the process that would prepare the coastal area for mass tourism (Alexandru, 2010: pp. 62–65). However, some regions were spared from the plan, particularly those located at the extremities of the coast, such as the area south of Mangalia, where 2 Mai and Vama Veche are located, and north of Năvodari, towards the Danube Delta and the present-day border with Ukraine. There are some advantages related to spending holidays in rural areas such as 2 Mai. These tourist–host relations are the basis for a type of humane tourism, which managed to survive past 1989 (Taşcu-Stavre, 2016: pp. 113–115).

First, even in the 1960s, there were few alternatives to the traditional guest-house, in spite of the aforementioned systematisation plan. The fact is that this plan would have required up to 15 years in order to be fully implemented, an optimistic prospect considering that it would not be completed until well into the 1980s (Alexandru, 2010). Such endeavours to transform the coastline in order to make way for mass tourism were common in all communist countries with sea access (Ghodsee, 2005; Grandits and Taylor, 2010). This delay, coupled with an increase in demand for littoral housing, served to maintain the tourist flow to rural areas, and is evidenced by statements taken during interviews conducted by Liviu Vasile (2011). One such statement comes from Paul Drogeanu:

> I was born in '48. I haven't been in 2 Mai as a child, I went there after finishing high school, during the first year of college (…) Staying in guest-homes in villages was a sort of answer to the total lack of infrastructure for real tourism, and for small budgets. Even if the new resorts were built during the 60s and even when there was post-nationalized Mamaia, a lot of people still went to old Costineşti, the village, and then to Schitu and they kept going down towards the south.
>
> (Paul Drogeanu in Vasile, 2011: p. 10)

Second, rural tourism allowed for the continuation of older habits, such as that of travelling to the seaside in large groups of friends and organising parties. Thus, the guest-house and its backyard would serve as a premise for social interaction and for spending time in a pleasant manner. This fact is exemplified by several statements made by locals, such as: 'In general, for people of the 70s, but also for those that came before and after, 2 Mai parties were encores of what took place in Bucharest on Saturdays…' (Paul Drogeanu in Vasile, 2011: p. 113) and 'there wasn't a day that went by without there being a party in one or more backyards. So I would host it today, you would host it tomorrow; there was this constant movement between backyards and sometimes on the beach' (Vintilă Mihăilescu in Vasile, 2011: p. 115). We can thus observe how the guest-house is slowly replacing the inter-war era hostel. One more reason for this transition is that guest-houses were a more attractive offer for families with kids, as they would have a more ample playground compared with hotels: 'There you would meet up with families you knew, many young couples with small children' (Trişcu in Vasile, 2011: p. 13).

Third, guest-homes offered a way out of the mundane and the routine of a society fractured by financial issues and the loss of individual freedoms. This is also evidenced by tourist accounts:

> The groups were small, 4–5 families at most, because you wouldn't have the courage to talk with others. Each group with their home, it was intimate.

> We would never stay in the same home with anyone new, (there would be) only us. This was our understanding with our host.
>
> (Ileana Lucaciu in Tîrcă, 2004: p. 73)

In spite of this, the backyard became a place of free discussion on various subjects, ranging from music to society, in a time in which such interactions were rather discouraged:

> Naturally, the evenings were reserved for this kind of non-conspiratorial gatherings; it was simply the pleasure of spending time together not only focusing on a bottle of alcohol but also on ideas, and there was a very rich pool of ideas (…) of course that these (conversations) also touched upon politics, critical attitudes, political jokes, and basically any form of resistance that was being practiced, all without any anxiety.
>
> (Eugen Ciocan in Tîrcă, 2004: p. 74)

Vintilă Mihăilescu, on the other hand, claims that:

> (What was happening here) was known but it was (allowed as) part of the general policy after 1967–1968, namely the idea of allowing 'valves' to exist. This has always been a part of the strategy used by Communist Parties everywhere. Everything was indeed being monitored, but not everything was forbidden.
>
> (Vintilă Mihăilescu in Vasile, 2011: pp. 221–222)

Last but not least, rural tourism (and the two settlements discussed in particular) allowed for various subcultures based on the concept of outdoor holidays, such as campers, nudists and others who craved a reconnection with nature, to flourish during the 1970s, mostly as a reaction against mass tourism. Maria Gheorghe remembers asking a tourist, 'Why do you stay in a tent and not in a house?', they replied 'That's how we like it, waking up to the sunrise, being near the water, without depending on anyone' (Tîrcă, 2004: pp. 52–53). Thus, the opportunity of staying in a tent on the beach or very close to it brought a new type of tourist to the rural seaside. As Camelia Pârjol describes:

> You wake up when the light enters your tent (…) I would come out dragging a chaise-longue after which I would prepare my coffee, it was an entire ritual, and you had this feeling of freedom that emptied your mind. I can't imagine any other place where I could go to with my tent and still sit on the beach. Not even in a camping spot, since my schedule would be dictated by others. This is the only place in which I can relax completely and feel good. (…) Nobody can convince me that going to the seaside means staying in a hotel.
>
> (Tîrcă, 2004: p. 76)

The tourist–host relationship in Vama Veche

Things were quite different in Vama Veche. Even if the inter-war era brought about the same number of tourists as in 2 Mai, the similarities stop after the Second World War. With a few exceptions, tourism in Vama Veche has completely different and distinct characteristics compared with the 2 Mai. Tourist–host relationships are much more sporadic as tourists generally follow a self-organising method, such as Tabăra Clujenilor or resort to renting rooms in 2 Mai and then commuting to Vama Veche (Taşcu-Stavre, 2016: pp. 116–118). This trend was fuelled by communist-era restrictions, which reduced the benefits obtained from tourism by the community in Vama Veche, especially when compared with 2 Mai. These restrictions were applied to control access to the village and to regulate temporary residence, under the motivation that Vama Veche was a border settlement. One such law stated that non-residents arriving in Vama Veche had to announce the authorities as to what the purpose of their visit was, as well as where they could be found during their stay. Although this law did not limit the locals' right to receive guests, it did prevent the creation of strong bonds between the host and the tourist, such as those in 2 Mai (Taşcu-Stavre, 2013: p. 1215). The situation was made worse by an administrative decision that called for the dissolution of the village, which obviously impacted any medium- and long-term investment plans for the area, whether for infrastructure or for the residents' homes (Taşcu-Stavre, 2015: p. 181).

In essence, the pre-1989 era marked not only a difference in how the locals handled tourism but also in how cohesive the two communities were. In 2 Mai, relations within the community were constantly good, while Vama Veche's community was plagued by the departure of a significant part of its residents and the arrival of foreigners looking to settle down in the village, which ultimately led to a decrease in social capital. Most of the area's depopulation took place in the second half of the 1980s, after news of the village's dissolution became public. While agriculture is still the main source of income in both settlements, 2 Mai has a considerable financial advantage brought on by tourism, which acts as an additional source of revenue (Taşcu-Stavre, 2011: p. 148).

2 Mai and Vama Veche after 1989

The summer of 1990 opened a series of opportunities for Vama Veche to start increasing its share of tourists. However, due to a lack in legislative framework (a characteristic of the transition era) most of the tourists that discovered Vama Veche completely bypassed the hostels and guest-houses, opting instead for a sort of self-catered accomodation in the form of beach housing via tents (Taşcu-Stavre, 2016: p. 136). Miruna Tîrcă's research reveals that 2 Mai's community was also impacted during this time. She makes the following observations regarding the shift in tourist flows in the two settlements:

> The initial years after the Revolution were marked by the considerable popularity of this place (2 Mai) [...]. However, they were followed by an

> exodus of the masses towards Vama Veche in the second half of the 90s, which led to an unprecedented development of the area. In 2 Mai things were refocused, probably due to the aforementioned exodus…
>
> (Tîrcă, 2004: p. 89)

A fundamental part of Vama Veche's success before the turn of the millennium was its beach, which became a sort of no man's land due to the fact that it was completely unrestricted, allowing not only access but also the possibility of setting up tents (Taşcu-Stavre, 2015: p. 182). The lack of restrictions was doubled by the lack of any attempts to organise or tax this type of activity. This led to Vama Veche's transformation into a very low-cost option for anyone travelling to the seaside, since there were basically no housing fees. Of course, the conditions were sorely deficient, having no toilets, no running water, no food vendors and no shade. This did serve as a discouraging factor among some tourists in the early 1990s, leaving those who braved these conditions to become a homogenous group. The situation is well illustrated in a series of interviews done by Simina Guga in Vama Veche (2006):

> When I was little I thought it was a bad idea to stay there because there was no place to buy food from; Vama wasn't even a village but rather a hamlet, with a few scattered houses and some tents. Some people were strumming a guitar and there was no pub. I did like the sand, though, as it was very fine and I also enjoyed the waves, which were always larger than those in 2 Mai.
>
> (30-year-old tourist, in Guga, 2006: p. 87)

As such, if we were to summarise the characteristics of tourism in the two villages we would come to the conclusion that 2 Mai had 'backyard tourism' while Vama Veche had 'beach tourism' (Mihăilescu, 2005: p. 73).

Due to the large influx of tourists, both settlements were faced with the issue of limited housing and the need to develop an adequate tourism infrastructure. Once again, the approaches used by each of the local authorities differed. In 2 Mai development took an incremental route, based on a continuous adjustment of the supply and demand ratio, by first using up all available space within the village limits and then performing a moderate expansion of territory. In Vama Veche's case, however, development was mostly chaotic, based on the immediate expansion of village limits and intensive construction projects, thus being overly intensive and extensive regardless of the actual demand (Taşcu-Stavre, 2013: p. 1253). The repeated expansions led to a significant increase in territory, basically enlarging the settlement to several times its original size.

Because tourism in Vama Veche during the 1990s was largely based around self-made accommodations on the beach, it was inconsequential to the welfare of the locals. Many locals from Vama Veche decided to sell their newly-acquired real estate (obtained after the redistribution of communist-era nationalised land), paving the way for non-locals to enter the market (Taşcu-Stavre, 2016: pp. 146–148). The lack of any coherent development plan, added to obsolete regulations, caused the appearance of a tourism infrastructure that discarded local customs and deformed the image of the settlement. Local authorities did nothing but encourage this type of development, usually by continually expanding the village limits and by approving an excess of building authorisations, ultimately leading to a sort of proto-urbanisation (Taşcu-Stavre, 2016: p. 169). The dissatisfaction of those still residing in Vama Veche is evident in the statements they make:

> The village was abandoned. Everybody goes to the seashore and stays there with a pocketful of money. They only come here once the beach and surrounding areas become overcrowded and we have to lower the prices, otherwise we might end up with an empty house.
>
> (55-year-old local, in Guga, 2006: p. 116)

This statement summarises the situation of locals who could not face the rising competition. Excluding locals with lower income from the tourism development process is a common practice also seen in other tourist areas in Romania (Iorio and Corsale cited in Neumeier and Pollermann, 2014: p. 275). Thus, instead of helping solve local development issues, we can observe that the exclusion of those with less financial power may actually cause new issues.

Then, in 2003, something miraculous happened. An attempt to evacuate the beach of all makeshift accommodations and ban camping was met with an overwhelming amount of opposition from the tourists, an event that would kick-start a series of changes for Vama Veche. The protest culminated with a concert (*Stufstock*) attended by about 20,000 people, who would create the core of the movement known as 'Save Vama Veche'. Through the following period, this movement became the unofficial voice of Vama Veche's tourists, thus becoming an important player in the local community (Taşcu-Stavre, 2011: p. 195). Perhaps the most notable achievement of this group was its dedication towards the sustainable development of the area. As early as September 2003, the 'Save Vama Veche' movement notified the Prime Minister's Control Corps about the violation of urbanism regulations, obtaining permission to draw up a new urban plan. At the same time, the movement gained legal status through the founding of the Bio-Cultural Areas Conservation Association, whose goal is preventing the destruction of the southern Romanian littoral by taking action in three areas: sustainable development of the village, environmental protection and cultural expression (particularly by organising a yearly alternative music festival). The urban plan was finalised during the autumn of 2005 and is one of the most complex plans aimed at the rural area because it contains not only a set of urbanism regulations but also a sociological study, a local development strategy and a morphological and typological analysis of the village (Taşcu-Stavre, 2015: p. 190). Unfortunately, the 2005 plan was only briefly followed, allowing for the further deterioration of the village's overall appearance, especially around the outskirts. In spite of this, some success was still achieved by creating partnerships aimed at protecting the surrounding natural area and by preventing Vama

Veche from becoming a mass tourism resort (Taşcu-Stavre, 2011: p. 201). This success is owed in equal parts to the mobilisation of both tourists, as well as locals.

It is our belief that rural tourism was less challenged in 2 Mai because of the community's previously discussed social cohesion. However, Vama Veche's community remains largely scattered in smaller groups. The erosion of social norms among the village's residents means that the situation is no better than that of the 1980s, as can be seen in the following interviews: 'We don't often visit other people from the village. Everyone minds their own business, tends to their own house, and to their own tourists' (55-year-old local, in Guga, 2006: p. 97). Most of the animosity is caused by the presence of foreign entrepreneurs who created businesses for themselves and thus take a share of the benefits brought on by tourism. They are viewed as strangers who came and purchased their way into the village and its way of life: 'People over here are very mean. I have never seen as much malice as there is in this village. Maybe if they were united they might have had more accomplishments and there wouldn't be as many Bucharesters around' (30-year-old local, in Guga, 2006: p. 97).

Conclusions

The first observation is that history matters; establishing steadfast relationships between tourists and their hosts, as well as building trust and reciprocity within a community is a long-term process. The strengthening of the local social capital in 2 Mai after the revolution served to block foreign entrepreneurs from entering the market and keep the benefits of tourism within the community. Vama Veche's turbulent development, on the other hand, greatly diminished the impact of tourism upon the welfare of the locals. Second, not any form of rural tourism is sustainable by default. Vama Veche's post-2000 development stands as an example towards the contrary. The lack of firm legal regulations and the laissez-faire attitude of the authorities led to the alteration of the environment. The locals are not able to compete with foreign capital, brought by non-locals and international hotel chains, thus losing from the start in the competition for tourists.

Perhaps the most interesting conclusion is that tourists, through their ability to govern themselves, can actually serve as a force for promoting and protecting sustainable development. Their newly-found influence upon local development strategies is a drastic change as their voice was not heard up to that point. This is all the more important since a coherent development plan must consider all those it will affect. The village 2 Mai stands as an example of how a unified community can implement an incremental strategy aimed at infrastructure development solely through local capital. This combination allowed them to successfully traverse the transition period. The benefits brought on by tourism have almost entirely been directed towards the locals because they had the know-how required to adapt their offer to the expectations of tourists, a skill they acquired through long-term direct contact with them.

A common element that made 2 Mai's sustainable development possible and may lay the groundwork for a similar development in Vama Veche, is the fact that both settlements hold a special significance. They were perceived from very early on as alternatives to the mainstream or as refuges (particularly during the communist regime) and have since drawn in tourists with their stories of freedom, the beauty of the surroundings and the unique atmosphere. This narrative, referred to as 'tourist gaze' by Urry ([1990]2002), is further enhanced by the fact that tourists who choose these two settlements as their holiday destinations consider themselves to be part of the local communities (the 'doimaist' of 2 Mai and the 'vamaiot' of Vama Veche). As such, the efforts made to save the area and its communities came naturally to tourists, since they view the two settlements as also belonging to them. The vamaiots are tourists who discovered Vama Veche during the 1990s and, noting its state of degradation, considered it their duty to act. Their effort did not go unrewarded, as they, together with the local community, managed to prevent a chaotic and unspecific development of the area. The examples of 2 Mai and Vama Veche present two different approaches to the issue of cultural sustainability: while the first one preserves the environment by adopting the tourist into a family, inspiring a sense of membership, the second one is mostly an escape from norms into the freedom of a 'sloppy' landscape. In both situations, the guests need the preservation of the environment, and are ready to intervene if needed. Their main concern is to not over-industrialise the area by developing forms of traditional tourism.

We can thus state that the development if the two communities is rooted in the pre-1989 stories of 2 Mai and the experience of the vamaiots after the fall of the communist regime, respectively. Cultural factors also played a role in mapping out their development, under the form of the narratives that help maintain an idyllic view of the two settlements. Lastly, the harmony between the views and beliefs of the locals and the tourists meant that together they managed to successfully oppose outside initiatives that pushed for change. As such, neither the state (during the communist regime) nor the free market (after 1990) could impose any radical changes in the local development trajectories of 2 Mai and Vama Veche. But there remains one big question: how long will the communities, both inclusive and exclusive, be able to resist hotel chains and modernisation of the area for the sake of natural beauty?

References

Alexandru, M. (2010) Litoralul ca experiment de urbanism postbelic. *Urbanism* 5–6: 62–65.

Ap, J. and Crompton, J. (1998) Developing and testing a tourism impact scale. *Journal of Travel Research* 37(2):120–130.

Birkeland, I. (2015) The potential space for cultural sustainability: place narratives and place-heritage in Rjukan. In: E. Auclair and G. Fairclough (eds) *Theory and Practice in Heritage and Sustainability: Between Past and Future.* Routledge, London: 161–175.

Bubulete, D. (2010) Vocaţie turistică, şansă şi ratare. *Urbanism* 5–6:78–82.
Burns, G. L. (2004) Anthropology and tourism. past-contribution and future theoretical challenges. *Anthropological Forum* 14(1):5–22.
Butler, R. W. (1999) Sustainable tourism: a state-of-the-art review. *Tourism Geographies* 1(1):7–25.
Dessein, J., Soini, K., Fairclough, G. and Horlings, L. (eds) (2015) *Culture in, for and as Sustainable Development. Conclusions from the COST Action IS1007 Investigating Cultural Sustainability*. University of Jyväskylä, Jyväskylä, Finland.
Easterling, D. S. (2004) The resident's perspective in tourism research a review and synthesis. *Journal of Travel and Tourism Marketing* 17:45–62.
Ghodsee, K. (2005) *The Red Riviera: Gender, Tourism, and Postsocialism on the Black Sea*. Duke University Press, Durham, United States.
Grandits, H. and Taylor, K. (2010) *Yugoslavia's Sunny Side: A History of Tourism in Socialism (1950s-1980s)*. Central European University Press, Budapest and New York.
Greenwood, D. (1972) Tourism as an agent of change: a Spanish Basque case. *Ethnology* 11(1):80–91.
Guga, S. (2006) *Impactul turismului asupra populaţiei gazda. Studiu la nivelul comunităţii locale din satul Vama Veche*. Unpublished BA thesis, Department of Sociology, University of Bucharest, Romania.
Horlings, L. G. (2015) Values in place; A value-oriented approachtoward sustainable place-shaping. *Regional Studies, Regional Science* 2(1):257–274.
Kambites, C. J. (2014) Sustainable development: the 'unsustainable' development of a concept in political discourse. *Sustainable Development* 22(5):336–348.
Lanfant, M-F., Alcock, J. and Bruner, E. (eds) (1995) *International Tourism: Identity and Change*. Sage Publications, London.
Mănescu, M. (2010) O lege neştiută a litoralului. *Urbanism* 5–6:68–73.
Mauss, M. (1997) *Eseu despre dar*. Polirom, Iasi, Romania.
Mihăilescu, V. (2005) Limanu. Spaţii sociale şi dezvoltare locală. *Societatea Reală* 3.
Neumeier, S. and Pollermann, K. (2014) Rural tourism as promoter of rural development – prospect and limitations: case study findings from a pilot project promoting village tourism. *European Countryside* 6(4):270–296.
Ostrom, E. (1986) An agenda for the study of institution. *Public Choice* 48:3–25.
Ostrom, E. (1990). *Governing the Commons: The Evolution of Institutions for Collective Action*. Cambridge: Cambridge University Press.
Retegan, E. (2010) Balcic, un moment de graţie irepetabil. *Urbanism* 5–6:83–90.
Smith, V. (1989) *Hosts and Guests: The Anthropology of Tourism*. University of Pennsylvania Press, Pennsylvania, United States.
Soini, K. and Birkeland, I. (2014). Exploring the scientific discourse of cultural sustainability. *Geoforum* 51:213–223.
Taşcu-Stavre, M. (2011) *Abordări instituţionale ale tranziţiei din România O analiză a schimbării instituţionale din Vama Veche şi 2 Mai*. Unpublished PhD thesis, Department of Political Science, National School of Political Studies and Public Administration, Bucharest, Romania.
Taşcu-Stavre, M. (2013) Tourism and local development in Vama Veche and 2 Mai. *CSK 2013 – Challenges of the Knowledge Society Conference, 17–18 May 2013, Bucharest* 1249–1258.
Taşcu-Stavre, M. (2015) Tranziţie şi dezvoltare locală în Vama Veche şi 2 Mai. In: A. Miroiu and I. P. Golopenţa (eds) *Acţiune colectivă şi bunuri comune în societatea românească*. Polirom, Bucharest, Romania:173–194.

Taşcu-Stavre, M. (2016) *Abordări instituţionale în studiul tranziţiei postcomuniste O analiză a transformărilor din 2 Mai ş2 Vama Veche*. Cetatea de Scaun, Tîrgovişte, Romania.

Taşcu-Stavre, M. and Bănică, C. (2014) Old and new in Vama Veche and 2 Mai. *Urbanism. Arhitectură. Construcţii.* 5(3):73–82.

Tîrcă, M. (2004) *Poveşti de la 2 Mai*. https://issuu.com/miruna10x/docs/povesti_din_satul_2mai (Accessed 30 November 2017).

Tisdell, C. (ed.) (2000). *The Economics of Tourism*. Edward Elgar, Cheltenham, United Kingdom and Northampton, United States.

Urry, J. ([1990]2002) *The Tourist Gaze*. Sage Publications, London.

Vasile, L. (2011) *Un fel de piua: 2 Mai şi Vama Veche*. Tipografia AdiCenter, Iaşi, Romania.

WCED. (1987) *Our Common Future*. www.un-documents.net/our-common-future.pdf (Accessed 30 November 2017).

12 World heritage and cultural sustainability

The farmers and fishermen of Vega, northern Norway

Karoline Daugstad and Knut Fageraas

Introduction

There are a number of perspectives on how to conceptualise cultural sustainability within the theoretical framework of sustainable development, ranging from a general statement about the way it builds a bridge with other dimensions of sustainability – its social, economic and environmental aspects – to more specific definitions of cultural vitality and viability (see Birkeland, 2008; Soini and Birkeland, 2014). It is not about a fixed state of affairs, although it is said to imply some sort of authenticity, but a continuing process of change towards positive development (cf. Stefanovic, 2000). For this chapter, an understanding of John Hawkes' (2001) conception of cultural sustainability is applicable; in short, it is about a society's ability to cope with the challenges and possibilities in a way that reflects the values and aspirations of its citizens. Hence, in our usage it points towards desired changes that are not in conflict with the cultural values that people attach to a place, their sense of traditions and heritage. The concept of tradition we use more or less in the same way as people we have interviewed, referring to cultural habits with long continuity. Heritage, not so often used by the interviewees, is defined, as it will appear in the following, in line with leading theories in the field of cultural heritage studies.

Auclair and Fairclough (2015: p. 1) put cultural heritage at the core of the sustainability discourse and practices. They demonstrate that 'the cultural values that people attach to a place are enmeshed with issues of memory, identity and aspirations', which they see both as central for people's wellbeing and as important elements in enhancing sustainable development (ibid.). Heritage is defined by heritage theorists as acts of remembering that work to create ways to understand and engage with the present (e.g. Smith, 2006: p. 2). Laurajane Smith emphasises that heritage is ultimately a cultural practice, performed through and affecting social relations – with real consequences for people and surroundings (ibid.: pp. 3–15). In the framework of cultural sustainability, and in accordance with Auclair and Fairclough, we see heritage as a productive cultural practice in line with citizens' identity-based values, memories and aspirations.

Such aspirations can be manifold. People relate differently to a particular place or a local community and do not necessarily share the same values, views and priorities regarding cultural heritage. Hence, people will impact on, contribute to and make use of the cultural heritage attached to a place in different ways. As Smith (2006: p. 13) outlines in her book *Uses of Heritage*, there are a great variety of uses of heritage, ranging from political usage to how it is understood and experienced in people's everyday life. In this study, based on the World Heritage site of The Vega Archipelago in northern Norway as a case study, uses of heritage are primarily analysed in the different ways representatives from the two main industrial sectors, farmers and fishermen, are getting involved with and engaged by World Heritage values. It includes ways of making economic profit, contribution to landscape management and voluntarily work organised by the special interest organisations for the preservation of the eiderdown tradition. Exploring how people working in the different sectors relate to cultural heritage is important in order to understand cultural sustainability at community level, and, on the more applied side, to generate useful knowledge for both policy-makers and those implementing public policies.

Vega was classified in the World Heritage List in 2004 as a 'cultural landscape' as it reflects the ways in which generations of fishermen/farmers over the past 1500 years have maintained a sustainable living in an inhospitable seascape near the Arctic Circle (UNESCO, 2004). The cultural practice of eiderdown production, crucial to people's subsistence in the past and still performed on a small-scale, was a key argument for Vega's World Heritage status. Eiderdown production was seen as representing a symbiotic relationship between culture and nature: people built small shelters for the eiders and protected the birds during breeding and in return they obtained, processed and sold the soft and highly cherished down.

In this chapter, our attention is directed towards how the recent United Nations Educational, Scientific and Cultural Organization (UNESCO) status and its promoted values are utilised, understood and appreciated locally by farmers and fishermen. Our approach was chosen on the basis of prior knowledge about the differences in social, economic and not least the environmental conditions for farming and fisheries at Vega and involves four research questions:

- How do the community's farmers and fishermen relate to Vega as a World Heritage site?
- Do they actively engage with the World Heritage, and if they do, in what ways?
- How can these relations or engagements be understood in the context of cultural sustainability?
- What role does the sector's different natural resource-basis and environmental conditions play?

In order to answer these research questions, we build on 18 semi-structured interviews recorded at Vega in spring and autumn 2009 as part of the research project 'Cultural Heritage as an asset for economic added value, selection processes from a coast-inland perspective' (see Daugstad, 2012; Fageraas, 2013; Flø, 2013; Krøgli *et al.*, 2013). The main aim of the project was to investigate how heritage was seen or used as an asset for economic development, i.e. how it was contributing to the 'heritagisation process' (cf. Harvey, 2001; Daugstad and Kirchengast, 2013). People employed in a range of key professions in the community (farmers, fishermen, tourist operators, politicians, bureaucrats and managers) were interviewed along with people who participated in legitimising, mobilising and utilising heritage. Some of the interviewees, amongst them farmers and fishermen, were employed in more than one of these professions and were politically active as well as being members of the interest organisations for preserving the World Heritage values. We draw on all of our interview material in this chapter, although predominantly the interviews with farmers and fishermen.

Background

Vega has a population of 1250 people inhabiting a few of the many islands in a vast archipelago that reaches far off shore to the continental shelf in the North Sea. Most of the archipelago was included in the World Heritage Area, except the two main inhabited islands that were given status as a buffer zone. Eider-down production is presently practised only on a few of the small outermost islands, but was customary on most islands in the archipelago in the past as it comprised a substantial part of people's income. 'Fisher-farmers' (smallholders making a living from a combination of fishing, small-scale farming and subsidiary economic activities) dominated the economic activity on Vega until the 1970s (Floa, 1999: p. 31). However, Vega transformed during the twentieth century due to structural changes in the primary industries into a two-tier society of full-time farmers and fishermen. The permanent settlements that existed on the outer islands were abandoned as many residents moved to the main island or to the mainland in search of better living and employment conditions. On the main island of Vega, the settlement pattern consists of fishing villages in the north and farming in the south. However, while the southern areas became the social, economic and political stronghold of the community, the north, where most of the former fisher-farmers from the outer islands settled, became socially, politically and economically marginalised (Fageraas, 2013).

In general, the Vega community experienced negative developments in the post-war era, caused by centralisation, population decline and environmental degradation. Fish stocks collapsed due to over-fishing and over-grazing of the kelp beds by sea urchins, while the eider population fell steadily to a tenth of its previous size. Furthermore, overgrowth caused by less livestock grazing threatened the open cultural landscape. Despite concerns that UNESCO status would demand the development of conservation plans with restrictions on marine as well as on-shore resource use, locals hoped that the UNESCO status would work as a catalyst for economic development, counteract population decline and – important to its local enthusiasts – help preserve the remains of the cultural practice of eiderdown production. Some also expected the designation to contribute to the primary industries by enhancing the marketing status of conventional economic activity within both farming and fishing. The interviews suggest that the UNESCO-listing has indeed revitalised the local community and strengthened its viability. However, the effects on farming and the fisheries have been highly divergent.

During the process of evaluating Vega prior to its nomination for World Heritage status the advisory expert from UNESCO concluded that the scope of the site had to be narrowed. One of the conclusions was that the 'fishing practices are largely historic and the traditions based on memories' (Ogden, 2002: p. 13). The practice of producing eiderdown, in contrast, was seen as a unique and rare example of a sustainable relationship between people and wildlife (ibid.: p. 6). The priority given to this rare land-based practice at the expense of practices related to the marine sphere has, since the nomination in 2003 and the entry on the World Heritage List in 2004, been accentuated by heritage experts, local enthusiasts and tourism operators. In the heritage discourse the outer islands became invariably termed 'down sites', no matter how much the settlements previously relied on fishing. Nevertheless, the physical remnants of the fishing villages in the archipelago with quays, warehouses and navigation buildings were classified as World Heritage, and the site is presented by UNESCO as a seascape, emphasising people's historic dependency on marine resources (UNESCO, 2014). However, not all land-based practices were given priority. World Heritage values do not include modern farming and consequently the productive agricultural areas of Vega were excluded from the World Heritage Area (Ogden, 2002: p. 12; Fageraas, 2013; Fageraas, 2016; pp. 94–95). Despite this, our results suggest that those related to this excluded form of economic activity may have benefited more from World Heritage status than most others – particularly fishermen.

Farming on Vega is almost exclusively based on grass-fed livestock production. Structural change and a shift from extensive to intensive practices during the last half of the twentieth century led to both an increase in productivity and landscape change (Floa, 1999). This is most evident in the southern areas of the main island where fields were merged into larger units and parts of previously outlying land (heaths and moors) brought into cultivation. In the northern areas where fisher-farmers survived the longest, there was little change in farmland structure and only a small increase in the extent of agricultural land (Krøgli *et al.*, 2013). Most of the outlying land/outfield areas on Vega are subject to overgrowth, due to less free-range livestock farming and a dramatic drop in fodder collection in the outfields (ibid.). However, the UNESCO-listing placed the development of a management plan for landscape maintenance and restoration of the World Heritage cultural landscape high on the agenda. The funding of the specific measures needed to implement the management plan came from state authorities via the local World Heritage Foundation and national agri-environmental schemes administered by the municipality. These provided farmers the opportunity to contribute to the upholding of World Heritage values related to cultural landscapes through schemes supporting grazing, mowing, restoration of fences and paths, etc. However, some of them also showed an interest in preserving the built cultural heritage and old cultural practices as well as in participating in the tourism business.

A progressive agricultural sector

The farming industry on Vega is widely perceived to be intensive, modern and progressive – a perspective that was emphasised by politicians, representatives from the fishing and farming sectors and others commenting on the conditions in the primary industries. Statistics support this perception as they show that Vega is one of the most prominent municipalities for pork and dairy farming (Vega Municipality, 2014). There are also a number of co-operatives of two to four farmers involved in joint investments in large, high-tech robotic cow systems. Even if the structural changes have radically reduced the number of farmers, agriculture is still the dominant employer, with 22 per cent of the population involved in farming (ibid.). In addition to favourable conditions for farming (productive farmland, agro-economic structure and technological developments) the active social environment among the farmers seems to have contributed significantly to creating a strong agricultural sector. The interviewees, local historical accounts, newspaper articles and information about the organisational life at Vega provide insight into the active social environment that farmers enjoy. Moreover, a relatively large recruitment to local, regional and national politics and management from the farming sector has probably contributed to its development in a progressive way, and at the same time reflects the sector's dominance in social, economic, environmental as well as cultural terms.

When asked what major changes the Vega community has experienced in the last 50 years, all farmers emphasised landscape change. The open grazed landscape of Vega of the past was seen as aesthetically pleasing, while the more closed landscape of today was referred to in negative terms. The spread of Sitka spruce, an alien species introduced in the 1950s and 1960s, was mentioned as particularly unwanted. The disappearance of plant and bird species due to the replacement of traditional agrarian practices by modern intensive farming methods was mentioned as having had a severe impact on the landscape. As a counter-measure, agri-environmental schemes in the wake of the UNESCO status, have been directed to the farmers involved in grazing the cultural landscape in the World Heritage Area. This was seen as an important means of slowing down the overgrowth.

Not all of the farmers were involved in grazing the World Heritage cultural landscape. One interviewee was concerned about creating an 'A' and 'B' team in farming as a result of the agri-environmental payments. The A-team in this context were farmers who were paid to let their animals graze in the World Heritage Area while the B-team were those who were not and thus missed out on the economic benefits as well as the positive status (for maintaining open landscape) such measures implied. This division of A and B was arbitrary as eligibility for participation in the World Heritage management was dependent on having some of the limited suitable grazing land, not on a desire to participate in agri-environmental provision.

Interviewed farmers mentioned the positive effects the UNESCO status had had on Vega's reputation. A number of potential benefits were suggested, such as making Vega a more popular place to live, slowing down the population decline and increasing tourism potential. Prior to World Heritage status a few farmers were already renting out simple accommodation for visitors. Now, more farmers are engaged in such services, first and foremost by rebuilding their old sea-warehouses. After the award of the UNESCO status several other kinds of tourist ventures were started. One couple, from one of the larger farms on the northern part of the main island, bought a small island property in the World Heritage Area, and renovated and rebuilt the houses to reconstruct a former fisher-farmer holding (complete with grazing) as a tourist initiative. They saw their initiative as part of the World Heritage effect on the community and emphasised that they would not have started grazing in the World Heritage Area or established the tourist initiative without economic support. The couple are one of the clearest examples of how farmers have become engaged in the World Heritage and participation in landscape maintenance schemes.

A depressed fishing industry

Compared with the agricultural sector, the fishing industry at Vega is depressed and in decline. The number of fishermen is much lower than in the past and hardly any of them are fishing their traditional areas on the Helgeland coast. Local fishermen were given a lower priority by the government who favoured deep sea fishing vessels. 'We are a dying breed', one of the interviewed fishermen noted, adding: 'there is no recruitment to the fisheries'. According to him the quotas set for the Helgeland region fisheries are too small to be shared, so to have someone with you on the boat is not economically viable. He saw a one-man fishing operation as being lonely, and, with just one crew-member on board, rather unsafe. This worked against recruitment in the sector. In 2009, when our interviews were conducted, the last of the many fish landing sites at Vega was closed. It was, however, reopened later the same year through a joint effort by the municipal council and the local professional fishermen's union and business organisation (Vega Fiskarlag). Despite this, the fishing industry appeared incapable of making any noteworthy progress according to the interviewed fishermen.

The fishermen we spoke to saw their industry neither as modern or traditional. They had not invested in large fishing vessels and did not see themselves representing a fishing tradition. They could have been typical representatives of the coastal fisheries in Norway as it has been practised during the twentieth century, with their fleet of 'Sjarks' – the characteristic small one-man fishing boats. Fishermen also showed little interest in the sector's old practices and traditions mentioned in the UNESCO documents. One of the interviewees said:

'The fisheries have not been valued highly (...) the status of the profession has been low' while another (a descendent of a fishing family but not a fisher) expressed concern that the industry had already been lost and would soon disappear. Many of the interviewees were critical of the way the down tradition had been given higher status in the World Heritage site than fishing and the marine sphere. They argued for greater emphasis on the fishing practices and traditions, referring to the nomination text and UNESCO documents.

The active fishermen interviewed did not express any particular interest in the UNESCO status. One fisherman, although appreciating the economic benefits, claimed that it was just 'old rubbish' that was preserved in the name of World Heritage, and that strict restrictions prevented people building what they really needed. Neither did this interviewee feel included in the World Heritage values. He emphasised it was the archipelago and the fisher-farmer that actually had significance as World Heritage but associated the fisher-farmer mostly with farming and the subsidiary activity of down production. Another fisherman, a pensioner, also held rather negative views of UNESCO status because it placed too many restrictions on private property. None of these fishermen were directly involved in the work to support traditional activities or the securing of the cultural landscape. However, one had later become a member of the special interest organisation supporting the down producers. At the time of the interview this interviewee was running a tourist enterprise, taking tourists in the archipelago to visit the World Heritage Area by sea. Several other fishermen and boat-owners were also involved in transporting tourists in the archipelago. Nonetheless, the interviewed fishermen thought that despite the obvious economic benefits, Vega would have been just as well off without UNESCO status. Even the fisherman who ran the rather professional tourist enterprise was not at all positive about World Heritage status and claimed that it had no direct effect on his business.

Discussion

The interviews revealed a significant difference between the farmers' and fishermen's views of the impacts of the World Heritage status, how they became engaged in World Heritage and what potentially positive effects they saw for themselves. While the fishermen perceived the status to be of little positive value both to their sector and to the community, many farmers saw possibilities for new income and also benefits for the whole community by slowing down population decline, increasing the attractiveness of the place and offering new employment opportunities. This complemented the farmers' aspirations to find additional income opportunities as well as interesting recreational activities. The fishermen's attitude towards the UNESCO status, on the other hand, mirrored the negative development and challenging future for coastal fisheries, related to disadvantageous policies, their social and cultural status, as well as the environmental degradation of the marine ecosystem and over-exploitation of fish stocks.

There is a general perception, forwarded by national authorities as well as UNESCO, that World Heritage is synonymous with economic added value (e.g. Miljøverndepartementet, 2012: p. 38; UNESCO, 2015). According to UNESCO, World Heritage is of crucial importance to society through its great potential to achieve social, economic and environmental goals (UNESCO, 2015). The nomination text for the inscription of The Vega Archipelago on the World Heritage List from 2004 also raised these expectations (Miljøverndepartementet, 2003: p. 52). Recent research has, however, concluded that this is not necessarily the case. The cultural historian Herdis Hølleland, referring to several research projects and consultancy reports, explains that a narrative has developed of heritage's regenerative possibilities which can lead to a sense of disappointment when the expectations do not materialise (2013: p. 230). To benefit from such status relevant actors need to be motivated beforehand and an outline of development possibilities needs to be clearly drawn (ibid.: p. 231). This may partly explain why, compared with the fishermen, farmers were more actively engaged by the World Heritage cultural values and made use of the UNESCO status for economic gain. At the heart of such motivation is a progressive perspective on their own industry.

However, the farmers' positive attitude and their engagement with the World Heritage status was also due to the way they benefited from and actively partook in landscape maintenance. Cultivation of arable land and livestock grazing in outfield areas gave the farmers an opportunity that was not an option for the fishermen. The farmers could contribute to cultural landscape management by having their livestock brought to the outer islands, and quite a few farmers have done exactly that. At present 700 sheep and cows are grazing the World Heritage cultural landscape (Vega Municipality, 2016). Such measures for landscape management are not at all new to farmers as agricultural policy from the 1970s onwards has increasingly focused on the multifunctional role of farming and the agrarian cultural landscape as heritage, economically supported by national agri-environmental schemes (Jones and Daugstad, 1997; Rønningen, 1999; Daugstad *et al.*, 2006). The existing system of agri-environmental schemes in Vega have after the UNESCO status been targeted towards managing and restoring the cultural landscape of the island realm, and thus function as an incentive for farmers' engagement with the World Heritage.

One particularly interesting difference between the farmers and the fishermen is in the way they related to the World Heritage values. The archipelago in all stages of the site's preparation, nomination and designation as World Heritage was described as a seascape with a rich fishing history. Whereas the fishermen failed to identify with World Heritage many farmers did, despite the fact that the agricultural sector's intensive operations were said to be inconsistent with the UNESCO status. Paradoxically, the occupants of farming smallholds in this region were historically so dependent on fishing that the men in most households could be termed full-time fishermen (Slettedal, 2009: p. 28). This was acknowledged in the local heritage discourse to such a degree that the World Heritage Area prior to the UNESCO listing had largely been associated with the fishing industry. It was (and still is) a gendered landscape – a male domain. However, this was now changed. As men historically spent most of the year fishing, land-based resource activities such as eiderdown production were left to women (cf. Elstad, 2004). This women's domain became the core value of Vega's World Heritage, celebrating as the UNESCO status was meant to do, the cultural *land*scape of the island realm and of women's contribution to down production (UNESCO, 2004). Hence, in the context of the World Heritage status, the site was no longer the seascape that fishermen could identify with. Not surprisingly, it is mostly women who are occupied in the heritage-based revival of former down sites and tourist initiatives based on the World Heritage (Sundli, 2011; Fageraas, 2013).

The difference in attitudes to heritage between fishermen and farmers at Vega must also be understood in a national context. Despite the omnipresent fishing activity with its immense significance for all human settlements along the Norwegian coast, and with great economic importance to state finances through centuries, it has not been valued as national heritage in the way farming has (cf. Daugstad, 2000; Jones, 2008: p. 283). Through the national Romantic period of the nineteenth century, the Norwegian farmer and the cultural landscapes of the inland valleys and mountain areas became iconic symbols of Norwegian identity. This seems to have impacted on conceptions of what constitutes valuable cultural expressions and landscapes to date, although coastal culture and its distinctive landscapes have been increasingly recognised as important heritage in recent decades. It is most likely that this bias has affected the conception of what is valuable at Vega, and, subsequently, how farmers and fishermen view the UNESCO status. The local historical accounts clearly show this bias towards emphasising the history of farming at the expense of the fisheries (Fageraas and Skar, 2013). Generally, heritagisation seems to be a positive process at Vega. It becomes, however, a particularly productive force when merged with the already progressive agricultural sector stimulated by a solid social, cultural, economic and environmental basis.

Given the depressed situation in the fisheries sector it is somewhat surprising that the fishermen did not seek to use the opportunities that World Heritage status can provide. The fishermen could (and there are good examples of this), participate in the tourism industry or establish their own tourism initiatives. Even if the farmers, like many others, were sceptical early on about being part of a World Heritage site, those we interviewed showed greater interest towards engaging with the UNESCO status. This may be connected to the way that World Heritage status corresponded with the farmer's values and identity, rooted as it is on land-based resource-use and animal keeping. However, the positive attitude towards World Heritage among the farmers was not confined to those in the 'A-team' who had access to subsidies through the uptake of agri-environmental schemes. Generally, the farmers seemed better prepared for participation in the heritagisation process, the work on landscape maintenance as well as participation in the tourism business. Without their progressive thinking and appreciation of World Heritage it seems unlikely that the cultural landscape of this vast island pastoral realm could be maintained.

Conclusions

Overall, the UNESCO status has been a positive development for Vega, bringing new possibilities to the local communities. To benefit from such status, however, it seems necessary that it is in line with peoples' cultural values and aspirations, i.e. it must be culturally sustainable. However, as evident in the case of Vega the cultural sustainability must not be seen in isolation to the social, economic and environmental basis of peoples' livelihoods. On Vega, it was the farmers who saw the potential of UNESCO status. The fishermen, in contrast, have experienced economic depression along with environmental problems, a resource crisis and social degradation resulting in a negative discourse in the sector about its conditions and future scenarios. Furthermore, the difference between the two sectors' appreciation of their heritage as well as the World Heritage status seems to have been influenced by a national heritage ideal. Heritage production in Norway has for nearly 200 years favoured heritage related to farming as representing the authentic national history and iconic landscape features. Vega's twofold character of farming in the southern areas and fishing villages in the northern parts is a microcosm of the conflict between land-based versus marine cultural values across the country. In addition, the farmers had the advantage of an agricultural policy that supported involvement in the maintenance of the cultural landscape through agri-environmental schemes. The fishermen's lack of engagement with the World Heritage reveals that UNESCO status does not always have positive effects for a local community and all its industries. The UNESCO-listing of Vega reinforced the existing division between the agricultural and fishing sectors in the community by strengthening the former, while the latter were still associated with social, economic and environmental decline.

There are two key findings from this analysis with implications for cultural sustainability. First: World Heritage status affected the farming and fishing industries differently as a result of differences in the two sectors' vitality and viability. Second: differences in the farmers' and fishermen's heritage engagement is connected to the prevailing policies in the sectors and their social, economic and environmental bases – which have had divergent impacts on the community's cultural sustainability. World Heritage as a land-based cultural practice celebrated for its sustainable interplay between nature and culture was something that farmers could identify with, but fishermen could not. The farmers had the advantage, through their conventional economic activity, of possessing a way to engage with nature that corresponded more with the World Heritage concept at Vega. Furthermore, through their engagement the farmers were able to optimise some of their aspirations towards new income possibilities and recreational activities. The World Heritage was also seen by farmers, like many others in the community, as a potential means of securing the viability of the local community as a whole, while the fishermen tended to see it as a threat.

The different outcomes for the fishing and farming sectors on Vega illustrate that the heritagisation processes do not necessarily have positive effects on local industries and, therefore, on the cultural sustainability of a society. While the status generally enhanced the cultural status of the farming sector, in the fishing sector there were only a few enthusiasts in the local community who worked to highlight the fishing practices and traditions so that they could be more appreciated as part of the site's World Heritage status. This could contribute to strengthening the cultural basis for the sector, which could have a significant impact on the social, economic, and eventually, the environmental basis of the industry. At present, there are positive tendencies in the fisheries sector related to the rebuilding of fish stocks and re-vegetation of the marine ecosystem of the archipelago. Moreover, there is an evolving public movement in the north of Norway in favour of the coastal fisheries and in support of the local fishing communities along the North Atlantic coast. This implies that government policies concerning logistics and quota systems have to be revised accordingly. If this leads to an improvement in the natural and economic basis of the sector, it would also strengthen its cultural and social sustainability, thus, potentially contributing to sustainable development.

Acknowledgements

This project was funded by the Norwegian Research Council's 'Environment2015' programme.

References

Auclair, E. and Fairclough, G. (2015) *Theory and Practice in Heritage and Sustainability: Between Past and Future.* Routledge, London.

Birkeland, I. (2008) Cultural sustainability: industrialism, placelessness and the re-animation of place. *Ethics, Place and Environment* 11(3):285–299.

Daugstad, K. (2000) Mellom romantikk og realisme: om seterlandskapet som ideal og realitet. Doctoral thesis. Department of Geography, Norwegian university of science and technology (NTNU), Trondheim, Norway.

Daugstad, K. (2012) Verdiskaping og kulturarv. *Kulturarven* June:44–47.

Daugstad, K. and Kirchengast, C. (2013) Authenticity and the pseudo-backstage of agri-tourism. *Annals of Tourism Research* 43:170–191.

Daugstad, K., Rønningen, K. and Skar, B. (2006) Agriculture as an upholder of cultural heritage? Conceptualizations and value judgements – a Norwegian perspective in international context. *Journal of Rural Studies* 22:67–81.

Elstad, Å. (2004) *Kystkvinner i Norge.* Kom forlag, Kristiansund, Norway.

Fageraas, K. (2013) Verdensarvens forandringer på Vega: kulturell verdsetting langs nye og gamle skillelinjer. In: G. Swensen and T. S. Guttormsen (eds) *Å lage kulturminner – hvordan kulturarv forstås, formes og forvaltes.* Novus, Oslo: 287–335.

Fageraas, K. (2016) Housing Eiders – Making Heritage. The Changing Context of the Human-Eider Relationship in the Vega Archipelago, Norway. In: K. Bjørkdahl and T. Druglitrø (eds) *Animal Housing and Human-Animal Relations. Politics, Practices and Infrastructures.* Routledge, London and New York: 82–99.

Fageraas, K. and Skar, B. (2013) Frambringelser av dun- og stølstradisjoner – Vega og Valdres i lokalhistorisk litteratur. in B. E. Flø (ed.) *Kulturarv og verdiskaping i eit kyst-innlandsperspektiv*. Norsk senter for bygdeforskning, Trondheim, Norway: 17–37.
Floa, O. (1999) Vega – Landbruksøya. In: I. E. Næss (eds) *Vega gjennom 10 000 år*. Vega kommune, Vega, Norway: 27–32.
Flø, B. E. (ed.) (2013) *Kulturarv og verdiskaping i eit kyst-innlandsperspektiv. Report 2/2013*. Norsk senter for bygdeforskning, Trondheim, Norway.
Harvey, D. C. (2001) Heritage pasts and heritage presents: temporality, meaning and the scope of heritage studies. *International Journal of Heritage Studies* 7(4):319–338.
Hawkes, J. (2001) *The Fourth Pillar of Sustainability: Culture's Essential Role in Public Planning*. Common Ground Publishing, Melbourne, Australia.
Hølleland, H. (2013) *Practicing World Heritage: Approaching the Changing Faces of the World Heritage Convention*. PhD thesis. Institutt for kulturstudier og orientalske språk, University of Oslo, Oslo.
Jones, M. (2008) The 'Two Landscapes' of the North Norway and the 'Cultural Landscape' of the South. In: M. Jones and K. F. Olwig (eds) *Nordic Landscapes, Region and Belonging on the Northern Edge of Europe*. University of Minnesota Press, Minneapolis, United States and London.
Jones, M. and Daugstad, K. (1997) Usages of the 'cultural landscape' concept in Norwegian and Nordic landscape administration. *Landscape Research* 22(3): 267–281.
Krøgli, S. O., Dramstad, W. and Skar, B. (2013) World heritage and landscape change – heritage buildings and their changed visibility in the coastal landscape of Vega, Norway. *Norsk geografisk tidsskrift*, 69(3):121–134.
Miljøverndepartementet. (2003) *Vegaøyan – The Vega Archipelago. Norwegian Nomination 2003 – UNESCO World Heritage List*. Norwegian Ministry of Environment, Oslo
Miljøverndepartementet. (2012) *Ny, helhetlig verdensarvpolitikk*. Norwegian Ministry of Environment, Oslo.
Ogden, P. (2002) *World Heritage Site Nomination. The Vega Archipelago, Helgeland, Norway. Report of Advisory visit: Peter Ogden (IUCN)*. June 2002. Unpublished.
Rønningen, K. (1999) Agricultural policies and countryside management. A comparative European study. Doctoral thesis. Department of Geography, Norwegian University of Science and Technology (NTNU), Trondheim, Norway.
Slettedal, S. (2009) *Steinalderøya i endring: en historisk studie av Vegaøyenes utvikling etter 1950*. Master's thesis in history. Norwegian University of Science and Technology (NTNU), Trondheim, Norway.
Smith, L. (2006) *Uses of Heritage*. Routledge, London.
Soini, K. and Birkeland, I. (2014) Exploring the scientific discourse on cultural sustainability. *Geoforum* 51:213–223.
Stefanovic, I. L. (2000) *Safeguarding Our Common Future: Rethinking Sustainable Development*. New York State University of New York Press, New York.
Sundli, K. (2011) *Omsorg eller kvinnovasjon?: mulig sysselsetting for kvinner på Vega i dag*. Master's thesis. Institutt for sosiologi og samfunnsgeografi, Universitetet i Oslo, Oslo. www.duo.uio.no/bitstream/handle/10852/15401/Sundli.pdf?sequence=2&isAllowed=y (Accessed 13 December 2017).
UNESCO. (2004) *Decision adopted at the 28th session of the World Heritage Committee (Suzhou, 2004)*. World Heritage Centre, UNESCO, Paris.
UNESCO. (2014) *Vegaøyan – The Vega Archipelago. World Heritage Centre, UNESCO*. http://whc.unesco.org/en/list/1143 (Accessed 4 November 2012).

UNESCO. (2015) *World Heritage and Sustainabile Development, World Heritage Centre, UNESCO*. http://whc.unesco.org/en/sustainabledevelopment/ (Accessed 19 November 2015).

Vega Municipality. (2014) *Jordbrukstjenesten*. www.vega.kommune.no/jordbruk (Accessed 7 January 2016).

Vega Municipality. (2016) *Skjøtsel i verdensarv*. www.vega.kommune.no/skoetsel (Accessed 23 August 2016).

Part III

Methodologies for cultural sustainability

13 Narratives, capabilities and climate change

Towards a sustainable culture

Nathalie Blanc and Lydie Laigle

Rethinking climate change adaptation using a narrative and capability perspective

In this chapter, we explore how narrative methodologies can be used to untangle the complex 'natural–cultural' construction of the climate change. Referring to a capabilities approach that explores the constraints and resources that people have in their daily lives, we analyse how the formulation of relationships, knowledge and experiences with the environment can influence the ability of citizens to adapt to climate change. We contend that learning about adaptation can be achieved by exploring ordinary stories of everyday life in particular. The main question is whether the exploration of capabilities through stories can be a path to a sustainable culture, meaning a co-emergent nature–culture, a contextualized conception of bio-physical-chemical processes. We need to recall that, for now, scholarship on the connections between environment, sustainability and culture is quite scarce and needs to be further studied (Parra and Moulaert, 2011). It has been acknowledged that culture is a lynchpin to the principle of sustainability since it is through culture that our relationship with nature and the human community is constructed and functions (Alexander, 1987; Stefanovic, 2000; Birkeland, 2008). As such, culture has been envisaged as the fourth pillar of sustainable development (Hawkes, 2001) in a context in which economic and environmental crises demand new ways of thinking and living (Soiini and Dessein, 2016).

We develop our thesis in four sections. The first section takes a broad look at capabilities and narratives in connection with the cultural question. The second argues that climate expertise and cities' plans rarely address in these terms the issue of adaptation to climate change. The third section examines different narratives based on lived experiences. The first narrative is drawn from a discussion that took place in the context of the Rio+20 summit. The second narrative involves climate changes as they are experienced by Inuit people on Baffin Island. The third narrative deals with ordinary situations in French cities. Finally, the fourth section presents an adventure scenario scripted by a science-fiction writer. This scenario narrates a scientist's adaptation to a very primitive situation in Washington following upheaval caused by climate change. We conclude by drawing a few lessons from the narratives.

Capabilities, narratives and sustainable culture

In recent years, capability-based analyses (Sen, 2010; Nussbaum, 2011) have gradually begun to be applied to environmental issues. Such analyses are based on the interplay between the (natural and social) possibilities offered by an environment, on the one hand, and on the capacity of individuals or groups to harness such possibilities for carrying out basic human functions or converting resources into action, on the other. This type of interpretive framework places the focus on the things that individuals or groups are likely to mobilize in their (societal and environmental) milieu to ensure their subsistence, health and mobility. Building on Sen (2010), Nussbaum (2011) has used the notion of capabilities to posit that it is not so much the possibilities to function that are influencing factors (e.g. the possibility to eat to one's fill, confront environmental change, etc.), but rather those 'that allow concerned individuals or groups to find the capacities to do so'. It is as such that Nussbaum insists on the ethical, sensory nature of our relationship with an environment: 'relationships with other species and the world of nature are a human capability, but one in which the other entities count not merely instrumentally but also as parts of that relationship' (Nussbaum, 2011: p. 158). These relationships shape us as beings and define our ethical relationship with others. Capabilities represent possibilities grasped by individuals or groups to have a transforming relation with their environment, in accordance with ethical principles in a given social, economic or political situation (Nussbaum, 2011).

Why examine capabilities based on narratives?

The methodological decision to use narratives is based on the importance of narration since it reveals our ethical relationship with the natural and cultural environment by expressing our way of being in connection with the environment (Bate, 2000). A pragmatic definition places narratives in a referred sequence of events, which represents a break from everyday order (Mondeme, 2014). The narrative structures the order of these new or wished-for events. What can be produced as narrative is an interpretation of the course of events which arouses interest. In addition, putting something in narrative form is part of the process of adapting to these new facts. Studying narratives is one way of looking at how new types of capabilities are forged out of the possibilities offered by an environment. Today, the public debate is largely dominated by a scientific-technical-political narrative that in part obscures ordinary narratives. By scientific narrative, we mean the scientific literature involved in Intergovernmental Panel on Climate Change (IPCC) reports, social and climate sciences publications that influence debates in Conference of Parties (climate negotiations, etc.) and play a role in establishing public policies at the different levels. But narratives can reveal how the cognitive and emotional registers of relationships with the environment change and how individuals incorporate such a change into their practices: narratives offer insight into the adaptation process in action, how the individuals transform their environment through new practices (through their capacity to act).

One defining feature of stories is their ability to connect very heterogeneous events and phenomena in time and space through causal connections or co-presence effects in a set of events. The more heterogeneous and rich the elements that contribute to a story, the more the narrative plays an important role in the construction of a homogeneous temporal space. Narratives present a scripted relationship with the environment and coax out capabilities (the existence or not of capabilities). In climatic narratives, a narrative includes the concrete details of ordinary life in connection with a sensory universe: this is the case for natural elements such as smells, colours and temperature changes. For certain populations, the knowledge built up during the construction of a narrative, i.e. in pragmatic mode, contributes to 'a knowledge that undergoes continual generation and regeneration as people interact with the environment: observing, learning, and adapting' (Berkes, 2008: p. 172). This goes hand-in-hand with a view of narratives as a way of accessing the knowledge of populations and the ideas they have of themselves in a given situation. Anecdotes help people to understand climate change in the context of their ordinary lives. We must not forget that climate on a human scale includes details that root it in the everyday lives that are shaped by natural phenomena (e.g. rain, the seasons, the smell of grass when the sun heats up, the flowers that grow in the spring, etc.).

From this perspective, narratives offer insight into how complex information involving science, culture and morality are included in the way our lives play out. Narratives are not simply lists of events; rather, they are constructed sets of knowledge (with a start, an intrigue, a sequence and consequences) destined to be shared with others or placed in the public arena. It is as such possible to analyse narratives by identifying the intrigue, determining the elements in the sequence and identifying the actors involved, including elements from the natural and built environment. It is also possible to understand how people or groups of actors redefine their identity with the help of such narratives, by testing the coherence of the connections between scientific, cultural, factual and emotional elements (Bremond, 1973). This plot-building process highlights multiple relationships between possibilities and capacities. Which relationships with environments (e.g., natural, artificial) are expressed through the different narratives? What types of practices develop in terms of adaptation to climate change by inhabitants themselves: e.g. the greening of cities, water collection, etc.? What capabilities and typology of drivers for adaptation from the perspective of inhabitants emerge from such narratives? How can these narratives offer insight into the local natures-cultures? This is especially true for climate change, whose definition as a phenomenon associated with human activities and excessive energy consumption is largely dependent on demonstrations that are particularly abstract and overly complex for the general public.

Climate plans and adaptation to climate change

Although adaptation to climate change deals with how populations adapt to evolving climatic conditions, it is still focused primarily on attenuating the impacts of such change on ecosystems and urban spaces. There are a broad range of approaches for understanding the notion of adaptation and these can be grouped roughly into the following two categories:

- IPCC approaches, primarily used by climatologists and ecologists for whom adaptation is a process involving the adjustment of ecosystems and living spaces to changing climatic conditions. These include variations in climate leading to breaks in the ecosystem chain and adverse effects on living spaces which experience extreme situations such as storms, flooding, drought, etc. Within this context, adaptation refers to the ability to limit the detrimental effects of climate change on living spaces and, in some cases, to seizing on opportunities for the adaptability of natural areas;[1]
- geographical and anthropological approaches which view adaptation as based on the interaction between social systems and long-term environmental changes (Adger, 2000: p. 2009).

It is mainly the first set of approaches that has been used in analyses of the adaptation of cities to climate change (Hoornweg *et al.*, 2011). Most of the research supported by the World Bank (Mchrotta *et al.*, 2009) and United Nations (UN) bodies (OECD, 2009; UNHabitat, 2011) at the scale of cities and in different continents of the world has focused on limiting major risks (e.g. flooding, the destruction of infrastructure and technical systems), their chain effects on 'urban modus operandi' and the vulnerability of city dwellers (e.g. supply problems, health risks), as well as related protective measures (e.g. information systems, warning systems and evacuation systems). Current climate plans are the result of these measures and approaches. As a result, cities have mainly linked adaptation to protection from climate change impacts and risks. This is also reflected in the scientific literature: adaptation privileges protection against climate change effects more at the expense of long-term environmental changes and visions. This explains why what is currently called adaptation mainly refers to a set of measures that contribute to enhancing the physical resilience of cities to floods and storms, and to reduce vulnerability of citizen to climate variations.

But some researchers and academics argue that this interpretation is too restrictive for analysing the challenges to human development posed by the adaptation of cities to climate change (Moser and Stein, 2011). For Adger (2001: p. 925), 'this range is limited compared with the spontaneous reactive adjustments in resource use and livelihoods that will be required by every individual whose livelihoods are directly or indirectly weather-dependent'. This implies a need to understand human development dimensions of climate change by considering what has been broken or lost in the relationship between city dwellers and their built environments, as well as what could be retrofitted or restored through experience and collective action.

Narratives of lived experiences

Several examples can contribute to the discussion. The first narrative involves the ethical dimension of the relationships with the environment. This is an illustrative example to better understand the ways in which a dialogue between scientists and inhabitants can be built.[2] The debates during the Rio+20 summit on adaptation to climate change in the Salomon Islands (2012) placed IPCC representatives, UN legal experts, non-governmental organizations (NGOs) and citizen delegates from the islands in opposition. The IPCC predicts a major increase in the rise of seawater levels and thus advocates for adaptation based on the gradual evacuation of the atoll. UN legal experts, for their part, recommend creating climate refugee rights for the inhabitants of these islands, and the NGOs and inhabitants raised important issues about reclaiming their relationship with the environment:

> having refugee status is one thing, but will the UN negotiate agreements with host countries?; will then this mean that we won't be able to choose our host country?; in any case, we do not want to become refugees as there is nowhere else in the world that is home to us; refugee rights are a non-right for us to stay on the land where we were born and that shaped us as people; we demand the right to protection without being torn from the islands; have you thought about the possibility of reconstructing a lagoon, a solution to recreate the ecosystem of the marine environment that would allow us to migrate inland?; have you thought about the creation of an international fund to conduct research into exploring this type of adaptation and taking the steps necessary to respect the marine environment, protect food crops and enable the expansion of the cities located on the highlands?[3]

It is worth noting that Brazilian Amazonian Indians, who live near medium-sized cities, expressed virtually similar issues and demands. This first example illustrates dialogue between different stakeholders in the context of an international conference. The different facets of this exchange were constructed in relation to each other and produced a narrative.

For the second example, we draw on narratives provided by the Inuit of Baffin Island in the Arctic Ocean (Fast *et al.*, quoted in Lejano *et al.*, 2011). In this example, there is no commensurability between the inhabitants' narratives and the scientific narratives. This incommensurability is not so much due to the facts themselves but to how they are written into the course of ordinary lives. In this sense, ordinary knowledge can be treated as a knowledge-practice-belief complex (Berkes, 2008). For Ingold (2000), practice is the backbone of knowledge. Narratives allow the meaning of different practices to be connected and to build their coherence in an intergenerational perspective:

> Ice breaks off earlier than in past years, and then as soon as ice leaves bowhead [whales] come in. Ice forms later than before, around mid

> November, and it seems to have difficulty forming or freezing on the shores. From the 1960s to the 1990s it used to form without any difficulty in middle of October – a month earlier than it does now. The sea ice is less predictable so hunters need to be more careful when they are travelling.
>
> The number of icebergs has decreased a lot in the last couple of decades. They have decreased dramatically even in my own lifetime. Inlets used to be full of old ice but this never happens anymore. Even our travel used to be restricted by icebergs, but now only wind restricts us. The biggest change seen is that this area used to have ice all the time but now ice breaks up a lot. That didn't use to happen. Even people from Qikiqtarjuaq [a remote village on the north side of Baffin Island] can't travel there anymore. Only the inlets freeze over now, and there are no more transit routes on the sea ice. We have noticed when we go caribou hunting that some rivers that get their water from glaciers never freeze over.
>
> Ice is so strange nowadays. It is more like lake ice than salt water ice. Freshwater is getting in there. The sea here has less salt than before. Last year my father noticed this. My father cooks his seal meat with sea water and noticed there was not enough salt in the water … Another example of changes happened last summer (2009) when I stayed outside all day with my daughter. After it became dark we went back in and we both got really sick from the sun. It is too warm here now – especially last summer. Even though I like the warm weather it was unbearable because it was too warm.

This narrative illustrates an intricate interweaving of practices and knowledge. There are many anecdotes that work to connect climatic observations with the course of ordinary life giving it credibility. The ice that used to miraculously take shape no longer does so and the sea has as such lost part of its agency. The way the anecdotes are placed in the flow of the story – shaping the narrative with their coherence, dramatic storyline and progression – is of course how the story's intrigue is created. The natural elements are there to verify and even pinpoint the changes.

This kind of narrative is obviously different from those told by inhabitants of very large metropolises. But our previous observations on air quality nonetheless reveal a narrative-creation process that is disconnected in its construction from the scientific explanation of facts related to air pollution. Indeed, climate representations are connected to our representations of the environments in which we live and the ways of living in these milieus. As such, the meaning given to all environmental elements is rooted in the very specific context of each individual situation. Our previous studies on air quality in Strasbourg (Blanc *et al.*, 2011) and on the notion of pollution showed that those interviewed did not rely much on scientific information or on the information provided by the hospital visited by some of them (asthmatics). Instead, they relied more on their senses. The following quote from an interviewee shows how not only smells but also colours can provide an indication of air quality and affect the perception of air quality in an environment.

> For example, the Rhine port, over there, you can see the walls, they've turned all black, dirty walls, pollution, and in the bars it's the same, the bars that are too smoky, you can't breathe in them, the ambience is not good, you cannot spend an enjoyable evening... (...) To experience a good ambience, there's the visual aspect, what you can see visually, whether it's the walls, things that are dirty, things like that, how some things feel... When you touch something in a place that's polluted, a tree leaf, for example, there's something on it, strange matter, a kind of oil... You can feel that it has been polluted. And then, basically, the smells. There are factory smells. There's an enormous one that you can really smell a lot, it's a kind of malt and hops smell, I don't know exactly how to describe the smell... Given the scope of this answer and the attention to his environment paid by the interviewee, the interviewer then asked him how he would define the term atmospheric pollution. Surprised, the interviewee tried to find the right words: A definition? (Silence) How I would define atmospheric pollution? One definition could be: the air is not pure; there might be too much CO_2 or carbon dioxide (carbon dioxide is CO_2, right? I'm not sure, I didn't take chemistry); what our body needs is not necessarily in the air, there are more of other substances, other things that are not necessarily good for our bodies.

This excerpt illustrates one way of connecting heterogeneous events that tie pollution to environmental health problems or, more precisely, to the way things are experienced physically. This sensory perception is also what allows pollution to be experienced; it embodies a narrative that is associated with autobiographical details and gives a plot to the different components that comprise the narrative.

The understanding of meteorology, of a climate evaluated on a daily basis, can also occur through the bodily senses based on a global representation of the environment (Haouès-Jouve, 2010). This is ambience. A climatic ideal would ensure that the balance of nature was maintained when the seasons were threatened with disappearance (Albert-Llorca, 1991). It is important to look at how everyday activities evolve according to such perceived climatic ideals. For individuals, and city dwellers in particular, green spaces provide clues that reveal variations and changes in nature. Such clues are combined with intermediary objects (e.g. a thermometer or the size of a plant or the date at which some species appear in certain places) to create a narrative and confirm an interpretation. Adaptation to climate change involves a degree of comparison between before and now, as well as between here and elsewhere, i.e. in the city and outside the city, in this neighbourhood and outside the neighbourhood. The measures transmitted by these objects are debated, narrated and compared with lived experiences and often allow science to be discredited in favour of a subjective confirmation of one's own perceptions of the climate (seasonal changes) and weather. When it comes to practices, they seek to adapt to the environment; stopgap changes to regular behaviour (for example, having a nap) are improvized rather than trying to get the environment (notably built) to adapt, unless such details can be taken into account when a house is built. Influencing the environment therefore involves adapting to the opportunities offered by different environments: wooded green spaces, for example, provide an ideal urban location for meteorological and pollution regulation. When those interviewees mentioned policies for adapting to climate change, they notably talked about the planting of trees and the creation of green spaces. Living beings are constantly evolving and therefore allow a unique framework to be built for understanding environmental change and for its narration.

This insight into the way people connect with their environmental milieu through a series of narratives, metaphors and causal relationships not only offers a few key means of interpreting the interactions between humans and their environments, but also offers clues to what we might expect from a close reading of situations of adaptation to climate change.

Science-fiction adventure

There are numerous narratives in literature, as well as in the visual arts and cinema,[4] that offer representations of climate change. Many of these also address the issue in the urban sphere. The most common narratives of this kind involve guilt, punishment and redemption. Humanity is guilty of having neglected the fragile nature of the earth and living beings. Climate change is portrayed as a form of punishment. From now on, we need to do what science asks of us.

In three novels – *Forty Signs of Rain* (2002), *Sixty Days and Counting* (2003) and *Fifty Degrees Below* (2005), Kim Stanley Robinson has addressed the topic of ecological catastrophe and climate change (global warming). In the trilogy's final volume, after a catastrophe, Frank Vanderwal, a National Science Foundation scientist, decides to live in a large downtown Washington DC park and must adapt to open-air life. He camps out in the trees and experiences climatic vagaries as a return to real life:

> The leaves were beginning to turn, the autumn spectrum invading the green canopy with splashes of yellow and orange and red and bronze. As a Californian Frank had seldom seen it, and had never imagined it properly. He had not understood that the colors would be all mixed together, forming a field of mixed color, like a box of Trix spilled over a lawn – spelling in its gorgeous alien alphabet the end of summer, the passing of time, the omnipresence of mortality. To all who took heed it was an awesome and melancholy sight. He let down Miss Piggy, descended into this new world. He walked absorbed in the new colors, the mushroomy smells of decay, the clattering susurrus of leaves in the wind. (…)
>
> He saw just where he was, moment to moment, and ran without awareness of the ground, free to look about. Joy to be out on days so fresh and sunny, so dappled and yellow. Immersion in the very image and symbol of change; very soon there would come an end to his tenuously established summer routines, he would have to find new ones. He could do that; he was even in a way looking forward to it. But what about the gibbons? They were

> subtropical creatures, as were many of the other ferals. In the zoo they would have been kept inside heated enclosures when temperatures dropped...
>
> (pp. 177–178)

The life of Frank Vanderwal in a Washington park, made exceptional by recent flooding due to climate change, is described in the excerpt above both in terms of his newfound proximity with the natural world, and through his realization of the beauty of the seasons. His own survival will require him to attune his body to the rhythms of the seasons and to the intense cold that is starting to set in. Another question is raised: what will happen to the animals that escaped from the zoo during the recent catastrophe, especially to those exotic species? This quote is particularly interesting since it combines several aspects of environmental change:

> climate change, the seasons, the passing of time and even the climates on the face of the earth since the dawn of time via the representation of exotic species incapable of surviving in this environment. Indeed, the protagonist runs into an aurochs in the same park, a genetically reconstructed animal...
>
> (p. 179)

What does this depiction of a sudden effort to adapt to climate change in an American city tell us? That the effort may be part of a desire to return to mankind's natural state, i.e. to be in close contact with the seasons and natural rhythms forgotten in large cities. Moreover, this narrative, like Roland Emmerich's 2004 catastrophe film *The Day After Tomorrow* provides a good example of the idea that cities themselves are particularly likely to fall victim to climatic catastrophes. Such punishment corresponds with a representation of urban space as human space that is at the root of numerous contemporary problems. Our goal here is not to go into detail about this narrative, which has publicly been widely criticized, but rather to get a better understanding of how it is connected to ordinary narratives of life in the city and climate representations (Adger *et al.*, 2009).

What lessons can we draw?

The first lesson we can draw is that a multi-narrative approach can provide insight into the diverse nature of adaptation to climate change, meaning to the sensory, symbolic and cognitive relationships with an environment that urban planning and adaptation techniques do not often address. This refers to how we envisage our relationship with the world and the interaction between society and the environment, which is the crux of current controversies. The second lesson is that such narratives connect heterogeneous events that illustrate new relationships between events (from the melting of the world's major glaciers to meat consumption, etc.) and this shows the extent to which such narratives are political in the sense that they provide new answers to address the crises we face. But who are the actors of these responses, in a context in which national states appear to be failing? It is hard to name them if we cannot accept ordinary narratives as veritable alternatives to the scientific accounts of climate change. It is, however, important to nuance observations that distinguish between scientific accounts and ordinary narratives. Of course they differ: whereas the actors involved do not describe unique features when talking about climate change, they do describe different sets of facts associated with different systems to measure and observe them. Scientific accounts do not establish an identity bond with the narrator. This separation comforts the thesis according to which modernity is characterized by a move away from traditional knowledge built on the intergenerational transmission of practical experience and collectively held values and on a move towards types of knowledge that rely on positivist epistemology based on measures, the testing of theories and the use of rules to test evidence-based findings (Ingold, 2000). But this separation is in part artificial since different types of knowledge are necessary both for scientists and laypeople (Latour, 1991). Further, the language of vulnerability employed today does not encourage assigning the power to act to those people designated as the victims of changes to come. The narrative sphere of climate change therefore needs to preserve the conditions of a new world that combines and reconciles the unique narrative sphere and the objectified sphere of scientific accounts. We first need to ask how destabilizing can climate change be? What is at stake? Our technology and its development, our economic institutions? Our lifestyles? Our political institutions? Our identity, our survival?

In terms of the relationship with nature, we cannot afford to leave climate change to the scientific realm. It needs to be part of the course of ordinary lives. It is as much a natural phenomenon as it is a cultural phenomenon. Perhaps – and this is a pointer for future research – references to nature are what allow all cultural facts to be rooted in the environmental sphere. The environment, therefore, is the construction from which possibilities emanate for individual and collective life. The environment is the anchoring point for the development of skills and capacities for action. It is a milieu in which humans are involved, that they help shape and that shapes them in return. It is a shared world of humans and non-humans, of culture and nature. Exploring the co-construction of societies and their environments through the intermediary of the capabilities bound up in narratives provides a way to delve further into co-evolutionist approaches. Up to now, human development approaches have focused on the environment as a place to live that offers resources more than a foundation in cultural life. Conversely, classical environmental approaches (dealing with nature protection and conservation) find it hard to focus on human development and cultural issues more specifically. Capability-based analyses (Sen, 2010; Nussbaum, 2011) are among the approaches in the field of human development that are focusing on the multiple dimensions of the relationship between environment and human beings and, therefore, on the idea of a co-emergent nature–culture. The natural–cultural lens – i.e. the meanings given to the environmental productions that actors individually and collectively interiorize (Geertz, 1973) – makes such examination possible. Nature–culture is as such a product of interpretations of the world that generates reflexivity.

Notes

1 According to the IPCC, adaptation includes 'an adjustment in natural or human systems in response to actual or expected climatic stimuli or their effects, which moderates harm or exploits beneficial opportunities', and the capacity for adaptation includes 'an adaptive capacity' (in relation to climate change impacts) which consists of the ability of a system to adjust to climate change (including climate variability and extremes) to moderate potential damages, to take advantage of opportunities, or to cope with the consequences (in IPCC (2007) Climate change, 2007: Impacts, Adaptation and Vulnerability, Contribution of Working Group II to the Fourth Assessment Report of the IPCC. www.ipcc.ch/pdf/assessment-report/ar4/wg2/ar4_wg2_full_report.pdf (Accessed 1 December)).
2 These examples were notably debated during side-event discussion sessions at the Rio+20 summit in June 2012.
3 Interview done by the authors at RIO+20 summit with Melchior Mataki who addressed Salomon Islands' stakes to UN Dialogues (see https://sustainabledevelopment.un.org/content/documents/1154219FINAL%20Solomon%20IslandsSIDs_National_Report_endorsed%20by%20Government%203July2013.pdf; Accessed 1 December 2017).
4 This is also true in the field of cinema. See for example the analyses by Nathalie Magné (2009) Le catastrophisme climatique dans le cinéma grand public. *Ethnologie Française* 4:687–695.

References

Adger, W. N. (2000) Social and ecological resilience: are they related? *Progress in Human Geography* 24(3):347–364.

Adger, W. N. (2001) Scales of governance and environmental justice for adaptation and mitigation of climate change, *Journal of International Development* 13:921–931.

Adger, W. N., Dessai, S., Goulden, M., Hulme, M., Lorenzoni, I., Nelson, D. R., Ness, Wolf, J. and Wreford, A. (2009) Are there social limits to adaptation to climate change? *Climatic Change* 93:335–354.

Albert-Llorca, M. (1991) *L'ordre des choses. Les récits originaux des animaux et des plantes en Europe.* CTHS, Paris.

Alexander T. M. (1987) *John Dewey's Theory of Art, Experience: The Horizons of Feeling, and Nature.* SUNY Press, New York.

Bate, J. (2000) *The Song of the Earth.* Harvard University Press, Cambridge, United States/

Berkes, F. (2008) *Sacred Ecology.* (Second edition). Routledge, New York and London.

Birkeland, I. (2008) Cultural sustainability: industrialism, placeless-ness and the re-animation of place. *Ethics, Place & Environment* 11(3):283–297.

Blanc, N., Waldwogel, C. and Glatron, S. (2011) Le développement urbain durable au prisme des politiques urbaines de prévention de la pollution atmosphérique: quelle place pour le citoyen aujourd'hui? In: G. Pinson, V. Béal and M. Gauthier (eds) *Le développement durable changera-t-il la ville? Le regard des sciences sociales.* Presses universitaires de Saint-Etienne collection Dynamiques Métropolitaines, Saint-Etienne, France: 299–315.

Bremond, C. (1973) *Logique du Récit.* Seuil, Paris.

Geertz, C. (1973) *Interpretations of Culture: Selected Essays.* Basic Books, New York.

Haouès-Jouve, S. (eds) (2010) *Formes urbaines, modes d'habiter et climat urbain dans le périurbain toulousain. Rapport de recherche, programme PIRVE. CNRS-MEEDDAT.* https://halshs.archives-ouvertes.fr/halshs-01019268 (Accessed 13 December 2017).

Hawkes, J. (2001) *The Fourth Pillar of Sustainability. Culture's Essential Role in Public Planning.* Cultural Development Network & Common Ground Press, Melbourne, Australia.

Hoornweg, D., Freire, M., Marcus, J. L., Perinaz, B. T. and Belinda, Y. (2011) *Cities and Climate Change: Responding to an Urgent Agenda. Urban Development Series. World Bank.* https://openknowledge.worldbank.org/handle/10986/2312.

Ingold, T. (2000) *The Perception of the Environment: Essays on Livelihood, Dwelling and Skill.* Routledge, New York.

Latour, B. (1991) *Nous n'avons Jamais été Modernes. Essai d'anthropologie Symétrique.* La Découverte, Poche/Sciences humaines et sociales, Paris.

Lejano, R. P., Tavares, J. and Berkes, F. (2011) *Climate Narratives: What is Modern about Traditional Ecological Knowledge ?* http://socialecology.uci.edu/sites/socialecology.uci.edu/files/users/pdevoe/climatenarratives.pdf (Accessed 8 March 2013).

Mchrotta, S., Natenson, C. E., Omojola, A., Folorunsho, R., Gilbride, J. and Roesenzweig, C. (2009) *Framework for City Climate Risk Assessment, Buenos Aires, Delhi, Lagos, New York.* World Bank Commissioned Research, Marseille, France.

Mondémé, T. (2014) *Fiction et usages cognitifs de la fictionnalité. Kepler, Cyrano, Fontenelle.* PhD Dissertation. University of Versailles Saint-Quentin, Versailles, France. www.theses.fr/2014VERS007S (Accessed 13 December 2017).

Moser, C. and Stein, A. (2011) Implementing urban participatory climate change adaptation appraisals: a methodological guideline. *Environment and Urbanization* 23(2):463.

Nussbaum, M. (2011) *Creating Capabilities. The Human Development Approach.* Harvard University Press, Cambridge, United States.

OECD. (2009) *Integrating Climate Change Adaptation into Development Co-operation, Policy Guidance.* www.oecd.org/environment/cc/44887764.pdf (Accessed 1 December 2017).

Parra, C. and Moulaert, F. (2011) La nature de la durabilité sociale: vers une lecture socioculturelle du développement territorial durable. *Développement Durable et Territoires* 2(2).

Sen, A. (2010) *The Idea of Justice.* Penguin Books, London.

Soiini, K. and Dessein, J. (2016) Culture-sustainability relation: towards a conceptual framework. *Sustainability* 8(167).

Stanley Robinson, K. (2002) *Forty Signs of Rain.* Harper Collins, London.

Stanley Robinson, K. (2003) *Sixty Days and Counting.* Harper Collins, London.

Stanley Robinson, K. (2005) *Fifty Degrees Below.* Harper Collins, London.

Stefanovic, I. (2000) *Safeguarding our Common Future. Rethinking Sustainable Development.* Albany, New York.

UNHabitat. (2011) *Global Report on Human Settlements, Cities and Climate Change.* www.unhabitat.org (Accessed 1 December 2017).

14 Artistic actions for sustainability in a contemporary art exhibition

Ásthildur Jónsdóttir and Chrystalla Antoniou

Introduction

Contemporary art exhibitions have the potential to play a key role for cultural sustainability as they have unique assets to build bridges between different community members, as well as encouraging self-awareness, values and decision-making. Many contemporary artists deal with issues that are disregarded in mainstream culture and politics, but which may be very welcome in educational settings as such issues are suitable for stimulating discussion, awareness and learning. In this chapter one art exhibition in Iceland is examined for the potential it offers in understanding the importance of sustainability and the ethical issues involved in a society's development.

The exhibition 'Challenge' took place at the Árnes Art Museum in Hveragerði, outside Reykjavik, in Iceland, from January to May 2015. The museum, mostly publicly funded, runs various shows of contemporary as well as modern art in its four large exhibition rooms. The museum director approached one of the authors of the chapter, Ásthildur Jónsdóttir, and asked her to curate an exhibition based on sustainability. The resulting exhibition was composed of two participatory artworks and associated workshops. Participatory art originates from the relationship between humans and the social context of creating art. In the participatory approach, the audience is engaged directly in the creative process, allowing members of the audience to become co-authors, editors and observers of the work. Participatory art works have the potential to create a dynamic collaboration between the artist, the audience and their environment (Bishop, 2006). Many visitors came and saw the resulting exhibition, attended associated workshops and guided visits for the public. The events broke attendance records for the museum. The visitors included local residents, travellers, school groups and groups of art teachers.

The exhibition and related activities were fundamental parts of Jónsdóttir's doctoral research which investigated the potential of art in education for sustainability (Jónsdóttir, 2017). Learning for sustainability involves gaining a holistic view of a situation while working towards an understanding of it. Many Nordic scholars put a strong focus on environmental awareness through art education. One inspiration is Helene Illeris, whose works in critical art education focus on aesthetics and environmental protection with a strong relation to values and virtues, aiming at changing society through a transformative pedagogy based in liberation, creativity and consciousness (Illeris, 2012). Jónsdóttir used action research and art-based research methods in her work. The activities at the art museum were assessed through a case study (Stake, 2003) based in an action research model (Kemmis and Wilkinson, 1998). Interviews were conducted with local art teachers and the museum director, as well as with workshop participants.

The aim of this chapter is to describe and explain how an art exhibition can raise awareness of sustainability issues by exhibiting diverse contemporary artworks that deal with different aspects of sustainability. The chapter provides examples of the benefits of promoting sustainability through art exhibitions, and suggests a model that has the potential to be replicated anywhere in the world. In the next section, the selection of artworks is described.

'Challenge': the art exhibition and the selection of artworks

Jónsdóttir selected works by 26 contemporary Icelandic artists that included photography, painting, performance and installations. The selected works indicate a firm connection to the local environment dealing with sustainability and ethical issues involved in a society's development.

The purpose of the workshops and the guided tours was to focus viewers' attention to discussions of environmental issues from the perspective of society. It was an important goal to create settings where visitors had an opportunity to participate in the activities in the exhibition. Participation and communication is the building block for a society of shared responsibilities. From the beginning, when designing the exhibition and planning the theoretical framework of the exhibition, it was a conscious decision to create settings that would open up possibilities of connecting to many-faceted values in society, encouraging solidarity and shared values between generations. Selecting works that have the potential to explain how human creativity is often in close contact with culture, and therefore cultural sustainability can be characterized both by utility and maintaining aesthetic experiences and values.

The selection of the artworks was framed by the wish to show how sustainability is affected by a range of environmental, economic, cultural and social factors which may interact or overlap with each other. Here, it was stressed that changes within one factor can affect another and change can only be sustainable if it takes into account all these factors (Hawkes, 2001). Focusing on educational value, the exhibition aimed at providing an atmosphere that would raise questions relating to the wicked problems of sustainability (Rittel and Webber, 1973). Wicked problems of society often have more than one solution, and a solution in one place and time is not necessarily a solution in another.

Culture was looked at as one of the fundamental aspects of sustainability in relation to environmental, social and economic viewpoints. When curating the exhibition, the selected artworks were linked by the idea of wanting to provoke viewers to consider their joint personal responsibility and help them reflect on values and virtues regarding sustainability (Kagan, 2012; Macdonald and Jónsdóttir, 2014).

The topics of the artworks selected ranged across a wide spectrum of sustainability issues (Jónsdóttir, 2015). The chapter does not allow for a detailed reflection of the selection of all the artworks but there are, however, some important issues that can be highlighted. For example, some of the works exhibited deal with how nature and natural resources are invaluable, providing services that humans cannot live without – services that are important components of a sustainable society (Orr, 2003). Some artworks ask whether sustainability concerns refer to a struggle for a balance between the 'good life' of human beings and the integrity of nature. These are important issues as we know that an imbalance has lead to exceeding the earth's environmental limits (Sampford, 2010; Háskóli Íslands, 2012).

Other works reflect on the effect that humans have on the environment due to society's demands for increased economic growth and the demand for more energy. With Iceland as reference, some artworks question the fast-growing tourist industry and the effects of increased pressure on the natural environment. Two of the works present clear references to nationalist ideas and invite the viewer to ponder the directions in which society has developed and the increased emphasis on the myth of the 'pure nation', as well as the emphasis on cultural stability.

The exhibits aimed to provoke critical thinking and encourage viewers to take a stand on the issues discussed, even demanding their participation. One example of an artwork of this category asked questions about how we utilize our resources and the consequences of inaction. For example, the photographic work *Revelation III*, by Hrafnkell Sigurðsson, shows the unsustainable use of materials by humans with references to the culture of packaging. In the work a plastic bubble-sheet is drifting down to a depth of 20 m in an Icelandic lake. The diameter of the plastic is of the approximate size necessary to wrap the artwork (Figure 14.1).

The works raised questions about consumption and its consequences. Stimulated by the artworks, viewers were invited to reflect on their daily consumption. Consumption is a complex phenomenon and the culprit is seldom one person (Jónsdóttir, 2015). Inaction can be expressed as laziness, lethargy or sloth, leading to a waste of resources.

Some of the works were chosen with the aim of encouraging people to reflect on values and the relationship between humans and nature. The untitled work by Libia Castro and Ólafur Ólafsson is one example, showing the artists wearing Icelandic national costumes, it deals with self- and national-identity and gender roles. On the one hand, a man wears a woman's costume, and on the other, a foreigner wears the national dress. At the same time, by posing in front of an aluminium plant, they raise questions about whether contemporary society has forgotten its connection to nature. In this way they elicit an ethical perspective, encouraging people to reflect on life and culture in connection with heavy

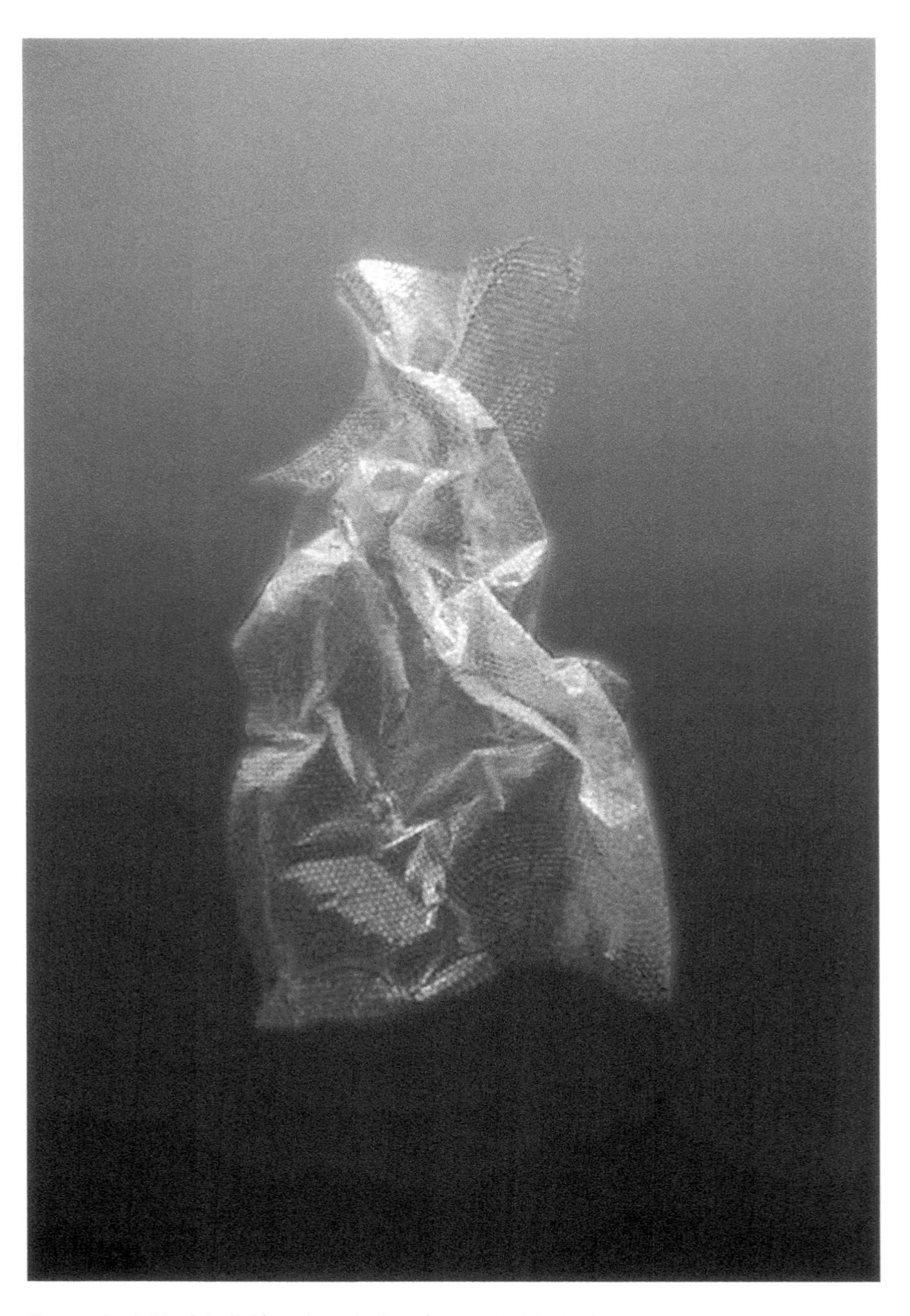

Figure 14.1 Hrafnkell Sigurdsson's *Revelation III*, 2014, photograph, 144 cm × 96 cm.

industry in Iceland. Reflection was invited as to the cost to the environment resulting from harnessing natural resources. This work created a dialogue with other works exhibited that raised questions regarding human beings' connection to nature (Figure 14.2).

Learning from artwork: the role of place

The main focus in this and the next section is to discuss some theoretical perspectives of the exhibition as a learning process based in arts-based environmental education, which can be viewed as one tradition within a broad programme of education for sustainability. Art activities offer unique ways of interpreting and signifying aesthetic experiences. Both through looking at and making art, people can develop their ability to come closer to reality and their inner self. At the same time, such activities feed and guide human sensibilities for reality and life. Art activities invite a more indirect and unforeseen learning process to take shape. Different kinds of learning take place when humans connect to the natural world through art compared with connecting to it via knowledge developed from scientific methods (van Boeckel, 2014).

Some contemporary artworks are well suited to help us approach the issues we face regarding sustainability through diverse perspectives and issues such as ecology, the environment, equality and philosophy. Such artworks raise questions of who we are, what we prioritize in our lives, what our relationship is to

Figure 14.2 Libia Castro and Ólafur Ólafsson's untitled portrait of the artists wearing the Icelandic national women's costume (peysuföt and upphlutur), 2000, photograph, 50 cm × 75 cm.

the world surrounding us, how we behave and the impact our behaviour has on our environment and on our society. The impression or emotion created by artworks can be long-lasting. The arts make vivid the fact that words in their literal form and numbers are limited in their ability to represent the world, i.e. the limits of our language do not define the limits of our cognition (Eisner, 2009).

Many countries and a wide range of schools and educational traditions are now oriented towards United Nations Educational, Scientific and Cultural Organization's (UNESCO) learning pillars for sustainable development, which focus on gaining a holistic view of a situation while working towards an understanding of it (Jónsdóttir, 2011; UNESCO, 2012). Such learning goes beyond raising awareness by addressing underlying issues and values that lead to unsustainable practices in our daily lives and by challenging some of the assumptions that underpin day-to-day practices.

Artists, in whatever medium they work, often create works that are closely related to the social context and are influenced by current affairs. Artists' works can explore ideas, concepts, questions and practices that examine the past, describe the present and imagine the future (Hicks and King, 2007). Teaching critical thinking is often part of education for sustainability, increasing the competence of students in identifying values and understanding the importance of taking action and being an active participant in a community (Breiting *et al.*, 2005). Art projects that engage with sustainability offer a combination of critical and creative thinking, often focusing on perceiving and exposing social and political contradictions, and thereby empowering viewers and participants to transform oppressive conditions.

Artwork can help a viewer interpret, research and create art that deals with concepts related to sustainable development, use different kinds of materials in a sustainable manner and maintain and develop a technical knowledge and understanding of materials. As in the other Nordic countries, the focus in Iceland since the mid-1990s has been on encouraging students' exploration of their own fascination with popular culture through a quest for alternative, open-ended and reflexive conceptions of art education in relation to concepts such as curiosity, fascination, polycentrism and performance (Illeris and Arvedsen, 2011). With its diverse educational approaches art education has the potential to engage students in learning about sustainability.

Starting in the middle of last century, scholars began to develop a curriculum that is founded on and related to the environment, starting with environmental education and later developing with a focus on place-based education (Gruenewald and Smith, 2007; Birkeland, 2014; Somerville and Green, 2015). Scholars have developed ideas on place and locale that involve people and the communication that occurs within a place (Knapp, 2005). It has been useful for educators to use a place-based approach to create settings that give people a particular and personal interest in society and the land (Gruenewald, 2003; Jónsdóttir, 2013) and to provide a good basis for working with sustainability. Meaningful education provides students with the opportunity to work on projects that create connections between the place of the curriculum and the place of the students, to one another and their own experiences. Students are encouraged to think critically when the particular qualities of the local environment are valued and questioned in relationship to assumptions about progress and human relationships to nature. In this way, teaching becomes responsive to ecology and local culture as the learning experience is explicitly rooted in the location of the learner (Graham, 2007).

An experiential and cultural approach to sustainability in art exhibitions

Sustainability has been related predominantly to its environmental aspects and this relationship has been well documented in literature on education for sustainable development, which covers many research traditions and educational practices (Sandell *et al.*, 2005). The broad concept of sustainability requires interwoven contributions from various disciplines to cover a broad range of knowledges, values, skills, attitudes and practices.

An experiential approach based in the educational principles of John Dewey (1938) makes it possible to go beyond unilateral approaches of sustainability that are tied to particular scientific aspects – often limited to either ecology or the social sciences. An experiential approach operates in terms of the deeper and larger issues of education offering possibilities for learning from direct experience. One relevant approach focuses on the cultural perspective. Eagan *et al.* (2002) highlight the importance of understanding the influence of culture through facilitating cultural communication when investigating and assessing issues related to the environment and sustainability. Even though the Brundtland Commission's report (WCED, 1987), which put forward a key definition for sustainable development, showed little attention to culture, recognition of its key role in sustainability appears to be growing and the academic sustainability agenda has widened, incorporating a broader cultural perspective into the former narrow scientific and technical focus (Brooks and Ryan, 2008).

The ways in which culture is approached in the framework of sustainability vary. For example, for Hawkes (2001) culture forms a separate fourth pillar in the three-pillar model of sustainability composed by the environment, the society and the economy, whereas for Worts (2011), culture is the foundation for the rest. Dessein *et al.* (2015) have presented a more complete model that represents three different roles that culture adopts in the sustainability framework, namely the self-standing, the mediating and the transformative. The self-standing role refers to culture as an autonomous pillar but linked with the other three well-established pillars, the ecological, social and economic. The mediating role is defined by culture for sustainable development as a situation in which culture adopts a connecting role, acting as a driver of sustainability processes. Lastly, the transformative role of culture for sustainable development gives culture an evolutionary role for creating sustainability. The different approaches are evidence of the academic efforts to find a position for culture in the framework of sustainability and show the recognition of its relevance and significance on a theoretical level.

On a practical level, art exhibitions and contemporary art in particular, have a pivotal role to play. Contemporary art exhibitions have the potential to engage people with all aspects of sustainability, from multiple perspectives and with alternatives paths (Kagan, 2012). Contemporary art exhibitions that intend to promote sustainability indicate that settings in museums and galleries can be created and shaped to shed light on various issues. For example, instead of displaying impartiality in ideas, practices and activities of the past an exhibition can promote environmental learning by highlighting the causes of environmental damage (Barrett and McManus, 2007: p. 332). Museums in particular have the potential to develop new audiences, engaging young people in innovative ways, according to the philosopher Bourriaud (2002). When institutions such as art museums actively solicit engagement and contribution from visitors they can make a significant impact on the health and vitality of the organization (Simon, 2010).

The existence of learning resources and informal educational infrastructure is highly significant, but not sufficient if individuals are not able to effectively and efficiently utilize them, and if they do not have guidance in knowing how to mix and match them (Falk, 2005). Therefore, it is important to analyse if and how teachers' awareness, readiness and skills are crucial when analysing learning outcomes concerning education for sustainability when using contemporary art exhibitions as learning resources and infrastructure. It is reasonable to argue that teachers need guidance, training, collaboration and experiences through which their skills can be enhanced. A curator can create a setting for teachers, students and the general public and facilitate active participants in the exhibition. When making educational use of the exhibition, sustainability issues can be considered through an artistic lens.

In the next section, the art exhibition 'Challenge' is analysed. The analysis focuses on the close partnership which was developed with local schools and which placed the learning process within the community, thus reflecting the concepts of collaboration, collectivism and shared responsibility in a concrete manner.

Analysis of the art exhibition 'Challenge'

The remainder of the chapter describes the results of the analysis of the exhibition. Each participant acknowledged that the exhibit had been beneficial for their professional life.

One of the artworks was called *Our Nature – My Wishes for the Future* (Figure 14.3). In that project the artist invited young people from the South of Iceland to take part in creating artwork in the form of a book. In the book-art the participants discussed their vision of the future and their hopes for future generations. Each participant was invited to create a page in the book-art with the collective aim of fostering a sense that art can be a dynamic part of our lives, and provide a lens through which each and every one of us can examine our perspectives on life. This participatory art was not just something that the visitors stood still in front of and quietly looked at; instead they co-created it.

Figure 14.3 *Our Nature – My Wishes for the Future* and workshop view at the exhibition 'Challenge', 2015.

Source: Ásthildur Jónsdóttir.

The role of *Our Nature – My Wishes for the Future* was to provide a context for dialogue between young people and the exhibition's visitors about the art exhibition as a whole. It included the voices of the local children that visited the exhibition with their schools and took part in making the book-art after looking at and interpreting the messages they found in the exhibition. The book-art created a space which fuelled the students' interest in those elements of our society that might be improved. The students had the opportunity to freely express their opinions, allowing each and every one to develop his/her position on issues by listening, reflecting, exploring and assessing arguments. All the participants offered strong connections to their own lived experience. The book-art thus provided a potential to empower communities and strengthen the public's awareness of environmental issues, as well as to enhance the influence that the public, through civic action, can have on the decisions of those in power.

It was not possible for all schools in the county to bring the students to the museum. The artist brought the book-art project out of the museum and visited two schools that had expressed interest in taking part in the project. One of the art teachers expressed gratitude for that effort:

> It is so important for the schools to be exposed to artworks in their daily schooling. In our village there is only one sculpture and a few older artworks inside the school. To get artists to come into our school and work with us on contemporary issues is very valuable.

Before starting their creative practice, the students were shown photos of the artworks exhibited and given space for interpretation and discussions. By creating a page for the book, each student took on the responsibility of completing a project that explored issues concerning their own community. They identified natural elements in their environment that they considered important to conserve, and expressed their wishes for a better future. One student explained it in this way:

> I wish for future generations to be able enjoy clean beautiful waterfalls; I wish that the children of the future will be able to play outdoors; I wish for peace on earth; I hope future generations will learn to enjoy the birds of the sky.

Other exhibition visitors were also actively participating by making their own pages for the project, thus adding to it during the actual exhibition. The approach used in the school was based on the notion of place-based education, where the students created meaning that can be related to personal experience in their own locality. The participants had access to a variety of materials, so that each one participant found a way for personal expression and experimentation. One of the teachers described her students' experience:

> The work provided my students the chance to be the centre of the experience at the art exhibition. Together they created knowledge by reflecting on the artwork shown in the exhibit. Their awareness of nature, that is normally tacit, became more concrete.

The participatory nature of some of the works in the exhibition and the workshops gave the museum the potential to create a two-way communication model establishing a sense of trust and respect in its audiences, taking on the characteristics of a 'forum' (Cameron, 1971). Another teacher who visited the exhibit with her family said: 'The participatory art making engaged the students so that they become a part of the artistic process in some way. The book-art allowed the spectator to help complete the piece, making the students a part of the team'. A teacher who later created similar work with all the students in a big school in Reykjavík where she works as an art director stated:

> I felt it was the issue of diverse students' observation that became the key factor in determining the success of this project. I think works like these are important for museum guests so they will feel personally included in the museum when they see people like themselves and their children represented.

One of the participating teachers noted that students reported proudly in school how their work was an important part of the exhibit. Another teacher, who visited the exhibition with a group of women from her neighbourhood, noted:

> They all felt so proud of how the children's observations were 'spot on' discussing issues that are very important for our community. I am not sure if

children from Reykjavík would have the same connections. Our children are used to being more connected to nature.

This comment showed the importance of the local dimension. The role of place and the students' interpretation of it played an important role in how they experienced the processes and participation in the art-book. Working with the home-place as a teaching resource has great potential in a place-based education and has the potential of creating place literacy (Birkeland and Aasen, 2012; Birkeland, 2014). Another teacher explained the importance of bringing her students' artworks out into the community: 'The kids take their own works more seriously and show them more respect when they are exhibited in a context like this'.

Other museum activities and workshops

During the time the exhibition was running, creative activities in workshops were offered. One of the four big rooms in the gallery was designed as a workshop and the book-art described above was exhibited there. When designing the exhibit, a wishing wheel was created to foster the concept of learning to care, allowing visitors to contribute their wishes for the future. That gave them the possibility of reflecting on their own wishes in their daily habits with the hope, which concurs with Hay (2006), that we need to change ourselves in order to make lasting changes to the world. The workshop space was always open for visitors, some of whom came many times. An older lady attended three of the workshops and said she felt part of the exhibition. Some of the schoolchildren came during their leisure time to revisit their work and create more works.

A course was given to the art teachers in the county before the exhibition opened, to assist them with planning on how they could include this exhibit in their practice. The Art Teachers' Association of Iceland was invited to visit the exhibit and discuss the connection to the national curriculum where sustainability is among the six fundamental concerns. The teachers were satisfied and said it was easier for them to understand what is expected from them in the curriculum framework. Guided talks were also frequently offered with the aim of provoking a dialogue, which would shed light on issues related to the links between nature and culture, in reference also to social and economic aspects.

Some of the workshops were specially targeted at families with a focus on recognizing the value of, and integrating where possible, traditional knowledge and intergenerational considerations. Other target groups such as women, senior citizens and art teachers had different themes and foci. The workshops were offered to build the public's awareness and practical knowledge of sustainability. That was done by encouraging discussion and sharing stories connected to the artworks in the exhibition.

Closed workshops were also offered for schools, providing diverse approaches to education for sustainability by creating artistic activities aimed at understanding how natural, cultural, economic and social systems work and are interdependent. With these activities, the Árnes Museum focused on the integrative role of promoting and implementing sustainability in Icelandic society. With this exhibition, the museum concentrated on building links with greater vitality to their community and engagement, becoming a place where conversations take place and through which change is initiated.

When organizing the workshops Elliot Eisner's (2009) principles were kept in mind, making the setting a means or tool to reconceptualize personal identity as well as connect to culture and society – to engage with the values of others and to participate and contribute through embodied knowledge. Different forms of knowledge, old and new, became a focus of the workshops. Knowledge was understood as local knowledge, which refers to knowledge that is unique to a given culture or society, originating from place-based life modes. Different artefacts were looked at and their common aspects were discussed and considered. The creators based their work on knowledge from their own backgrounds, experiences and prior understandings with the hope that it would lead to something good. The participants in many of the workshops were asked to reflect on the artworks in the exhibition and to create an artefact that could help them remember their hope for a better world with greater empathy, equity and tolerance. One of the visitors, an art teacher expressed:

> This exhibition has stayed with me ever since I saw it. I think it is great when artwork reminds you of who you are and helps you to sharpen your values in life. When organizing my teaching for this term, this exhibit was on my mind.

One of the workshops reflected on the world's over-consumption of plastic. The participants discussed plastic consumption in society and reflected on the negative consequences of over- consumption. The participants, who had all been asked to bring with them used 'worthless' plastic bags, learned a technique to iron together many layers of old plastic bags and left-over fabrics. From the new fabric they sewed multipurpose bags, most of which the participants aimed to use as grocery bags. One of the participants noted:

> It was amazing how everyone that participated and had brought in worthless plastic bags that normally would end up in the garbage started to think of them differently. They all wanted to take them back and use them. When I was organizing my teaching for the fall semester I drew from this idea where I have my students use this technique to create bags that we will sell for charity. This also strengthens the concepts that our actions matter.

One of the workshops was held at the same time as the town's flower festival, housed in the only horticultural school in Iceland. The focus of the workshop was to create mandalas. The mandala is a profound and universal symbol of continuity, integration and interconnectedness because in the beginning is the end and in the end is the beginning. All kinds of flowers, plants and natural elements were selected and laid out as material for creation. The participants were given an explanation of the nature of mandalas and how everything, within and around us, is composed of mandalas, the circle being the template of creation. With images put up in the workshop, the space and the principles that provide the foundation for all mathematics, science, geometry, biology and of natural and manmade architecture were explained (Cunningham, 2002).

The different workshops, the participatory works and the 'Challenge' exhibition as a whole give evidence of how academic efforts can support the creation of an exhibition based on a framework of education for sustainability. When interviewed, the museum visitors recognized the exhibition relevance and significance as a driver of sustainability in their lives, both professionally as well as personally. One of them stated:

> Visiting this exhibition and a workshop for art teachers not only gave me many ideas and insights on how to address sustainability in my classroom, it also gave me a better understanding of this complex phenomenon personally. I'm more concerned about respecting nature in my daily consumption.

All the workshops offered in connection to the exhibition engaged the participants both individually and collectively in the creative, expressive, inclusive and responsive processes of the arts as they developed confidence in themselves as creators. They realized there could be many answers to the same problem. This is the key distinction and dimension of making art and engaging in a design process, and according to Eisner (2002), one of the principal points in teaching art.

Conclusion and reflection

The aims of the project were achieved since the art educators that took part in some of the workshops have reported on how they have continued to develop their understanding of education for sustainability. Some art teachers have reflected on how useful they have found it to use the exhibition catalogue when discussing sustainability. The visitors of the exhibition and the participants in the workshops were able to interpret the artworks based on their prior lived experience. In the exhibition the viewers used the opportunity to consider and even debate the artistic reflections of sustainability wicked problems. The artworks questioned assumptions that are generally accepted as true without looking for counter-arguments. The exhibition created an arena to help visitors raise questions, creating a space for discussing tensions within the world and exhibiting works that themselves are connected to their experiences.

The exhibition 'Challenge' created conditions where visitors and workshops attendees were active participants on the different platforms offered. The Árnes museum took on a role as an advocate for sustainability by inviting the general public, educators and families to be active participants and find their personal connection to sustainable development. All art teachers interviewed agreed that the exhibition delivered transformational learning both for them and their students that aroused increasing interest in sustainability.

Responses to issues of sustainability have implications for the field of art education and can influence trends and changes in the environment of education for sustainability and art education. There is a general need for wide-ranging discussion and a focus on education for sustainability within society, including schools. In the assessment of the exhibition, Jónsdóttir felt that the diverse voices of the artists involved and direct contact with them were missing. These reflections led to two exhibitions inspired by 'Challenge' being opened in New York in 2016. One entitled 'Art for Action: Icelandic art in the service of sustainability' was held at the United Nations and the other, entitled 'Borrowed Time', in Scandinavia House. Here, she included recordings of the artists' reflections and thoughts about their own works so museum guests could listen to them during their visit.

The concrete examples given in this chapter may inspire more curators, artists and teachers to take a step towards working with the arts as a means for promoting sustainability through a unifying approach working with the nature–culture interface. Museums, both because of their collections and because of their role as community gathering places, can be forces for intercultural communication and understanding of sustainability.

References

Barrett, J. and McManus, P. (2007) Civilising nature: Museums and the environment. In: G. Birch (ed.) *Water Wind Art and Debate. How Environmental Concerns Impact on Disciplinary Research*. Sydney University Press, Sydney: 319–344.

Birkeland, I. (2014) *Kulturelle hjørnesteiner*. Cappelen Damm, Oslo.

Birkeland, I and Aasen, A. (2012) Ecopsychology and education: Place literacy in early childhood education. In: M. J. Rust and N. Totton (eds) *Vital Signs: Psychological Responses to Ecological Crisis*. Karnac Books, London: 105–117.

Bishop, C. (2006) *Participation: Documents of Contemporary Art*. Whitechapel Gallery/ The MIT Press, New York.

Bourriaud, N. (2002) *Relational Aesthetics*. Les presses du reel, Dijon, France.

Breiting, S., Mayer, M. and Mogensen, F. (2005) *Quality criteria for ESD schools: Guidelines to enhance the quality of education for sustainable development*. Austrian Federal Ministry of Education, Science and Culture. http://seed.schule.at/uploads/QC_eng_2web.pdf (Accessed 20 August 2015).

Brooks, C. and Ryan, A. (2008) *Education for Sustainable Development. Interdisciplinary Discussion Series Report*. Higher Education Academy, Southampton, United Kindom.

Cameron, D. (1971) The museum: A temple or a forum? *Curator* 14(1):11–24.

Castro, L. and Ólafsson, Ó. (2000) Untitled (Portrait of the artists wearing the Icelandic national women's costume) [Photograph 50 cm × 75 cm]. With courtesy of the artists.

Cunningham, B. (2002) *Mandala: Journey to the Center*. DK Publishing, London.

Dessein, J., Soini, K., Fairclough, G. and Horlings, L. (eds) (2015) *Culture in, for and as Sustainable Development: Conclusions from the COST Action IS1007 Investigating Cultural Sustainability*. University of Jyväskylä, Jyväskylä, Finland.

Dewey, J. (1938) *Experience & Education*. Simon & Schuster, New York.

Eagan, P., Cook, T. and Joeres, E. (2002) Teaching the importance of culture and interdisciplinary education for sustainable development. *International Journal of Sustainability in Higher Education* 3(1):48–66.

Eisner, E. W. (2002) *The Arts and the Creation of Mind.* Yale University Press, New Haven, United States.

Eisner, E. (2009) What education can learn from the arts. *Art Education* 62(2):6–9.

Falk, J. H. (2005) Free-choice environmental learning: Framing the discussion. *Environmental Education Research* 11(3):265–280.

Graham, M. A. (2007) Art, ecology and art education: Locating art education in a critical place-based pedagogy. *Studies in Art Education* 48(4):375–390.

Gruenewald, D. A. (2003) The best of both worlds: A critical pedagogy of place. *Educational Researcher* 32(4):3–12.

Gruenewald, D. A. and Smith, G. (2007) *Place-Based Education in the Global Age: Local Diversity.* Lawrence Erlbaum, Philadelphia, United States.

Háskóli Íslands. (2012) *Sjálfbærni- og umhverfisstefna.* (University of Iceland. Sustainability and environment policy). Háskóli Íslands, Reykjavik, Iceland.

Hay, R. (2006) Becoming ecosynchronous, Part 2. Achieving sustainable development via personal development. *Sustainable Development* 14:1–15.

Hawkes, J. (2001) *The Fourth Pillar of Sustainability: Culture's Essential Role in Public Planning.* Common Ground, Champaign, United States.

Hicks, L. and King, R. (2007) Confronting environmental collapse: Visual culture, art education, and environmental responsibility. *Studies in Art Education* 48(4): 332–335.

Illeris, H. (2012) Aesthetic learning processes for the 21st century: Epistemology, didactics, performance. *Journal of the International Society for Teacher Education* 16(1):10–19.

Illeris, H. and Arvedsen, K. (2011) Visual phenomena and visual events: Some reflections around the curriculum of visual culture pedagogy. *Synnyt/Origins Finnish Studies in Art* 2.

Jónsdóttir, Á. (2011) *Listir og sjálfbærni, Áhrifamáttur sjónlista í menntun til sjálfbærni (Art and sustainability. The potential of arts in ES).* http://netla.hi.is/arslok-2011 (Accessed 18 May 2015).

Jónsdóttir, Á. (2013) Art and place-based education for the understanding of sustainability. *Education in the North* 20(Special Issue):90–105.

Jónsdóttir, Á. (2015) *Challenge.* (Exhibition catalogue) Listasafn Árnesinga, Hveragerði, Iceland.

Jónsdóttir, Á. (2017) *Artistic Action for Sustainability: Potential of Art in Education for Sustainability.* Lapland University Press, Rovaniemi, Finland.

Kagan, S. (2012) *Toward Global (Environ) Mental Change Transformative: Art and Cultures of Sustainability. Volume 20.* Heinrich Böll Stiftung, Berlin.

Kemmis, S. and Wilkinson, M. (1998) Participatory action research and the study of practice. In: S. Kemmis, P. Weeks, B. Atweh (eds) *Action Research in Practice: Partnerships for Social Justice in Education.* Routledge, London: 21–36.

Knapp, C. E. (2005) The 'I-Thou' relationship, place-based education and Aldo Leopold. *Journal of Experiential Education* 27(3):277–285.

Macdonald, A. and Jónsdóttir, Á. (2014). Participatory virtues in art education for sustainability. In: T. Jokela and G. Coutts (eds) *Relate North: Engagement, Art and Representation.* Lapland University Press, Rovaniemi, Finland:82–104.

Orr, D. W. (2003) *Four Challenges of Sustainability.* School of Natural Resources, University of Vermont, Burlington, United States.

Rittel, H. and Webber, M. (1973) Dilemmas in a general theory of planning. *Policy Sciences* 4:155–169.

Sandell, K., Öhman, J. and Ôstman, L. (2005) *Education for Sustainable Development*. Studentlitteratur, Lund, Sweden.

Sampford, C. (2010) Re-conceiving the good life: The key to sustainable globalization. *Australian Journal of Social Issues* 45(1):13–24.

Sigurðsson, H. (2014) *Revelation III* [Photograph 144 cm × 96 cm]. With courtesy of the artist.

Simon, N. (2010) *The Participatory Museum*. www.participatorymuseum.org/read/ (Accessed 1 December 2017).

Somerville, M. and Green, M. (2015) *Children, Place and Sustainability*. Palgrave, Basingstoke, United Kingdom.

Stake, R. (2003) Case studies. In: N. K. Denzin and Y. S. Lincoln (eds) *Strategies of Qualitative Inquiry*. (Second edition). Sage Publications, Thousand Oaks, United States: 134–164.

UNESCO. (2012) *Exploring Sustainable Development: A Multiple-Perspective Approach. United Nations Decade of Education for Sustainable Development (2005–2014)*. https://sustainabledevelopment.un.org/content/documents/732unesco.pdf (Accessed 1 December 2017).

van Boeckel, J. (2014) *At the Heart of Art and Earth*. Aalto University, Helsinki.

WCED. (1987) *Our Common Future*. Oxford University Press, Oxford, United Kingdom.

Worts, D. (2011) Culture and museums in the winds of change: the need for cultural indicators. *Culture and Local Governance* 3(1):117–132.

15 Media aesthetic methodologies

Analysing media stories of nature and wildlife

Nina Svane-Mikkelsen

Introduction

Whatever we say or otherwise express reveals our relationship with the world around us and affects our surroundings directly or indirectly. Living in the epoch of the Anthropocene – a geological era where human activities have significant global impact on Earth's ecosystems (Crutzen and Stoermer, 2000; Castree, 2016) – the need to develop environmentally sustainable practices is becoming increasingly urgent. Addressing and challenging common conceptions of nature and wildlife is one approach that can help us to facilitate environmental sustainability.

Worldviews form the basis for our actions both on an individual and a collective level through political decision-making, economic dispositions and so forth. Ways of thinking of nature are inevitably linked to behaviour that affects the environment and thus to whether environmental sustainability is achievable or not. Our conceptions of nature can therefore represent a cultural barrier to change and, consequently, contribute to the major environmental problems of today such as climate change and biodiversity loss. The cultural vectors in this equation can be described as 'cultural carriers', a term borrowed from peace psychology (Warren and Moghaddam, 2011). Cultural carriers can be objects, practices, concepts or other cultural expressions that maintain certain normative meanings over time. They exert a powerful influence on human societies, often sustaining continuity through times of political, economic and legal change (ibid.). Hence, cultural carriers can be vehicles for maintaining a desirable or undesirable status quo. The aim of this chapter is to present ways to explore cultures of nature, as part of investigating and supporting cultural sustainability. This will be done by analysing popular stories of wildlife as examples of important cultural carriers that shape conceptions of nature and thus contribute to defining nature–culture interfaces on a global scale.

In modern Western society, mass media and other media are central arenas for establishing and negotiating our cultural interpretations of nature and wildlife. Nature and wildlife genres flourish in the media and are hugely popular, the television productions made by British Broadcasting Corporation (BBC) Natural History Unit being examples (BBC Studios, 2016). With more and more people living in big cities, people increasingly have more of their encounters with nature and wildlife through mass media and the internet rather than through direct physical contact.

Media and communication studies can contribute to sustainability by providing insights into the interface between culture and nature. For instance, media studies can provide a deeper knowledge of cultural interpretations of nature by making thick descriptions and carrying out content-analysis of how nature and wildlife are mediated. Media here are defined as technical and linguistic devices for communication. They have a significant cultural influence and operate across a variety of communicative architectures – e.g. newspapers, radio, etc. (Gentikow, 2006). In this chapter, the focus is on the visual media of documentary film and photography where stories of nature are explored through a media aesthetic analysis. The aim of the analysis is twofold. First, to explore examples of widespread and popular media stories of nature in order to illustrate how we frame nature. By studying how nature is understood in popular communication and how ideas of nature are expressed through sound and images, we can identify what kind of storytelling might support sustainable development and thus demonstrate (media)cultural possibilities. Second, through these concrete 'walk-through'-analyses, the chapter will show how media aesthetic analysis can be a useful analytical tool for researchers, politicians, non-governmental organizations and nature communicators of different kinds (e.g. media producers, teachers, museum employees and nature guides). In general, all people engaged with environmental issues can benefit from developing better understandings of the whats and hows of nature–culture interfaces within Western (popular) culture and the public sphere. Media aesthetic analysis can be applied to any cultural expression, so the area of application is extremely wide.

Introducing media aesthetic analysis

What is media aesthetic analysis exactly? It is a way of conducting aesthetic research and a qualitative analytical method with connections to visual culture studies. It includes the researcher in the analytical process and is particularly suitable for deep qualitative description and analysis of mediated communication. The method provides deep and critical reflections on cultural expressions and aesthetic everyday experiences, reflections that co-think the theme of the expression, the form of expression and the media technology. As the Norwegian media researcher Liv Hausken points out, media aesthetics provides a picture of the role the media's different modes of expression play in communicating the subject matter (2009: p. 8). The attention of the researcher is directed towards communication and mediation, the materiality of the communication, the communication technology and the media experiences that the given expression seems to play on or imply (ibid.: p. 9).

An important part of a media aesthetic project is to develop a language for that which you, at any time, want to shed light on (ibid.: p. 168). Media aesthetic method is about looking out for theoretical, aesthetic and practical challenges and openings (ibid.: p. 185). Taking on this approach we ask questions such as: what is told when nature is communicated? How is it done? How is the audience's attention regulated? What aesthetic grips are used? What media experiences are activated and how do these affect the meaning of the expression?

Doing media aesthetic analysis across different media types makes it possible to accentuate characteristics of the different media and expressions, and therefore there is an implicit invitation to look across different media types (ibid.). The researcher's eye gets sharpened and directed towards details, gets tuned in towards meanings and sets of problems that unfold as the analysis develops. New areas of focus and interest appear through the engagement with the empirical material at hand, through the detailed description of the media work that is explored. Along the way, the researcher gets an eye for and focuses on details the person in question does not normally see. This can pave the way for new directions where objects of analysis and foci of analysis become relevant along the way in the analytical process (ibid.). We can demonstrate how this works by analysing examples of nature stories, starting with wildlife photographs on show in the streets of Oslo in Norway, followed by the wildlife tradition of BBC and Sir David Attenborough.

Spectacular wildlife photographs by Steve Bloom

People walking the streets of Oslo in Norway could coincidentally run into a large number of monumental photographs exhibited outside on the street from June to October in 2007. A media aesthetic approach can be applied to this exhibition (hence the move to present tense).

A large number of photographs, each approximately 100 cm × 150 cm, is mounted on rectangular concrete pillars that are placed on the ground in a curved row (see Figure 15.1). The large colour photographs are typical wildlife shots. The motives are mainly beautiful scenery and close ups of '... wild animals in their natural surroundings' as it is written on a poster introducing the exhibition (Bloom *et al.*, 2007).

The photographs are impressive by their sheer size, glossy surface and technical perfection. It is easy to become intrigued by their beauty. A monkey is depicted surrounded by white steam, its greyish silverfish coloured fur blending smoothly with the soft tones of the damp landscape (see Figure 15.2). The monkey, which we can read is a Japanese Macaque, sometimes called a 'snow monkey', is sitting alone in water, and looks as if it is bathing and enjoying it. Its hand is placed on its fur, the fingers are slim and delicate and it is gently touching itself. The landscape around the animal is rocky, underpinning the grey nuances of the image with stony-grey tones. The steam coming from the water may also be from the sky. The impression is that heaven and earth is one. The beauty of the motive makes quite an impact. Taking a glance over the area it is clear that several photographs look almost like family portraits (like the portrait of snow monkeys seen in Figure 15.1) and several are close-up photographs of animals' eyes, as if the photographer is seeking to meet the animal's gaze, to get

Figure 15.1 Overview of Steve Bloom's exhibition 'Spirit of the Wild', Oslo 2007.
Source: Nina Svane-Mikkelsen.

as close as possible. What is the purpose of this? To seek close contact? Does the photographer think an animal's soul can be revealed this way?

On a large poster the exhibition is introduced and we can read that the title of the exhibition is 'Spirit of the Wild' and that Steve Bloom is the photographer. Bloom is exhibiting in collaboration with World Wildlife Fund (WWF) and an organization called CO+Life. From the poster we can read that CO+Life promote photographic projects involving the environment, nature, animals, human life and living conditions. Synergies between these elements are highlighted to support principles of sustainable development. CO+Life exhibitions aim to promote better knowledge of the earth and the world we live in, and of how we can influence the Earth's development and environment (Bloom *et al.*, 2007). So, the agenda is clear, this is work that is meant to support environmental sustainability.

When it comes to accessibility they have done a good job. A lot of people pass by, stop and look at the photographs. By making oversized images and exhibiting in public space they make the work accessible, but what are they saying more precisely? What culture of nature communication is displayed here?

Figure 15.2 Steve Bloom's photograph of a bathing snow monkey in the exhibition 'Spirit of the Wild', Oslo 2007.

Source: Nina Svane-Mikkelsen.

Monkeys and water

Bloom's photographic works in 'Spirit of the Wild' is accompanied by texts about the animals depicted and these are surprisingly romanticizing and anthropomorphic; they interfere with the experience of the photographs. For instance, the photograph of the bathing snow monkey is commented upon by Steve Bloom like this:

> A snow monkey appears through a translucent veil of rising steam. The hot steam is her sanctuary. Her small oasis in the vast chill. Immersed in the warmth, she gazes intently at her own arm. I, too, become drawn into her contemplation, discovering her long elegant fingers, perfectly formed nails, intricate folds on her knuckles; details like yours and mine.
>
> (Steve Bloom in Bloom *et al.*, 2007)

After reading this, the image of the monkey emerges as a story of a female (monkey) bathing, with 'monkey' in parenthesis. Bloom's choice of words like 'sanctuary', 'oasis', 'immersed' and 'warmth', 'contemplation', 'discovering' (her own body), 'elegant', 'perfectly formed' and 'intricate', combined with the widespread use of 'she' and 'her' and attention to the direction of the animal's gaze as inward and directed towards its own body, makes the description remarkably anchored in traditional gender roles, coupling traditional notions of femininity with this female animal. It is all about *her* beauty, pleasure and contemplation on *her* own body.

Looking for the same photograph in Bloom's book *Untamed* (Bloom, 2004: p. 145), we find it printed over a whole page without any text and over the next pages accompanied with other images of monkeys bathing at the same spot. In this presentation the story about these monkeys appears far less gendered. In the back of the same book there is a list of small bookmark-images with explanatory texts. The text following the image of the bathing snow monkey is also a lot more neutral than the text in the exhibition. In the book, the traditional language of biology is used: it is stated that a solitary snow monkey, 'Enveloped in steam, examines her hand intently' and that 'social improvement can occur within the troop due to these intelligent primates' ability to learn unusual skills such as washing their food, diving for shellfish and bathing in geothermal springs' and '(c)onsequently, a general social improvement can occur within the troop' (Bloom, 2004: p. 418).

It is perhaps hard to avoid genderization and romantification of animals in photography, but it is important to analyse this and its effects. By being reflexive, we can aim for variation and multiple nature and animal stories. There is for example some justification for allowing ideas of an animal's emotion and (self-) reflection to play a part in the description of higher primates such as monkeys and apes. Bloom's identification with and compassion for the animals is needed in order to develop more respectful behaviours towards them and the environment. More love expressed about our fellow creatures on this planet is a good thing. Bloom applies, however, very gender specific attributes and properties to the female monkey. It *is* an extremely anthropomorphic description, and maybe also depiction, of an animal. The image and text say a lot more about humans than about animals or nature. This is neither good nor bad, but we must not forget that this is true for any story we make about nature.

Perhaps monkeys' and apes' interactions with water echo something in us and reminds us of our own experiences with water? There are more photographs of higher primates and water in 'Spirit of the Wild': a chimpanzee is sitting in profile, the black fur and the dark skin in green grassy surroundings where other ape-bodies can also be seen as blurred contours in the background. It is sitting in and looking at water coming from above and the ape's long arm is reaching out, touching the water. The overall atmosphere in the picture is fresh and vital, mostly because of the fresh green colours and the clear running water (see Figure 15.3).

The chimpanzee and the snow monkey are portrayed equally anthropomorphized, but with very different connotations. Actually, after initially reading the text accompanying the snow monkey one tends to read the image of the chimpanzee as depicting a male because this photograph is presented in a much

Figure 15.3 Steve Bloom's photograph of a chimpanzee reaching for water in the exhibition 'Spirit of the Wild', Oslo 2007.

Source: Nina Svane-Mikkelsen.

more gender-neutral way – as man is in human culture. It is accompanied with a factual text about the high intelligence of chimpanzees, regarded as man's closest relative, and their need for protection. In the book version of 'Spirit of the Wild', this photograph is accompanied by a quote by the famous primatologist Jane Goodall (Bloom, 2006: p. 120) proposing the idea of religious feelings in animals. Goodall asks if it is not possible that the chimpanzees are responding with feelings like awe when experiencing what she calls the mystery of water: 'water that seems alive, always rushing past yet never going, always the same yet ever different' (Bloom, 2006: p. 120, quoting Goodall, 2000: p. 189). Goodall emphasizes that it was not until our prehistoric ancestors developed language that it was possible to discuss such internal feelings and create a shared religion (ibid.).

The posture of the ape, combined with the quote above that refers to existential feelings and reflections, triggers associations to a famous play where the thinker is male: 'To be, or not to be, that is the question' (Shakespeare, [1603/1604/1623]2005: act 3, scene 1, line 6). With references to Shakespeare's *Hamlet*, a play that focuses on heavy existential questions, the overall connotations of the image-text become philosophical. The monkey gazes upwards and outwards. One can ask why there are no descriptions of female gender here. Might it not be a younger female depicted? This is not specified in the thumbnail-text (Bloom, 2006: p. 127). In the earlier publication *Untamed*, the image of the chimpanzee is printed over a double page with no accompanying text. In the captions in the back of the book, the text is also not gendered (Bloom, 2004: p. 410).

Imagining the animal mind

Any reading of nature or nature-stories will involve anthropomorphism to various degrees. Goodall is inviting us to consider the possibility of high-level feelings and reflections in a pre-language ape-mind. She is asking a question and not claiming to read the mind of the ape. All in all, her text mirrors a respectful position. Bloom's photographic work belongs to a Jane Goodall tradition of animal and wildlife documentation where bonds between species are emphasized. A tradition where 'idealized feminine intimacy with nature, and a web of emotional relationships and fantasies are persuasive', as media scholar Cynthia Chris puts it (2006: p. 66). It is also a tradition of 'representations that still remain conventionalized within a genre that was then and is now largely the work of First World professionals in Third World settings' (ibid.).

Bloom's assemblage-stories of wildlife must be seen in relation to the development of Western natural history during the last three centuries developing in parallel with colonialism. Previously, wildlife and wild animals were most often demonized and large predators depicted as beasts (Orner, 1996). Whether animals are depicted as angels or demons, romanticized or demonized, it is still a tradition of deploying human (and monetary) values to the animal world – to the natural world – on a large scale. It is a tradition of exploitation and exotification. Bloom's photographs show deep and beautiful compassion for the animals depicted, but we must also ask what role these photographs play in society. His work appears today within contemporary consumerism where wildlife photographs and photographers play a distinct role, more often maintaining status quo rather than challenging it, more often embracing aesthetics and language that can be traced back to colonialism, rather than reinventing nature-stories.

The wildlife tradition of the BBC and Sir David Attenborough

Television documentaries on wildlife and nature are in the same tradition as Bloom's photographs. Sir David Attenborough is arguably the most famous wildlife communicator in the history of television. Through a lifetime he has told audiences about wildlife through numerous series of wildlife documentaries produced mainly by the BBC. He is a mentor for a tradition and an icon for and a shaper of popular Western views on nature.

Watching the episode 'Worlds Apart' from the older BBC wildlife series *The Living Planet* from 1984, it is striking how old it appears. The colours are somewhat bleaker than in newer nature productions. Cinematographic techniques have developed a lot over the last 30 years. Since then we have seen productions with amazing visual storytelling. We have seen films showing the world from different animals' perspectives, drawing on biological knowledge of their vision and use of high speed photography and mounted mini-cameras as well as 3D-modelling and other digital graphical tools. Compared with this, *Worlds Apart* appears slow and somewhat low-tech in its use of visual and audio effects, but we can see it as typical and cutting edge in the 1980s since the BBC is known for employing updated visual technologies in its productions. This is also clearly demonstrated in later landmark series, such as *Planet Earth* from 2006.

The episode 'Worlds Apart' starts with Attenborough's arrival on a remote island. There are several interesting features in this introduction: Attenborough is wearing khaki shorts and shirt and thus appears like a colonial Englishman on safari in a former colony. Attenborough is present on the screen with three unnamed, probably local, black people. They transport Attenborough to the shore of an island in a smaller rowboat. The three men are all rowing while Attenborough is scrutinizing the coastline, eagerly leaning forward in the front end of the boat. He is foregrounded, the three others are in the back. He reaches the shore, leans towards a tree, turns towards the camera and starts talking about the place, enthusiastically using engaging rhetoric with a lot of superlatives like 'spectacular', 'extraordinary' and 'extreme' (BBC and Attenborough 1984, timecode 00:31) and eager gesticulation. Attenborough appears a lot on-screen throughout the episode. Frequently a large stone, often on the beach, serves as a spot where he sits down to 'show-and-tell'. The choice of situation and the format of 'travel-and-quest' (Chris, 2006: p. 64), choice of clothing and postures, positions and roles of the different human actors, echo and reenact a history of Western colonialism, colonizing both natures and cultures. Attenborough is a Western white male and acting like a prototype of an explorer taking new landscapes under possession.

Distant natures and the disappearance of the presenter

In the later documentaries Attenborough appears less on-screen than in earlier series. For instance, the series *The Blue Planet* from 2005 and *Planet Earth* from 2006 is without, or almost without, footage of human beings altogether (BBC *et al.*, 2006). Here his direct participation is limited to the voice-over narration, which is very recognizable and gives the film a stamp of quality as a result of his reputation. But there is less talk and more music than in the earlier production, 'Worlds Apart', where music is only used a few times and kept short. What can we say about this development where the narrator is moved from on-screen to off-screen?

In the 2005 and 2006 series we see an almost pristine nature, untouchable, serene and far away, both in the sense of depicting remote geographical areas and because of a frequent use of distant views. We have a viewer-position high above earth instead of watching Attenborough as a presenter in the landscape, being hands-on with objects and living creatures. For example, in 'Ocean Deep', an episode in the series *Planet Earth*, we experience scenery footage, merely seascapes seen from high above, as a reoccurring point of departure for a number of minor stories in the episode. The camera returns to this high position on a regular basis which serves as a chapter overview and a site for change of subject: we dive down to a story of a new species, a different ocean and so forth. All the episodes in this series appear more like audio-visual symphonies, as works of art governed by aesthetic principles like colour, movement, rhythm, sound. A sensual collage with beautiful imagery and ambient music. The underwater footage has very deep focus and clarity, and when several species are present, they are often filmed, and the footage cut, with rhythm in mind, so their appearance together is dance-like, like choreography. Of course, the gliding underwater movements in this episode enhance the impression of rhythm of movement as an important element. An appealing example is when birds, shearwaters, are baiting a shoal of mackerel (BBC *et al.*, 2006: timecode 10:26). We see a bird close-up, almost touching the camera lens. The details in its feathers can be enjoyed, the water's movement and small bubbles around the feathers when the bird moves in the water, turning around itself, and, at the same time, we see, clear and sharp in the far background of the image, other birds and the shoal of fish in swarming formations. As Attenborough expressed it himself at the time of the launching of the series:

> This new series is more a celebration of our planet, not a lament about the state of it. (…) This landmark series takes viewers to the world's highest peaks, deepest caves and most remote deserts. The footage is simply without parallel.
>
> (Quote from text on the cover of the DVD-version of *Planet Earth*: BBC *et al.*, 2006)

Nature is 'there', not 'here'. It is celebrated as unchartered and untouched wilderness. And it is not the modest everyday nature that is of interest, it is the exceptional nature, undiscovered by (white) man.

Nature as no country for man and the city as a habitat

The concepts of nature and culture are closely tied together in language as opposites. This divide is deeply embedded in the tradition of wildlife film and photography. Quite literally, wildlife documentary rarely includes any depiction of people and their creations, cities, building or the like. Nature and culture are seen as two mutually exclusive worlds. Accordingly, in wildlife genres, we expect that there be no signs of human activity in the depicted landscape. This is true for both the BBC and Attenborough's productions and Steve Bloom's photographic work. They are devoid of any sign of human life on Earth, even when the images are shot in small sanctuaries or when the animal depicted is actually under human care far away from its original habitat. One example of this is the chimpanzee in the Monkey World Rescue Centre in Great Britain, reaching out to touch the running water (Figure 15.3; Bloom, 2004: p. 410, 2006: p. 127). But when it comes to expanding the notions of what counts as nature, Attenborough in 1984 already presents cities as habitats for animals and plants – in the final episode, 'New Worlds', of the TV series *The Living Planet*. One may argue that he still keeps a focus on the animal world as separated from human lives, just depicting the animal's adaptation to a new landscape, even if this is a cityscape. Depicting animal life, not the co-living of different actors existing within the same area.

Major strands of storytelling: symphony and show-and-tell

Attenborough is still active and important within nature storytelling today and both the afore mentioned show-and-tell-travel-and-quest style of 'Worlds Apart' and the symphony style of the *Planet Earth* series ('Ocean Deep') is still in use: Attenborough has written the manuscript for and narrates the voice-over for *Galapagos. Nature's Wonderland*, a production from 2013 for IMAX-theatres on show at Tycho Brahe Planetarium in Copenhagen from 08 February 2014 to the end of September 2017 (Tycho Brahe Planetarium, 2017, date unknown; Danish Film Institute, date unknown). This production clearly belongs to the sub-genre of nature symphonies, filling the huge auditorium at the planetarium with music and imagery (Attenborough *et al.*, 2014).

Furthermore, he has made a TV-documentary series where he again appears on-screen as presenter that shows-and-tells: in 2013 BBC and Humble Bee Film launched *David Attenborough's Natural Curiosities* (UKTV *et al.*, 2013). 'Stretched to the Limit' is the first episode of 21 episodes over three seasons produced so far. With this series Attenborough's storytelling is again developed further with a new take on the show-and-tell shows, now including detailed accounts of the history of science. Here Attenborough is also incorporating important driving forces in early natural history and the formation of early curiosity cabinets: curiosity and a focus on anomalies. For instance, the first episode elaborates on super-stretched body parts as extraordinary adaptations, presenting the giraffe's long neck and the chameleon's stretchy tongue as typical examples of such anomalies. He makes direct use of items from museum collections when following the footsteps of knowledge production in Western natural history.

In this series Attenborough is often sitting in a museum of natural history, and mostly in an old museum, not a modern one. It is an environment of dark wooden shelves and desks and old specimens in glass containers. This is a format that suits Attenborough's age, as he can sit down showing-and-telling, indoors in controlled surroundings. The adjustment of the format to his age is done with great charm. The combined focus on the history of science and on biology and zoology is interesting. Attenborough asks the questions scientists have asked in earlier times, using all sorts of props, for example the specimens they collected and historical paintings. In 'Stretched to the Limit' he provides answers to the questions of why the giraffe has such a long neck and the chameleon such a long tongue. Attenborough traces stories of how this knowledge came about and includes cultural historical perspectives. For instance, he tells the story of the transport of the first giraffe in France and Great Britain and emphasizes how the giraffe was an object of people's curiosity, being the first (and probably only) giraffe they ever saw. People gathered to see the animal wherever it arrived on its way through France to Paris, and as it was walked to its destination from Marseilles. We learn about the giraffe and how we got to know about the giraffe.

By telling stories about the wondering and wandering of early natural history this TV format positions the natural sciences within a historical and cultural setting. Seeing how natural history was shaped, the viewer develops an understanding of how natural history has been constructed in particular ways. Even though Attenborough does not ask directly how natural sciences today can contribute to environmental sustainability, the cultural perspective on natural history can contribute to a renewal of sustainability discourses and practices. By stressing heterogeneity and complexity, as is done here, by presenting natural history as a field in an ongoing process, historically anchored and still evolving, these productions embody a natural history that includes stories and discussions of what is sustainable culturally and environmentally. The productions are, however, governed by quite a strict focus on questions of biology, zoology, geology and geography, and a narrow understanding of these subjects, leaving social, political and cultural questions and implications to humanities and social science. With the recent acknowledgement of the Anthropocene as a geological era, this might change (Castree, 2016).

The stories in all the BBC series, narrated (and some written) by David Attenborough, are kept strictly within an overall framing of Western natural history, but they have nevertheless developed and changed over time. The BBC and Attenborough have managed to make landmark productions over decades. They are innovative, make use of the latest media technology and biological knowledge and provide cutting-edge storytelling within the quite strict boundaries of the genre.

Normative issues and the way forward

We have seen how aesthetic media analysis helps us to understand cultures of nature stories and enable us to be reflexive and critically engage in them. We can address what is mediated to us and our own readings of the works. The examples in this chapter have shown typical traits of popular blockbuster nature television and of prominent wildlife photography. Embedded values have been exposed and we have searched for pros and cons of these story cultures with regards to supporting changes in direction of environmental sustainability, as a first step in facilitating change.

As researchers within the field of science and technology studies have shown, science is embedded in value systems (Asdal *et al.*, 2007). In the era of the Anthropocene, normativity and normative questions must be discussed within the natural sciences. One important part of working with natural science, and the public communication of it, can be to expose and question the values embedded and work more openly and directly with the goals of sustainable development.

The photographs of Bloom and the BBC television series analysed here do not challenge traditional genre boundaries for what counts as nature or wildlife documentary. They display cautiousness when dealing with questions that involve political decision-making. Attenborough's narration does not include human agency or any descriptions of concrete processes of protecting the environment. Social, political and cultural factors are only part of the natural world depicted, as an effect on numbers and sizes (like numbers of whales left, areas left). This is in line with the National Geographic Society's stated policy of 'avoidance of controversy' (Chris, 2006: p. 61). Any reference in the BBC productions to issues that have a clear political edge, like dealing with pollution, global warming, loss of biodiversity or other environmental problems, are held in very general terms, as for instance David Attenborough's last summarizing words about the planet in 'Ocean Deep' demonstrate: 'We can now destroy or we can cherish. The choice is ours' (BBC *et al.*, 2006).

A rhetoric of the general is also symptomatic of the texts about environmental protection and animal protection in 'Spirits of the Wild'. On the other hand, Steve Bloom is very specific on the individual level, the level of the single animal. Here depictions and descriptions are almost personalized. Mass mediated nature stories can contribute to the development of cultural and environmental sustainability, media being an important part of the public sphere, an important communicative link between researchers, the public, government and non-governmental organizations. Blockbuster productions like those from the BBC Natural History Unit and wildlife photography like the work of Bloom, can facilitate an interest in and care of nature. This is not a rejection of Western natural history and nature communication, but a call for continuous critical reflection on stories of nature that contribute to shape our future nature–culture interface. Calls for planet protection made in nature productions often seem like routine expressions following the celebration of nature's beauty in a place distant from our lives. The problem with these general 'call-to-action statements' is that almost everybody agrees, but hardly anyone has any idea of how to save a planet. We want to cherish the planet with Attenborough, and we want to save wildlife together with Bloom. But how exactly? When? And who are we, exactly?

Wildlife does not exist in total separation of human activity and life zones. If we want to fight for a short Anthropocene, stories of a strict separation between nature and culture is not optimal. We need stories of nature that explore existing and emerging natures-culture interfaces that take cross-species interdependence much more seriously (Tsing, 2016). Nature stories can support individual responsibility and action by including human agency and local knowledge, giving detailed accounts of situated problems and solutions, allowing complexity in presentations of concrete cases of sustainable practices and experience. Such complexity will include depiction of co-existence of species, co-thinking environmental, social, economic and cultural perspectives. It also includes uncertainty and discussion, and engaging in policy-making in concrete cases.

We have to give up some clarity and simplicity in the nature stories and start following the complex and muddled – and promising – trails of time- and site-specific processes that have actually made a positive difference to nature and wildlife. Such stories make visible the mutual entanglement of species and environment as a first principle in a way that mirrors living in the Anthropocene. Stories that show doubts and ask questions can be cultural carriers (Warren and Moghaddam, 2011) by bringing forward what we do not know, instead of creating barriers through certainty and mastery. They are stories that may lead to change instead of maintaining a destructive status quo.

References

Asdal, K., Brenna, B., Moser, I. (eds) (2007) *Technoscience. The Politics of Interventions*. Unipub AS, Oslo.

Attenborough, D. (manuscript, narrator in UK version), Geffen, A. (producer) and Williams, M. (director). (2014) *Galapagos. Nature's Wonderland*. 40 minutes' documentary film for IMAX-theatres. Colossus Productions film in association with SKY 3D.

BBC Natural History Unit and Attenborough, D. (1984) 'Worlds Apart', episode 10 in the television series *The Living Planet*. The complete series DVD-collection 4-disc set.

BBC Natural History Unit, Discovery Channel and NHK. (2006) 'Ocean Deep', episode 11 in the television series *Planet Earth*, narrated by David Attenborough. The complete series DVD-collection 5-disc set.

BBC Studios. (2016) *Natural History Unit, British Broadcasting Corporation*. www.bbc.co.uk/production/factual/programmesandshows/natural-history-unit (Accessed 6 September 2016).

Bloom, S. (2004) *Untamed*. Abrams, New York.

Bloom, S. (2006) *Helt vildt. Spirit of the Wild*. Nyt Nordisk Forlag, Arnold Busck AS, Copenhagen, Denmark.

Bloom, S., CO+Life and WWF. (2007) *Spirit of the Wild*. Out-door exhibition in central Oslo (poster).

Castree, N. (2016) *An Official Welcome to The Anthropocene Epoch*. www.rdmag.com/article/2016/08/official-welcome-anthropocene-epoch (Accessed 6 September 2016).

Chris, C. (2006) *Watching Wildlife*. University of Minnesota Press, Minneapolis, United States.

Crutzen, P. J. and Stoermer, E. F. (2000) The 'Anthropocene'. *Global Change Newsletter* 41:17–18.

Danish Film Institute. (date unknown) *Forsiden / Filmdatabasen / Fakta om film: Galapagos: Naure's Wonderland*. www.dfi.dk/faktaomfilm/film/da/100417.aspx?id=100417 (Accessed 08 December 2017).

Gentikow, B. (2006) New Media as 'Cultural Techniques' and as Forums for Communicative Action Empirical Research and Constituents of a Theory. *Nordicom Review* 1.

Goodall, J. (with Phillip Berman) (2000) *Reason for Hope: A Spiritual Journey*. Warner Books Inc., New York.

Hausken, L. (2009) *Medieestetikk: studier i estetisk medieanalyse*. Scandinavian Academic Press, Oslo.

Orner, M. R. (1996) *Nature Documentary Explorations: A Survey History and Myth Typology of the Nature Documentary Film and Television Genre from the 1880s through the 1990s*. Department of Communication, University of Massachusetts, Boston, United States.

Shakespeare, W. (author), Andrews, R. and Gibson, R. (eds) ([1603/1604/1623]2005) *Hamlet*. (Second edition). Cambridge School Shakespeare, Cambridge University Press, Cambridge, United Kingdom.

Tsing, A. (2016) Response to: A New Nature. Commentary in Debate on Forum: A New Nature. *Boston Review*. https://bostonreview.net/forum/new-nature/anna-tsing-anna-tsing-response-new-nature (Accessed 07 September 2016).

Tycho Brahe Planetarium. (2017) Personal correspondence with secretary (Anne Bach), 08 December 2017.

Tycho Brahe Planetarium. (date unknown) *Forside/Billetter & filmprogram: Galapagos*. www.planetariet.dk/billetter-filmprogram/galapagos (Accessed 08 December 2017).

UKTV, Humble Bee Films and Attenborough, D. (2013) *David Attenborough's Natural Curiosities: Stretched to The Limit*. First episode originally transmitted 29 January 2013 in United Kingdom.

Warren, Z. and Moghaddam, F. M. (2011) Cultural Carriers. In: D. J. Christie (ed.) *The Encyclopedia of Peace Psychology, Volume 1*. Wiley-Blackwell Publishing Ltd., Oxford: 291–294.

Index

Page numbers in **bold** denote figures, those in *italics* denote tables.

For Product Safety Concerns and Information please contact our EU
representative GPSR@taylorandfrancis.com
Taylor & Francis Verlag GmbH, Kaufingerstraße 24, 80331 München, Germany

www.ingramcontent.com/pod-product-compliance
Ingram Content Group UK Ltd.
Pitfield, Milton Keynes, MK11 3LW, UK
UKHW021007180425
457613UK00019B/844